PSYCHOLOGICAL ASPE

The Amsterdam Academic Archive is an initiative of Amsterdam University Press. The series consists of scholarly titles which were no longer available, but which are still in demand in the Netherlands and abroad. Relevant sections of these publications can also be found in the repository of Amsterdam University Press: www.aup.nl/repository. At the back of this book there is a list of all the AAA titles published in 2005.

Miranda A.L. van Tilburg and
Ad J.J.M. Vingerhoets (eds.)

Psychological Aspects of Geographical Moves

Homesickness and Acculturation Stress

3✕a

Amsterdam Academic Archive

Psychological Aspects of Geographical Moves (ISBN 90 361 9597 7)
by Miranda van Tilburg and Ad Vingerhoets was first published in 1997
by Tilburg University Press, Tilburg.

Cover design: René Staelenberg, Amsterdam
ISBN 90 5356 860 3
NUR 770/882
© Amsterdam University Press · Amsterdam Academic Archive, 2005

Preface

The idea for this book grew out of a symposium on 'Homesickness and Acculturation Stress' held at the 13th World Congress of the International College of Psychosomatic Medicine in Jerusalem, Israel, in September 1995. The chapters of this book are based upon the papers and discussions of this symposium. Some of the authors were unable to attend the symposium, but contributed to the book to help us give a more complete picture of current research and thinking about homesickness and acculturation stress.

When we began our research on homesickness in 1991, we were surprised how little was known and written about this topic in the scientific literature. As our research developed and we tried to publish some of our results, we found – particularly in the United States – that research on homesickness was met with much skepticism. When talking about homesickness at conferences, many colleagues did not take our research, and even the topic, seriously. In the same vein, journal editors and reviewers gave evidence of many misconceptions. Many reviewers, although generally positive about our papers, remarked that they really saw no need to publish anything on this topic. One editor even returned a manuscript on adult homesickness, apparently unread and unreviewed, with the suggestion to send it to a journal that focuses on children.

At the same time, our research taught us that the magnitude of the problem was much bigger than expected. Among Dutch military conscripts, homesickness was the main reason for seeking psychiatric help. An announcement in a women's magazine yielded a response from over 300 hopeless women who felt themselves seriously incapacitated by their homesickness. They suffered from a high degree of homesickness, which dramatically affected their way of living and led to negative self-perceptions. Many of these women saw us as their last and only hope to 'cure' them of their homesickness, apparently not aware that we also knew very little about what they were precisely suffering from and how it impacted on their lives. This ignorance prevented us from offering them any real solution.

These experiences convinced us that it was important to combine research efforts on homesickness and related concepts, not only in the Netherlands, but internationally. The organization of the symposium on homesickness and acculturation stress may be considered an important first step. The papers and discussions at this symposium showed that research on homesickness and acculturation stress was very scattered. In addition, there was a lack of agreement on a definition, and the concepts were operationalized in many different ways. However, this made the conference very fruitful and diverse. We learned a lot from each other's research and were inspired by each other's ideas and ways of thinking. Consequently, the idea was put forward to combine the papers into a book. It is not our intention to give a complete overview of the current knowledge on homesickness and acculturation stress, but rather to show the diverse lines of research. An additional purpose is to stimulate further research and theorizing on homesickness and acculturation stress. We also hope that this book may contribute to a better understanding of the problems, not only for our colleagues but also for anyone else who is confronted with these issues professionally or personally.

The first four chapters of *Psychological aspects of geographical moves: Homesickness and acculturation stress* present an overview of homesickness, acculturation stress, and related concepts. Among others, the following issues are addressed: What is the precise nature of homesickness and acculturation stress? How are they related to other concepts, like depression, adjustment disorder, and culture shock? What are the major determinants and predisposing factors? Chapters 5 through 8 focus on aspects of homesickness and acculturation stress among specific groups, such as international students, migrants, and refugees. Chapter 8 looks at experiences of homesickness and acculturation stress in a non-western culture. Chapters 9 and 10 address homesickness in children and adolescents, with special emphasis on how youngsters cope with it. The next two chapters focus on homesickness and personality, with chapter 11 addressing normal personality accompaniments of homesickness, while Chapter 12 pays attention to the relationship between homesickness and personality disorders and attachment. Finally, chapters 13 and 14 deal with a specific temporary form of geographical move, namely, international tourism.

Preface to the second edition

When the opportunity arrived to publish a second edition of the *Psychological Aspects of Geographical Moves* we were excited and disheartened at the same time: excited to keep the momentum that we created almost 10 years ago going; disheartened because so little has been achieved in the last decade. The immigrant or displaced person remains an uncommon topic of scientific study. Only a handful of new studies have been published on homesickness since the first edition of the book. Acculturation stress has fared only slightly better. Even though these are popular topics for dissertations, few studies have been published in peer-reviewed journals and virtually none in the major (psychology) journals. The little research that has been published has generated too few hypotheses or insights to bring this field to a higher level of understanding. Even many authors of this book have moved on to other research topics. At the heart of the inattention to this important topic is the lack of funding and publishing opportunities in this field. And, surprisingly, also clinicians do hardly show interest, apparently unaware of the major impact of this condition on health and well-being. This is in sharp contrast with the ever increasing willingness and need to travel for study or job opportunities, as well as for vacations. The result is a dramatic increase in the numbers of people travelling all over the world. International students, soldiers stationed overseas, people displaced due to wars and natural disasters, businessmen and their families on international assignment, seasonal farm workers - all have to deal with the effects of a move from their homes and countries. In almost all cases, this generates considerable distress, not only on the side of the traveller/immigrant but often also for the receiving country.

The limits of a multicultural society are becoming increasingly noticeable. For example, in Europe there are increasing clashes between immigrant and resident groups, which often are associated with problems with integration. In addition, there is ample evidence that immigrants are less healthy than native-born citizens, which raises questions about the impact of adaptation and homesickness on physical and mental well-being. These developments show that the psychological effects of geographical moves do not just temporarily affect the moving individual and his family, but they can have long lasting effects on individuals, groups, and the society at large. Due to the paucity of research, the content of the first edition is still largely as valid as it was when we published it for the first time. Some of the authors have made minor or major updates to their chapters to include new findings. We hope that with the publication of this second edition we are at the start of a new era in which homesickness and acculturation stress finally receive the attention they need and deserve.

Miranda van Tilburg
Ad Vingerhoets
October 2005

Contents

Contributors

Maurice Eisenbruch
University of New South Wales, Centre for Culture and Health, Sydney, Australia

Liesbeth Eurelings-Bontekoe
Leiden University, Department of Clinical and Health Psychology, Leiden,
The Netherlands

Adrian Furnham
University College of London, Department of Psychology, London, UK

Shirley Fisher
Strathclyde University, Centre of Occupational and Health Psychology, Glasgow, Scotland

Irma Gruijters
Tilburg University, Department of Psychology, Tilburg, The Netherlands

Terence Hannigan
Stevens Institute of Technology, Student Counseling Services, Hoboken
New Jersey, USA

Dan Hertz
Hebrew University-Hadassah, W. Schindler Foundation for Medical Psychotherapy, Jerusalem,
Israel

Wendela Kuper
Tilburg University, Department of Psychology, Tilburg, The Netherlands

Marcel Monden
Regional Institute for Ambulatory Mental Health Care, Hoorn (West-Friesland),
The Netherlands; Health Care Special Services, Limmen, The Netherlands

Camille Randall
University of Kansas, Department of Psychology, Lawrence, Kansas, USA

Nanda Sanders
Tilburg University, Department of Psychology, Tilburg, The Netherlands

Paul Schmitz
University of Bonn, Institute of Psychology, Bonn, Germany

Christopher Thurber
Phillips Exeter Academy, Department of Psychology, Exeter, New Hampshire, USA

Hannie Thijs
Tilburg University, Department of Psychology, Tilburg, The Netherlands

Guus Van Heck
Tilburg University, Department of Psychology, Tilburg, The Netherlands

Miranda Van Tilburg
University of North Carolina, School of Medicine, Chapel Hill, North Carolina, USA

Eric Vernberg
University of Kansas, Department of Psychology, Lawrence, Kansas, USA

Ad Vingerhoets
Tilburg University, Department of Psychology, Tilburg, The Netherlands

Aafke Voolstra
Tilburg University, Department of Psychology, Tilburg, The Netherlands

1 The Homesickness Concept: Questions and Doubts

AD VINGERHOETS

Introduction

In today's world more and more appeals are being made to our adaptational capacities. The time of living and dying in the place where we were born in is long past. Current educational, professional, and – not in the least – recreational activities take us away far from our home environment and bring us into contact with other places and other cultures for shorter or longer periods. International exchange programs, dispatchment movements, migration, and international tourism make us spend less time in our familiar environment than we ever did before. In addition, we must not forget special and vulnerable groups, such as refugees all over the world, those who are forced to leave their home countries for whatever reason and people undergoing hospitalization and institutionalization. In short, modern man has to be prepared to break the bonds with the home environment and to adapt to new and, in many respects, demanding surroundings. Being separated from the familiar environment may induce a reaction complex with characteristic accompanying emotional, somatic, and behavioral elements and cognitions that may be labeled as 'homesickness.'

When reviewing the scientific literature on homesickness, it is amazing to see that – especially in American literature – hardly any attention has been paid to this phenomenon. Is the American culture not familiar with homesickness (in adults), because there one does not have real roots, as an American colleague once suggested? Or, alternatively, is homesickness taboo and not socially accepted in the U.S.A.? How can it be possible that Altman and Low (1992) published a volume (see also Giuliani & Feldman, 1993) entitled *Place Attachment*, in which the term homesickness was only mentioned on one single page? On the other hand, a search on the world wide web with homesickness as search term yields many hits in particular focusing on school camps and the transition of students to university. In addition, there are, also in American literature, sufficient indications that residential moves and migration may be associated with increased distress and risk of mental and physical disease.

For example, making a residential move is included in the Holmes Rahe (1967) Social Readjustment Rating Scale and other life events scales. Admittedly, though not top of the list: position 32 with 20 life change units, it is nevertheless listed. Moreover, there are impressive data suggesting that moving may bring about serious health problems, not only in children and the elderly, but also among adults. For example, Jacobs and Charles (1980) published a case-control study on life events and the occurrence of cancer in children. It was shown that as many as 72% in the cancer group (as compared to 24% in the control group) had experienced a residential move at some point during the two-year period preceding the onset of the disease. Adults also seemed to be at risk of developing mental (in particular depression) and physical diseases including diabetes mellitus and other such immune related disorders after a move (cf. Van Tilburg *et al.*, 1996a). A residential move thus increases a person's vulnerability to mental and somatic disease. However, this observation does not in itself justify devoting attention to a concept like homesickness, although it may be of help when it comes to better defining the population at risk.

If we feel that it makes sense to enrich the scientific world with the concept homesickness, and if we really want to make any progress in this field, it will be important to establish a consensus on the construct in order to pave the way for the development of assessment tools with adequate psychometric characteristics.

The aim of this chapter

What I want to do in this contribution is, to first of all give some good reasons for why we should investigate homesickness. Then, I will present the case study that made me become interested in this phenomenon. It is a case that raises some important questions concerning the specific nature of this phenomenon. I will further describe our first research efforts and my ongoing struggle with the construct. I shall expand on how my thinking has developed and which aspects of this made me feel confused about this intriguing concept. I will offer some speculative models that may be relevant for theorizing about the development of homesickness and attachment to places, and I will speculate how these relate. Of course, closely allied to the issue of conceptualization is the issue of measurement. How can homesickness be accurately measured? I will also briefly address the issue of pathological versus non-pathological homesickness. I will finish with some more questions; questions that I feel need to be answered before we can make real progress in this area.

Why do we study homesickness?

I think that there are several good reasons for making an in-depth study into homesickness and its related phenomena. Firstly, as just described, there is increasing migration all over the world. There is evidence that migrants often show higher medical consumption levels than comparable non-migrant populations. Although this is not to say that many other factors also play a role in the explanation of this phenomenon, problems of integration and adjustment should be examined as potential facilitating factors of ill health. In addition, a better understanding of the factors that promote or prevent the onset of feelings of homesickness may provide clinicians with knowledge, which would help in the development of effective therapeutic approaches. This is all the more important in the light of evidence that homesickness not only interferes with adaptation to new situations, for instance with migrants and refugees, but it does more as well. It may also seriously hinder reintegration when back in the homeland, because of overidealization, which makes the return often disappointing (cf. Begemann, 1988). Secondly, I feel that studying homesickness has the potential to contribute significantly to our understanding of stress processes and their role in the development of psychosomatic problems. It is especially the reversibility of sometimes dramatic psychiatric or somatic symptoms that offers unique opportunities for the study of psychobiological stress responses. After returning to the home situation, recovery can be speedy, dramatic and impressive (cf. Rosen, 1975). It would be most interesting to obtain a better insight into the possible accompanying psychobiological changes.

In short, investigating homesickness may be important for developing the necessary intervention strategies that are badly needed for improving the quality of life of migrant populations and refugees (De Vries & Van Heck, 1994; Hertz, 1988). It may also further our understanding of the more fundamental processes relevant to general research and theorizing on stress and emotions, in particular the vulnerability aspect.

A case study

A is a 16-year-old boy, who suffers from homesickness. Although he is able to deal with it rather well, it still negatively affects his ability to enjoy holidays. His entire life is characterized by a strong attachment to his home environment. Already as a baby of less than a year, he had crying spells when put in strange beds or cots. As a 3-year-old, he strongly protested when his mother left him with his grandparents or aunts, to visit his little sister who was hospitalized. His mother can remember him bursting into tears on waking each day and asking desperately where he was going to be taken today. Even sitting in a supermarket trolley and having his mother or father out of his sight for a few moments, was enough to make him cry. The playschool and early school years also yielded serious problems. When touring or making a trip, making jokes on being lost and unable to find the way back home was enough to make him feel desperate. Going camping with his soccer team at the age of eight did not last for long. The next morning, he was brought back home, severely distressed and in tears; he had not slept and had developed fever. Once home again, the recovery was remarkable and rapid. It also appeared that the boy felt very distressed when the father was absent for a few days. At the age of sixteen he still suffers from feelings of homesickness when away from home. It makes no difference whether his parents or his friends accompany him. Every morning, when being away from home, starts with these feelings and the accompanying desire to go back home. He now is aware that these feelings will wane and disappear during the course of the day, especially when he is engaged in activities. This 'coping' strategy allows him to go on holiday, although there are limits. More than two weeks away from home seems to be an insurmountable problem for him. He further knows that he must not withdraw but

4

must engage in social activities. The intensity of the feelings is not affected by whether he likes or does not like the new place and the company. Most of the time he really enjoys the holiday activities and being together with his friends, but there is nevertheless the strong desire to go back home. So, there is no latent desire or seeking to escape from adverse conditions. On the contrary, he is torn between the joys of a vacation and his inner urge to go back home.

This case brings up a couple of interesting and important questions. For example, what is the relationship between homesickness and separation anxiety? At what age can children develop homesickness, i.e., when are they aware not only of the presence of the mother but also of their own home environment? Is there a causal relationship between early childhood experiences and homesickness in later life? How does one become so strongly attached to the home environment? Is homesickness a unitary phenomenon or can different forms be distinguished. Finally, what are the therapeutic possibilities? Should homesickness be conceived of as a chronic condition, with which one has to live with, or can it really be cured? What are the possibilities for designing adequate interventions?

I will not address all of these questions, but I mention them in the hope that, in the near future, colleagues will devote attention to these developmental aspects. It was lack of knowledge and of empirical data that stimulated me to start working on this issue from the point of view of my own background, i.e., stress and emotion research. As often happens, however, the more I became familiar with the topic, the more I also became aware of the pitfalls and methodological problems inherently associated with the study of homesickness.

First research attempts

Together with my colleague Guus Van Heck and three psychology students, I started my first investigations in this area. One student, Aafke Voolstra, focused on homesickness and personality. Van Heck and colleagues report on these findings in their contribution to this volume. The second student, Irma Gruijters was interested in whether certain objective situation characteristics might be relevant for the development of homesickness. She provided volunteers with situation descriptions, which varied in the following three respects: (1) Distance: far away from home *vs.* rather close; (2) Duration: just a few days *vs.* a longer period; and (3) Company: alone *vs.* with intimates *vs.* with acquaintances. As was to be expected, least homesickness was reported in the situations that could be described as nearby, of short duration and with company. What was more surprising was that distance proved to be the least important factor. The absence of close people and duration appear to be far more relevant. The problem with this study is, of course, that the situations are just hypothetical. Nothing is known about the validity of these self-reports and to what degree these self-reports reflect implicit and personal, but not necessarily valid, theories rather than the actual behavior that will be displayed when being in such situations. Can one adequately predict how one will feel and behave in new and unfamiliar situations? Case reports cast doubt on this assumption. Homesickness may strike quite suddenly and unexpected, in experienced travelers or in someone who lives a happy life away from their home country, when exposed to a stressor (such as the death of parents).

The third student, Hannie Thijs, asked adult study participants to report homesickness experiences and examined these descriptions and responses to structured questions concerning the antecedents and behavioral, cognitive, and somatic reactions. These answers were also compared with the responses to the same questions concerning closely related feelings, i.e., sadness, anxiety, and desire, which in a pilot study emerged as most close to homesickness. To our surprise, some subjects in this investigation gave descriptions of longing for their youth or times past (what we would like to refer to as nostalgia rather than homesickness). Most subjects, however, indeed reported memories of moves, boarding schools, and holidays abroad, as situations in which they developed homesickness. However, in many cases it was explicitly emphasized that feelings of homesickness first emerged, after some kinds of problems had been experienced, such as conflicts with fellow travelers, accidents, etc. (see also the chapter by Van Tilburg).

This last observation again puzzled me. Was that 'real' homesickness or was it merely the desire to escape from adverse conditions? Organisms generally try to avoid or escape from adverse conditions, but is that an essential component of homesickness? I do not think so. As illustrated in the case study, the desire to go back home manifests itself also in situations appraised as pleasant. We thus found out that the term homesickness, at least in the Dutch language, appears to be applied to a wide variety of psychological states including separation anxiety, nostalgia and a desire to avoid or escape conflicts and other less enjoyable situations.

Is homesickness an unequivocal concept?

My confusion increased further when I spoke with a clinical psychologist (Bremer, personal communication) who pointed out that he distinguishes between two types of homesickness: the cat-type and the dog-type. The cat-type involves a strong attachment to places and to the physical environment, whereas the dog-type emphasizes strong bonds with persons. This terminology was chosen, because cats are generally believed to develop strong attachments to their physical environments. After a move a cat may run away and attempt to return to the former home. Dogs by contrast reportedly generally show more signs of distress when being separated from their owner and they apparently seem to appreciate being reunited with their owners.

Rümke (1940) introduced the term pseudo-homesickness, which refers to a pattern of homesickness-like reactions resulting from personality disorders and identified a fourth form in which the unbearableness of the new situation is the predominant aspect. Bergsma (1963) made a distinction between normal and pathological homesickness. He saw homesickness as a normal phenomenon, which can become pathological when it cannot be coped with adequately. According to this author, pathological homesickness can be divided into no less than eight subtypes: (1) primitive homesickness, found among primitive and mentally retarded persons who have excessively strong bonds with their environment; (2) infantile or symbiotic homesickness, prevalent among young children primarily connected to the mother figure; (3) neurotic homesickness, reflecting an ambivalent and discordant relationship with the parents; (4) hysterical homesickness, which is based upon a neurotic and discordant relationship with a hysterical mother, with whom the homesick person wants to identify him/herself; (5) mental deficiency homesickness, resulting from some sort of mental deficiency; (6) liberty homesickness, characterized by a predominant yearning for freedom; (7) 'zeewee,' a specific Dutch term describing the yearning for the sea, common among seamen living ashore; and (8) 'Hinausweh,' a German term meaning return-sickness, a form of homesickness that occurs when one returns back home from another place. However, since nothing is known about the empirical and/or theoretical basis of this classification, one may question the validity of this classification.

Meanwhile we continued and extended our research efforts. The first results emerging from Miranda van Tilburg's project definitely convinced me that there are individuals who seem to be really homebound. During vacations, they prefer to stay at home alone, while the rest of the family is on holiday. These individuals miss their house, their bed, and their own toilet very severely, when being away from home. Are they the real cat-types? Or do they suffer from a more general kind of agoraphobia? A basic difference between homesickness and agoraphobia is that depressive symptoms usually accompany homesickness, whereas phobias in general are characterized by increased anxiety and panic.

Some study participants had recently moved to another place. Often this concerned women whose husbands had a new (and, in objective terms, more attractive and better paid) job. However, in spite of the new and often nicer and more comfortable house, they failed to settle and keep longing for their previous environment. Was this the 'real' homesickness I was looking for, or was this more kind of adjustment disorder?

Fisher (1989) emphasized the importance of how the new environment is experienced. Important aspects are the extent to which individuals lack knowledge about routines and procedures resulting in loss of control and how the demands made by new roles are appraised. Some of our preliminary findings support this view. We found four independent factors on a questionnaire completed by 'homesick' (according to their own criteria) persons: (1) missing the physical environment; (2) missing people; (3) difficulty adapting to the new environment; and (4) difficulty with new routines and the new lifestyle. Should these findings be regarded as evidence in support of a classification in four subtypes of homesickness?

In addition, the just referred to distinction between 'normal' homesickness and 'pathological' homesickness is an issue that deserves further attention. Is it indeed reasonable to assume that homesickness is a normal and 'healthy' reaction to leaving the safe home environment, in much the same way as grief is a normal reaction to losing intimates or feeling depressed is the logical and normal reaction when one is diagnosed as suffering from a serious disease (cf. Averill & Nunley, 1993; Middletown et al., 1993)? Horowitz et al. 1993) presented a sophisticated model for the identification of pathological grief, which may be of help when trying to develop a corresponding decision model for homesickness. However, before a similar model can be developed for homesickness, more information should be available on the normal course of reactions to moves and separation. Are there, after relocation, also response phases, each of which might have a pathological variant? As far as is known, there is nothing in the relevant literature to indicate that such phases indeed exist. Therefore, it seems more appropriate to apply the decision rules used in determining clinical depression, in particular in the post-partal period. This kind of depression is also clearly linked to a specific and concrete event and, much similar like after a move, after childbirth the majority of the women show no signs of depression whatsoever. The differentiation between the normal and the pathological reaction may, for the time being, be based on the following aspects. A first criterion to be applied is the intensity of the reaction. One may assume that the pathologically homesick will show kind of hypersensitivity to leaving their home-place. The reaction is much more intense and dramatic than is the norm and it strongly interferes with normal functioning and role fulfillment in the new situation. A second criterion may be that there is undue prolongation and no reduction in the experiencing of symptoms and disturbances. Not only psychological and behavioral reactions should be considered but, given the sometimes intense somatic reactions, like loss of appetite, sleepiness, headaches and fever, these should also be taken into account.

Finally, I want to draw attention to the relationship between homesickness and adjustment, because the way investigators perceive this relationship may be extremely helpful when it comes to obtaining a better and more unequivocal definition of homesickness. Theoretically, each of the following three positions can be held: (1) homesickness results from a failure to adjust to the new situation; (2) homesickness is a psychological state that prevents or interferes with good adjustment, and (3) homesickness is more or less synonymous with failure to adjust.

To summarize, whereas I was initially convinced that homesickness was a real and easily to identify phenomenon, later on I had serious doubts. Is homesickness just a label people use when they are feeling distressed about living in any other place than the home-environment? My next impression was that there might be two or even more different types of homesickness. Would these different types all have a different etiology and/or ontology? When should homesickness be regarded as pathological? What is the relationship between homesickness and more or less related constructs like separation anxiety, agoraphobia, and adjustment disorder? Some of these issues will be dealt with in more detail in Van Tilburg's chapter.

Some putative basic models

In this volume ample attention is given to Fisher's homesickness model, which is based on psychological stress theory. Such an approach has certainly its merits and will stimulate further research. However, this model does not offer any insight and understanding into *why* people may become strongly attached to their environment and/or why individuals may have serious problems when confronted with the necessity to learn new routines, nor into *how* more stable personality features may influence these processes. Therefore, I would like here to present some explanations, based on ideas and data put forth by Debuschere (1984) on romantic love. Homesickness and love(sickness) obviously have much in common: (1) strong affective reactions arise when the individual is separated from the place or person; (2) the home cq. person is not replaceable or exchangeable; and (3) the cognitive and somatic sensations show remarkable similarity: obsessive thoughts, rumination, idealization, stomach troubles, lack of appetite, and sleeplessness.

The logical next question is whether theories on love can help us to explain homesickness. Debuschere (1984) discusses the following three theoretical views: (1) the emotion attribution theory; (2) learning theory; and (3) the opponent-process theory. In the following paragraphs I will briefly address these three models, add two more, and try to show that it may make sense to apply these models to homesickness as well. In addition, it is worth noting that some specific testable hypotheses can be derived from these models.

The emotion attribution theory states that general feelings of arousal will be interpreted and labeled according to cognitions guided by the concrete situation. An important assumption mainly based on the classic, but at present controversial work of Schachter and Singer (1962), is that specific emotions are not accompanied by specific psychobiological states, but rather are associated with quite undifferentiated physical arousal. In this view, physical arousal and 'being away from home' may be interpreted as 'homesickness,' whereas the same physical arousal and 'seeing a nice person' may be experienced as 'being in love.' A serious problem, however, concerns the source of the necessary physiological arousal? Where does the bodily arousal come from? Or, alternatively, is there no real physical arousal and is it just a matter of perceived arousal?

Perhaps it makes sense to extend this theory by taking into account the basic findings of the work of Pennebaker (1982) on symptom perception. This author points out that the threshold for perceiving bodily processes may be lowered, when there is no or little stimulation via other modalities. The assumptions of this theory can be summarized as follows: (1) individuals are limited in their information processing capacities and, as a result, select information; (2) proprioceptive (i.e., from within the body) and external information will thus compete and, as a consequence, attention will oscillate between both modalities; (3) perception is to some extent dependent on stimulus characteristics; the more intense the stimulation, the more likely it is that the stimulus will be perceived; (4) additionally, to some extent, perception is also dependent on cognition (which in turn can be influenced by personality traits, early (traumatic) experiences and mood). It may thus be hypothesized that individuals having suffered from a specific childhood experience (e.g., separation anxiety) in combination with certain personality characteristics are more sensitive to bodily symptoms, which subsequently come to be labeled as homesickness when being away from home. This model thus also explains why homesickness develops especially at quiet moments, like during meals, when going to sleep, or when waking up, when there is only limited distraction due to a lack of external stimulation.

The second approach is based on learning theory. It is tempting to speculate that there might be a generalization of negative feelings induced during early childhood when the child is removed from the mother which is carried over to situations in later life, characterized by separation from the home situation. This model may offer an explanation of how homesickness can develop in individuals who, in their childhood, have experienced traumatic separation, more or less similar to the famous little boy Albert who became conditioned to fear furry objects because of the previous association of the appearance of a rabbit with a loud noise which initially called for crying and other fear-induced behavior (Watson & Rayner, 1920).

Whereas in the models just described the emphasis is on negative childhood experiences, one may alternatively emphasize the positive feelings associated with being at home. An exemplary model in this tradition is the one formulated by Zajonc (1968, 1971) as his 'mere exposure hypothesis.' Central to this hypothesis is the notion that reinforcement is not a necessary condition for the occurrence of attachment. Zajonc argues that "the mere repeated exposure of an individual to a given stimulus object is a sufficient condition for the enhancement of his/her attraction toward it" and it does not make a difference whether the stimulus object is of the same species ("love"), a member of a different species, or an inanimate object. The author illustrates his discussion with several examples of imprinting and related phenomena in animals. However, he also presents evidence demonstrating that similar processes affect humans just as much and that these effects are not limited to a particular age group. It would be tempting to elaborate this model for homesickness and to formulate testable hypotheses on the process of attachment to the home situation.

Going a small step further, one may see a correspondence with addiction. Just as has been suggested for love, a homesick individual also may be considered to be addicted to the home situation. This hypothesis is mainly based on the opponent-process theory of acquired motivation as put forth by Solomon (1980). Briefly summarized, this theory states that repeated or continued exposure to affect-arousing stimuli, such as attachment objects, results in (1) diminished affective response to the presence of those stimuli (the 'A-state') and (2) a stronger response to their withdrawal (the 'B-state'). Because the B-process effectively opposes the A-state, a growth in strength of the former will by definition lead to a weakening of the latter.

Solomon further states that repeated exposure has a strong effect on the opponent-process system. Whereas the primary A-process is unaffected, the B-process is strengthened by use and weakened by disuse. This model has been applied to drug addiction, social attachment, love, craving for sensory experiences, and multiple separations in monkeys. Homesickness may be a valuable addition to this list of applications. Aldwin and Stokols (1988) have critically discussed this theory within the context of environmental changes.

Especially where the development of homesickness in the elderly is concerned, the work of Rowles and his co-workers is also most relevant. Rowles (1983, 1984) and Rubinstein and Parmelee (1992) have studied ageing in rural environments. They described how old people in rural settings tend to imbue local space with personal memories and social meanings all of which may produce strong emotional attachments to the home environment. These authors hypothesize that old people cognitively divide the physical environment into zones of decreasing intensity of involvement away from their homes. Emotional attachment is closely linked to the concept of *insideness*, which distinguishes proximate spaces from the more peripheral zones, which in turn may be denoted as the *outside* zones. Rowles identifies the following three components with regard to the inside-outside continuum: (1) a sense of being almost physiologically smelted into the environment, resulting from daily familiarity with the place's physical aspects and the routines and habits adhered to; (2) social insideness, which has to do with a sense of being known well and knowing many others well. This may make individuals feel secure and confident of receiving social support if it is needed; and (3) places in the neighborhood may assume a special meaning on the basis of personal history, because they are associated with significant and emotional events in one's life. To summarize, having an attachment to a place includes having an emotional bond with the place (possibly mediated by social ties), memories and other cognitive interpretations, which gives meaning to one's personal experience in that place. In addition, a sense of anxiety and distress may arise if one is removed from the place.

Brown and Perkins (1992) describe three stages we go through when we move away from a place to which we have become attached to: (1) pre-disruption, (2) disruption, and (3) post-disruption. Voluntary moves are often planned, which allows the individuals to prepare themselves for the change. Within this process one may distinguish between, on the one hand, loosening one's attachment and obligations to the former home environment and, on the other hand, anticipating and connecting with the new life. What is most important during the disruption phase is choosing and growing to like the new location. Involuntary perceived moves are generally viewed as more stressful. Remarkably, it is only in the post-disruption phase, that these authors explicitly mention homesickness, maintaining ties with the former home, and identifying with the new place. In their view homesickness thus differs from the distress caused in the disruption phase. Unfortunately, no further elaboration of their conceptualization of homesickness and how it relates to their other constructs has been presented.

The processes described here suggest that the etiology of homesickness may differ qualitatively and may result from any of the above described processes. The next question to ask is whether this also implies that manifestations of homesickness may be different, depending on their etiology. What also needs to be considered is what consequences this may have for the conceptualization of homesickness and, in particular, for the possibilities for treatment.

Research approaches and methodological issues

How can homesickness best be studied? Field studies have the potential to yield interesting data. There are currently many examples of situations in which people are more or less forced to move or to change their place of residence. In addition to the assessment of superficial psychological variables, it would be interesting to apply in depth-interviews and to collect psychobiological data, including hormone and immune measures.

Quasi-experimental studies in which homesick persons and non-homesick controls are randomly assigned to a 'home' and 'no-home' condition probably provide the best feasible alternatives for the study of homesickness. As far as is known such studies have until now never been conducted. In such a design, it is even more appropriate to apply psychobiological measures in a standardized way in addition to employing merely psychological measures.

Experimental approaches with humans are of course not possible. It would therefore be interesting to explore whether it would be feasible and make sense to develop animal models. The cat and dog reactions would suggest that these species might be interesting subjects for a study into the basic mechanisms of homesickness. However, I am not aware of any reports on homesickness or of possibly equivalent behavior of in the behavioral sciences frequently used species like rats or primates. Observations by Scott (1987) of two dogs suggest that dogs may indeed be capable of becoming strongly attached to their familiar environment, although it is not entirely clear how important the caretaker's role was in these cases. Brodbeck (1954) has also reported that puppies readily attach themselves to humans. In Scott's report, a sheepdog puppy, reared in his laboratory, was sold to a family at the age of six months. After five days the owners returned it because they were afraid that it was going to die, as it had not eaten, slept, drunk, or moved as long as it had been with them. Once back in the laboratory, it recovered within a few hours. There is also evidence suggesting that animal models (at least non human primates) lend themselves for the study of the psychobiological aspects of grief (cf. Laudenslager *et al.*, 1993). It thus seems reasonable to examine the possible validity of animal models for homesickness.

In ethology, it is well known that many species show territorial behavior and, for a wide variety of species, specific behaviors are interpreted as indications of site attachment. According to Ardrey (1966) establishing territorial boundaries serves three needs: (1) the need for security – in the heart of the territory; (2) the need for stimulation – at the periphery of the territory; and (3) the need for identity, i.e., identification with something larger and more permanent than the organism itself. With some animal species, behavior has been studied as a function of the distance from the own territory. Any significant differences in behavior might therefore be an indication of site attachment. It would be worthwhile to explore to what extent the insights obtained from such studies have relevance for the investigation of human homesickness. Working on the development of an animal model for homesickness in a multidisciplinary context appears to me to be a most interesting challenge.

The recent work with prairie voles demonstrating the important role of substances like oxytocin and vasopressin in forming lifetime bonds demonstrates that this venue indeed may result in important and interesting discoveries (Insell & Carter, 1995).

A final interesting approach would be the cross-cultural one. To what extent do people from other cultures know homesickness? And is there a difference, as might be anticipated, between dwelling hunters or nomads and gatherers.

Assessment issues

Independent of the choice of the best and most feasible research approaches and designs, a major problem is the assessment of homesickness and closely related the case definition. In the foregoing exposition I hope that I have succeeded in making clear that models and theories that facilitate the development of psychometrically valid and reliable measuring instruments, allowing the analysis of nomological networks, are badly needed. To date, there is still a lack of valid instruments to determine whether someone really suffers from homesickness. Assessing homesickness has some specific problems. Since the population in general appears to use the term homesickness in a very broad sense with different meanings, I have serious doubts as to whether it is a good idea to select items from the definitions provided by a sample of subjects who label themselves as homesick, such as done by Fisher for the development of her Dundee Relocation Inventory. The Homesickness Decision Tree (Eurelings-Bontekoe et al., 1994) is based on expert opinions. But this measuring device also has its limitations. If someone admits to suffering from homesickness when away from home on his/her own, but not when his/her family is with him/her, is that qualitatively or quantitatively different from someone who, even when his/her family is present, suffers from homesickness? Is it perhaps possible for the homesick to draw up a hierarchy of homesickness evoking situations in a similar vein to what is done with phobic patients (compare the method applied by Gruiters, described previously and see also the chapter by Van Heck et al.)? Another aspect concerns the time dimension, how and how fast does homesickness develop? Preliminary data from our own group (Van Tilburg et al., 1996b) suggests that some subjects even suffer from a kind of 'preparatory homesickness' that in some cases may wane when the individual is away from home for a few days. Should this condition alternatively be regarded as 'fear-of-depression,' more or less equivalent to the 'fear-of-fear' phenomenon in phobics? By contrast, others seem more like slow starters; they first develop their symptoms a few days after having left their home environment and their homesickness feelings gradually increase with passing time. The assessment issue thus concentrates in particular on the possible need of measuring (specific kinds of) homesickness as a psychological state and determining the proneness to develop homesickness in certain situations. In any case, it is clear that the development of new assessment tools should be theory based in order to facilitate progress in this rather new field.

Conclusion

It may be that the readers' expectations were rather high when they started reading this chapter. By now, they will realize that I have only put forth questions and that I fail to supply any answers. However, one should be aware that the study of homesickness is still in its infancy and there is little theory driven research, mainly because there is hardly any theory. Apart from Fisher's seminal work, little systematic research has been conducted to date. I feel therefore that it is important to start with very elementary and basic questions concerning the precise nature of the phenomenon, in order to establish a generally accepted definition on which the development of assessment tools can be based. I am not certain whether all these questions make real sense and are the most relevant, but perhaps they will direct us and help us to find the right questions and answers. I hope that this contribution will initiate a discussion on the basic issues and the most appropriate methodology for the study of homesickness. Stress research has taught us that neglecting theory may cause much confusion and it appears also to be a rather inefficient way of making progress in science. Better mutually tuned research efforts and the application of uniform measures may help us to further fathom this most interesting phenomenon.

Given the present state-of-the-art I would propose defining homesickness in a very strict way. For me, homesickness reflects problems with separation from the home environment. It interferes with adjustment to the new situation. By contrast, distress caused by adjustment problems in new environments should not be labeled homesickness. In order to avoid unnecessary ambiguity and confusion (recall the serious problems with the stress concept!), I would like to conclude by calling for attention to problems of definition. I look forward to fruitful discussion and the development of new and promising research plans.

References

Aldwin, C., & Stokols, D. (1988). The effects of environmental change on individuals and groups: Some neglected issues in stress research. *Journal of Environmental Psychology, 8,* 57-75.

14

Altman, I., & Low S. M. (Eds.) (1992). *Place attachment*. New York: Plenum.

Ardrey, R. (1966). *The territorial imperative*. New York: Atheneum.

Averill, J. R., & Nunley, E. P. (1993). Grief as an emotion and as a disease: A social-constructionist perspective. In: M. S. Stroebe, W. Stroebe, & R. O. Hansson (Eds.), *Handbook of bereavement: Theory, research, and intervention* (pp. 77-90). Cambridge: Cambridge University Press.

Begemann, F. A. (1988). *Hulpverlening aan vluchtelingen en asielzoekers*. [Psychosocial interventions for refugees]. Rijswijk, The Netherlands: Ministry of Welfare, Health and Culture, Center for Health Care for Refugees.

Bergsma, J. (1963). *Militair heimwee* [Homesickness in the army]. Unpublished Ph.D. thesis. Groningen, The Netherlands: Groningen University.

Brodbeck, D. J. (1954). An exploratory study of the acquisition of dependency behavior in puppies. *Bulletin of the Ecological Society of America, 35,* 73.

Brown, B. B., & Perkins, D. D. (1992). Disruptions in place attachment. In: I. Altman & S. M. Low (Eds.), *Place attachment* (pp. 279-304). New York: Plenum.

Chawla, L. (1992). Childhood place attachments. In: I. Altman & S. M. Low (Eds.), *Place attachment* (pp. 63-86). New York: Plenum.

De Vries, J., & Van Heck, G. L. (1994). Quality of life and refugees. *International Journal of Mental Health, 23,* 3-23.

Debusschere, M. (1984). Onderzoek naar verliefdheid in sociale psychologie: Een kritisch overzicht. [Research on love in social psychology: A critical review]. *Gedrag – Tijdschrift voor Psychologie, 12,* 1-20.

Eurelings-Bontekoe, E. H. M., Vingerhoets, A., & Fontijn, T. (1994). Personality and behavioral antecedents of homesickness. *Personality and Individual Differences, 16,* 229-235

Fisher, S. (1989). *Homesickness, cognition, and health*. London: Erlbaum.

Giuliani, M. V., & Feldman, R. (1993). Place attachment in a developmental and cultural context. *Journal of Environmental Psychology, 13,* 267-274.

Hertz, D. G. (1988). Identity – lost and found: patterns of migration and psychological and psychosocial adjustment of migrants. *Acta Psychiatrica Scandinavica, 78 (Suppl. 344),* 159-165.

Holmes, T. H., & Rahe, R. H. (1967). The social readjustment rating scale. *Journal of Psychosomatic Research, 11,* 213-218.

Horowitz, M. J., Bonanno, G. A., & Holen, A. (1993). Pathological grief: Diagnosis and explanation. *Psychosomatic Medicine, 55,* 260-273.

Insell, T. R., & Carter, C. S. (1995). The monogamous brain. *Natural History, 104,* 12-14.

Jacobs, T. J., & Charles, E. (1980). Life events and the occurrence of cancer in children. *Psychosomatic Medicine, 1,* 11-23.

Laudenslager, M. L., Boccia, M. L., & Reite, M. L. (1993). Biobehavioral consequences of loss in nonhuman primates: Individual differences. In: M. S. Stroebe, W. Stroebe, & R. O. Hansson (Eds.), *Handbook of bereavement: Theory, research, and intervention* (pp. 129-142). Cambridge: Cambridge University Press.

Middletown, W., Raphael, B., Martinek, N., & Nisso, V. (1993). Pathological grief reactions. In: M. S. Stroebe, W. Stroebe, & R. O. Hansson (Eds.), *Handbook of bereavement: Theory, research, and intervention* (pp. 44-74). Cambridge: Cambridge University Press.

Pennebaker, J. W. (1982). *The psychology of physical symptoms*. New York: Springer.

Rosen, G. (1975). Nostalgia: A 'forgotten' psychological disorder. *Psychological Medicine, 5,* 340-354.

Rowles, G. D. (1983). Place and personal identity in old age: Observations from Appalachia. *Journal of Environmental Psychology, 3,* 299-314.

Rowles, G. D. (1984). Aging in rural environments. In: I. Altman, M. P. Lawton, & J. F. Wohlwill (Eds.), *Elderly people and the environment* (pp. 129-157). New York: Plenum.

Rubinstein, R. L., & Parmelee, P. A. (1992). Attachment to place and the representation to the life course by the elderly. In: I. Altman & S. M. Low (Eds.), *Place attachment* (pp. 139-164). New York: Plenum.

Rümke, R. C. (1940). Over heimwee [On homesickness]. *Nederlands Tijdschrift voor de Geneeskunde, 84,* 3658-3665.

Schachter, S., & Singer, J. (1962). Cognitive, social, and physiological determinants of emotion. *Psychological Review, 69,* 379-399.

Scott, J. P. (1987). The emotional basis of attachment and separation. In: J. L. Sacksteder, D. P. Schwartz, & Y. Akabande (Eds.), *Attachment and the therapeutic process* (pp. 43-62). Madison: International Universities Press.

Solomon, R. L. (1980). The opponent-process theory of acquired motivation: The costs of pleasure and the benefits of pain. *American Psychologist, 35,* 691-712.

Van Tilburg, M. A. L., Vingerhoets, A. J. J. M., & Van Heck, G. L. (1996a). Homesickness: A review of the literature. *Psychological Medicine, 26,* 899-912.

Van Tilburg, M. A. L., Vingerhoets, A. J. J. M., Van Heck, G. L., & Kirschbaum, C. (1996b). Mood changes in homesick persons during a holiday trip. *Psychotherapy and Psychosomatics, 65,* 91-96.

Watson, J. B., & Rayner, R. (1920). Conditioned emotional reactions. *Journal of Experimental Psychology, 3,* 1-14.

Zajonc, R. B. (1968). Attitudinal effects of mere exposure. *Journal of Personality and Social Psychology, Monograph Supplement, 9,* 1-27.

Zajonc, R. B. (1971). Attraction, affiliation, and attachment. In: J. F. Eisenberg & W. S. Dillon (Eds.), *Man and beast: comparative social behavior* (pp. 141-179). Washington DC: Smithsonian Institution Press.

2 Culture Shock, Homesickness and Adaptation to a Foreign Culture

ADRIAN FURNHAM

Introduction

What is it like being a sojourner in a foreign country? Do 'foreigners' do as well as 'natives'? How well do they cope with the culture of the country in which they are studying? Is there much evidence of psychological distress among sojourners, be they businessmen, diplomats, missionaries, the military or students? Foreign and exchange *students* have been the topic of academic research for a very long time (Bock, 1970; Brislin, 1979; Byrnes, 1966; Furnham & Tresize, 1983; Tornbiorn, 1982; Zwingmann & Gunn, 1963).

Well over a million young people go abroad to study at a foreign university. The experience of studying in a foreign country leaves a powerful impression on young people that may last all their lives. For a few the experience is negative and they recall the loneliness, homesickness and rejection of the foreign country, but for most the experience is very enriching; so much so that some people prefer never to return home and to continue living in their new country. As a result of the increase in student movement much has been written on this topic (De Verthelyi, 1995; Jenkins, 1983; Kagan & Cohen, 1990; Neto, 1995; Searle & Ward, 1990).

The increase in studies on 'foreign' or international students is probably a function of a number of issues (Crano & Crano, 1993; Furukawa & Shibayama, 1993, 1994; Kagan & Cohen, 1990; Harris, 1995; Sandhu, 1994). This include the large increase in their numbers; the fact that a significant number fail, drop-out or have serious psychological and medical problems whilst abroad *and* adapting once they return; developing theoretical work on the experience of sojourners; and existence of specialist academic journals that focus on the issues associated with foreign student exchange.

But foreign students are not the only sojourning group worthy of research. More and more research has focused on the difficulties of businessmen and women and their families who go abroad. Studies on business people who have moved from one area or country to another have come up with evidence of unhappiness, distress and poor adjustment (Torbiorn, 1982; De Verthelyi, 1995; Furnham & Bochner, 1986). Of course, this is not always the case and, as research has shown, there are a large and complex number of variables determining the actual adjustment of particular individuals. At the same time, it is probably safe to say that overall, business people experience less difficultly than, say, students or other sojourners moving to new environments. There may be a number of reasons for this: business people are usually posted elsewhere for a set, specific and relatively short period of time; businessmen and businesswomen are posted abroad for a specific purpose, usually to deal with particular technical and managerial problems; business people have strong sponsorship, are given financial incentives for working abroad and often their lifestyle overseas is an improvement on what they have left behind; a tour abroad often increases opportunities for advancement on return; in contrast to students (and some migrants), business people tend to be older and are usually more mature; businesses often provide accommodation enclaves, 'old-hand' guides and a social-support network that insulates the sojourner against the initial difficulties and surprises of movement; because businesses are primarily interested in the work their employees do, the employees' time is carefully structured and scheduled. Finally, the social relationships both inside and outside the workplace are probably more likely to be on an equal footing for business people rather than for students.

However, rather than look at the experiences of different sojourning groups, this chapter will focus on the definition of a relationship between the related concepts of culture shock, homesickness, and adaptation (or acculturization).

Culture shock: an unexpected experience

The culture shock 'hypothesis' or 'concept' implies that the experience of visiting or living in a new culture is an unpleasant surprise or shock, partly because it is unexpected, and partly because it may lead to a negative evaluation of one's own and/or the other culture (Cleveland *et al.*, 1963).

The anthropologist Oberg (1960) was the first to have used the term. In a brief and largely anecdotal article he mentions at least six aspects of culture shock. These include:

1. *Strain* due to the effort required making necessary psychological adaptations.
2. *A sense of loss and feelings of deprivation* in regard to friends, status, profession, and possessions.
3. Being *rejected* by/and or rejecting members of new culture.
4. *Confusion* in role, role expectations, values, feeling and self-identity.
5. *Surprise, anxiety* even *disgust* and *indignation* after becoming aware of cultural differences.
6. *Feelings of impotence* due to not being able to cope with the new environment.

Researchers since Oberg have seen culture shock as a frequently occurring process of adaptation to cultural differences. Others have attempted to improve and extend Oberg's definition and concept of culture shock. Guthrie (1975) has used the term *culture fatigue*, Smalley (1963) *language shock*, Byrnes (1966) *role shock* and Ball-Rokeach (1973) *pervasive ambiguity*. In doing so different researchers have simply placed the emphasis on different problems – language, physical irritability, role ambiguity.

Bock (1970) described culture shock as primarily an emotional reaction that follows from not being able to understand, control and predict another's behavior. When customary experiences no longer seem relevant or applicable, peoples' usual behavior changes to becoming 'unusual.' Lack of familiarity with environment (etiquette, ritual) has this effect, as do the experiences of use of time (Hall, 1959). This theme is reiterated by all writers in the field (Lundsteldt, 1963).

Culture shock nowadays is seen as a temporary stress reaction where salient psychological and physical rewards are generally uncertain, and hence, difficult to control or predict. Thus a person is anxious, confused and apparently apathetic until he or she has had time to develop a new set of cognitive constructs to understand and enact the appropriate behavior. Writers about culture shock have often referred to individuals lacking points of reference, social norms and rules to guide their actions and understand others' behavior. This is very similar to the attributes studies under the heading of *alienation* and *anomie*, which includes powerlessness, meaninglessness, normlessness, self and social estrangement and social isolation (Seeman, 1959).

In addition, ideas associated with *anxiety* pervade the culture shock literature. Observers have pointed to a continuous general 'free-floating' anxiety which affects peoples' normal behavior. Lack of self-confidence, distrust of others and psychosomatic complaints are also common (May, 1970). Furthermore, people appear to lose their inventiveness and spontaneity, and become obsessively concerned with orderliness (Nash, 1967).

Most of the investigations of culture shock have been descriptive, in that they have attempted to list the various difficulties that sojourners experience, and their typical reactions. Less attention has been paid to explain for whom the shock will be more or less intense (e.g., the old or the less educated); what determines which reaction a person is likely to experience; how long they remain in a period of shock, and so forth. The literature seems to suggest that all people will suffer culture shock to some extent, which is always thought of as being unpleasant and stressful. This assumption needs to be empirically supported. In theory some people need not experience any negative aspects of shock; instead they may seek out these experiences for their enjoyment. Sensation-seekers, for instance, might be expected not to suffer any adverse effects but to enjoy the highly arousing stimuli of the unfamiliar. People with multi-cultural backgrounds or experiences may also adapt more successfully. For instance, Adler (1975) and David (1971) have stated that although culture shock is more often associated with negative consequences, it may, in mild doses, be important for self-development and personal growth. Culture shock is seen as transitional experience, which can result in the adoption of new values, attitudes and behavior patterns.

Thus, although different writers have put emphasis on different aspects of culture shock, there is agreement that exposure to new culture is usually stressful. Fewer researchers have seen the positive side of culture shock whether for those individuals who revel in exciting and different environments, or for those whose initial discomfort leads to personal growth. The quality and quantity of culture shock has been shown to be related to the amount of *difference* between the visitor's (sojourners', managers') culture and the culture of the country they are visiting or working in (Babiker *et al.*, 1980). These differences refer to the numerous culture differences in social beliefs and behaviors. The defining characteristics of culture shock are that it is unexpected, and for the most part, negative. Its effects may be long-lasting and ultimately beneficial.

Homesickness and the desire to return

References to homesickness occur in all languages over many centuries. In the eighteenth century, medical texts occasionally explained pathology in terms of homesickness. It is, of course, also experienced by people who move *within*, rather than *between* countries as they too have left their home. The key psychological features of homesickness appear to be a strong preoccupation with thoughts of home, a perceived need to go home, a sense of grief for the home (people, place and things) and a concurrent feeling of unhappiness, disease and disorientation in the new place which is conspicuously, not home. Home represents both people and places, and is specifically about the familiar, safe and predictable environment. It represents, in its mildest form, a longing to be back home, and in its most severe form, an obsession.

In a number of studies, Fisher investigated the causes and correlates of homesickness (Fisher *et al.*, 1985; Fisher & Hood, 1987). She found that 60%, of her mainly native sample of students at a small Scottish university, suffered from homesickness. In order to tease out the experience of the homesick vs. the non homesick she asked them various questions. She found no age, sex or home-environment factors (i.e., city vs. country) as good predictors of homesickness. Compared to those who did not report homesickness, however; the homesick students: lived further from home; were attending a university which was not their first choice; were less satisfied with their current residence; were less satisfied with present, relative to past, friendships; expect their friendships to be better in the future than at present.

Fisher's studies also found an association between homesickness reporting and a greater number of cognitive failures, poor concentration, handing in work late and decrements in work quality. These data suggest that homesickness is a potentially important phenomenon that may exercise a considerable influence on academic performance, at least over the short term.

More recently, Brewin *et al.* (1989) investigated some of the determinants of homesickness and reactions to homesickness in two samples of first-year English psychology students who had left home for the first time. Homesickness was found to be a reasonably common but short-lived phenomenon, and was predicted longitudinally by greater self-reported dependency on the other people and by higher estimates of the frequency of homesickness among students in general. Although homesickness was equally common in men and women, women were much more likely to discuss their feelings with others and to respond by being more affiliative. Greater anxiety and depression about homesickness were also associated with more confiding behavior. There was a suggestion that homesick male students who were more likely to seek out others with homesickness, perceived homesickness as more common.

Homesickness is clearly less debilitating than culture shock. The two concepts are related, but there are various differences between them. Culture shock nearly always involves movement to another country while homesickness does not; culture shock is usually unanticipated whereas homesickness is not; culture shock is pervasive whereas homesickness is less so; there are fewer long-term benefits from experiencing homesickness as culture shock; homesickness is nearly always conceived of negatively while culture shock is sometimes a pleasurable experience. Acculturation stress may be seen as a consequence of culture shock (and, to a limited extent, homesickness). It is essentially the stress that results from perceiving, experiencing and adapting to different culturally prescribed and proscribed norms. Acculturation stress is part function of the amount of culture shock experienced, but also a function of other individual difference variables. Indeed, personality (i.e., neuroticism), demographic and ability (i.e., intelligence, linguistic ability) factors may be the best predictors of both culture shock and acculturation stress in sojourners. The concept of adaptation usually refers to the process whereby individuals reduce acculturation stress and learn the 'grammar' of the new culture. The time taken in cultural adaptation is primarily a function of the degree of culture shock and acculturation shock involved.

To any research newcomer to this literature, the use of so many terms, at times synonymously, and at times with specific and distinct meaning, is difficult. Further, this problem is not confined to the English speaking literature.

There is clearly an overlap between these two concepts. People experiencing culture shock may or may not be homesick. Equally, the homesick need not be in a foreign culture to feel the longing to be back home.

Acculturation stress

Many terms are used in this diverse, yet fast-growing, literature to mean virtually the same thing. These include: cross-cultural *adaptation* (Anderson, 1994); socio-cultural *adjustment* (Searle & Ward, 1990); and acculturative *stress* (Sam & Berry, 1995; Smart & Smart, 1995). Different authors define and measure this stress quite differently. Thus, Sam and Berry (1995) measure it by negative self-evaluation, depressive tendencies and psychological and somatic symptoms. Others measure stress by a combination of psychological and socio-cultural adjustment questionnaires (Searle & Ward, 1990). Rogler *et al.* (1991) in a review specifically on Hispanic migrants into Mexico found that five measures of acculturation are frequently used: intergroup and intergenerational comparisons, language usage, self-report inventories, specifically developed scales and simply length of residence. They note that measures of distress in mental health status usually concern general adaptation and adjustment, psychological symptoms, delinquency or deviant behavior and alcohol abuse.

Sam (1995) developed a very simple ten-item questionnaire based on four distinct types of acculturation that had been identified: assimilation, integration, separation and marginalization.

"*Assimilation* is the outcome when immigrant group members choose to identify solely with the culture of the larger society and to relinquish their ties to their ethnic culture. *Integration* involves a strong identification and involvement with one's traditional ethnic culture, as well as that of the larger host society. *Marginalization* is characterized by a rejection and/or lack of involvement in one's own traditional ethnic culture, as well as the culture of the larger society. *Separation* entails an exclusive involvement in one's traditional cultural values and norms, coupled with little or no interaction with members and the culture of the larger society. These four acculturation attitudes are sometimes referred to as modes of acculturation" (Sam, 1995: 240).

Some researchers have reviewed the literature in an attempt to clarify some of the major issues surrounding this important but nebulous concept (Smart & Smart, 1995). They argue that there are seven critical features associated with acculturation stress. It affects physical health (deleteriously); affects decision making; impairs occupational functioning; contributes to role entrapment and status leveling; may contribute to strained and ineffective counselor-client relations; is related to lack of role models; and acculturation stress may be increased when there are minimal rewards for learning English/native language.

Anderson (1994), in a thorough review of this literature notes four rather different models used to understand adaptation. The first is the *recuperation* model, which focuses on the recovery from shock as the mechanism for accommodation to life in the new strange land. The second is the *learning process* model, which focuses on the learning of new skills. Communication theorists and behavioristically-oriented social skills trainers both focus on the acquisition of insights and behavioral patterns as the key to adaptation. The third model is the *psychological journey* model, which focuses on the stages and features from being at the fringe of a culture to being at the center. The fourth is the *equilibrium* model, which sees adaptation as a dynamic and cyclical process of tension reduction and change. To a large extent, these are adaptation models, which have concepts like tension, drive, need and uncertainty.

Anderson (1994) argues that each model has something, which is necessary but not sufficient for the process of change. Further, they may be over-simplistic and do not define their terms well. She distinguishes between adjustment, which is the reduction or satisfaction of short-term drives, while adaptation is that which is valuable for long-term survival. She argues that there are six simple principles for adaptation, such as: it involves adjustment and learning; it is cyclical, continuous and interactive, and implies personal development. She stresses the fact that the process involves affecting cognition *and* behavior. Further, the experience has the potential for being both positive and negative. Like Furnham and Bochner (1986), she would prefer that cultural adaptation be conceived not as a mental health concept, but as one of learning, development and competence, in response to new challenges.

Ward, who has carried out programmatic research in this area (Searle & Ward, 1990; Ward & Kennedy, 1993a,b; Ward & Searle, 1991), has also noted different conceptual models around the acculturation/adaptation concept. A complex phenomenon such as cross-cultural transition requires a framework that combines psychological, socio-cultural and external (socio-economic) variables (e.g., the level of development in the host country compared with that of the home country), to fully describe and understand it. However, since all these factors have been found to be of at least some predictive validity, they need to be integrated within a bigger theoretical framework. The failed attempt to find a simple and universal explanation gave rise to more systematic research, comparing types of sojourners (Berry *et al.*, 1987), or groups of sojourners that vary in cultural distance to the host country (Ward & Kennedy, 1993a,b).

According to this author the concept of a universal adjustment pattern for all cultural transitions, at first advocated by many (Church, 1982), has been discarded. Ward and Kennedy (1993b) argued that socio-cultural variables have been neglected to the disadvantage of both theory and research. Ward and colleagues have maintained that adjustment or adaptation during cross-cultural transitions can be broadly divided into two categories: psychological and socio-cultural (Searle & Ward, 1990; Stone-Feinstein & Ward, 1990; Ward & Searle, 1991). The former refers to feelings of well-being and satisfaction, while the latter is concerned with the ability to 'fit in' or negotiate interactive aspects of the host culture. Ward and Kennedy (1993) offer three additional points regarding psychological and socio-cultural adjustment. First, although inter-related, psychological and socio-cultural adaptation to cross-cultural transitions are predicted by different types of variables. Second, the predictors of psychological and socio-cultural adaptation may be distinguished as core and peripheral, that is, some predictors retain significance regardless of the motivations for the move (e.g., sojourners, refugees, etc.), or the groups' origins and destinations, while other predictors are situation and culture-specific. Thirdly, the magnitude of the relationship between psychological and socio-cultural adjustment varies according to specific groups and contexts. They suggest that the psychological socio-cultural distinction provides a basic framework for the integration of existing literature and for the future exploration of the process and outcome of culture contact and change.

＊ Ward and colleagues also emphasized that all contributing adjustment variables (e.g., social support, life events) should be distinguished into those which are culture-specific, and those, which are culture-general. Whereas some variables were found to be robust predictors of adjustment in all settings, other variables were shown to be more culture-sensitive. In addition, Ward and Kennedy (1993a,b) recommended distinguishing the measurement of adjustment into that of *psychological* adaptation (measured by mood), and that of socio-*cultural* adaptation (measured by social (competence). For psychological adaptation or adjustment, the following variables were found to be non culture-specific: locus of control, life changes, and social support (Ward & Kennedy, 1993a). Core predictors of socio-cultural adjustment are: culture distance (Furnham & Bochner, 1982), command of language and general knowledge about the host culture (Ward & Kennedy, 1993a).

Personality (e.g., extraversion) and host national contact are both good examples of culture-specific variables. While extraversion was found to facilitate psychological adjustment in a particular cultural setting (Searle & Ward, 1990), this personality trait also seemed to predict the well-being in other transition situations (Armes & Ward, 1989). Ward and Kennedy (1993a,b) concluded therefore that psychological adjustment was dependent on the 'fit' between sojourner personality and host culture. Host national contact, reported by some to have a positive affect on psychological adjustment (Church, 1982), is also said to have the opposite effect. Again, the amount of interaction with host nationals appears to be affected by such socio-cultural factors as command of language.

There appears to be some consensus that the concept of acculturation stress needs some careful and thoughtful analysis. It may be wise to disregard the concept altogether, because acculturation is not always stressful. Further, because clinical, cross-cultural, educational and organizational psychologists have all taken an interest in the acculturization process, they seem to have put their individual stamp on it. Consequently, it is possible to see a clinical or mental health interpretation being somewhat different from a learning or educational perspective. More recent papers have attempted to classify different approaches and categorize the important variables that play a part in the process (Furnham & Erdmann, 1995).

What causes culture shock and poor adaptation?

The extensive but varied educational psychological, psychiatric and sociological literature on sojourners' adjustment has been heavy on data but light on theory (James & Hastings, 1993). Various common-sense hypotheses have been found wanting while most researchers tend to be more exploratory than specifically theory testing. Ptak *et al.* (1995) reported the results of an interesting survey with 94 cross-cultural trainers with between 8 and 45 years' experience. They found that the experienced trainers disagreed about the components, approaches and philosophies of training that novices must address. The following questions indicate the specific areas of concern (Ptak *et al.*, 1995:449):

1. Should initial cross-cultural training programs be conducted before departure or after exposure to the new culture?
2. How do you balance your time with the need to transfer information (e.g., through lectures) and also prepare trainees for the emotional aspects of cross-cultural adjustment (e.g., experimental activities)?
3. Should simulations be a priority?

4. Should 'actor/entertainer' qualities be valued in a presenter?
5. How comfortable should participants be in the training setting?
6. Is learning to live in a new culture always an uncomfortable process?
7. Is a cross-cultural trainer also a counselor?
8. Where do you stand along the spectrum between using other peoples' ideas as your own and copyrighting material and ideas so that no-one can use them without authorization?
9. Should evaluations be standard procedure and do you consider culturally appropriate evaluations?

Furnham and Bochner (1986) have outlined and discussed at least eight possible explanations for the empirical data. As the cause implies cure, it seems most important to be clear as to what may be the major cause of culture shock.

a   Loss, grief and mourning

The concept of loss, and more particularly the work on grief, mourning and bereavement, has been applied to many areas of human experience. Migration (but to some extent all forms of geographic movement) involves being deprived of specific relationships or significant objects (Munoz, 1980). These include family, friends and occupational status as well as a host of important physical variables ranging from food to weather patterns. The loss may be followed by grief (a stereotyped set of psychological and physiological reactions, biological in origin) and mourning (conventional bereavement behavior determined by the mores and customs of society). Indeed it is the similarity between various documented symptoms of grief, and the *stages* or *phases* of grief, which have most interested researchers on migration and mental health. Because bereavement behavior is to some extent culturally determined, this may account for various differences in the reaction pattern of migrants and sojourners from different cultures.

However, there are a number of problems with the analogy between grief and migration. First, it is presumed that all migrants, sojourners and travelers experience negative, grief-like reactions, which is clearly not the case. Second, although the grief literature does take into account individual and cultural differences, it makes no specific predictions as to what type of people suffer more or less grief, over what period or what form the grief will take. Third, counseling for the grieving would seem highly inappropriate for migrants, who need information and support as much as therapy.

b   Fatalism (locus of control)

There is a considerable literature in personality and social psychology on a person's perceived locus of control. *Fatalism* is therefore the generalized expectation that outcomes are determined by forces such as powerful others, luck or fate and is the opposite of *instrumentalism*, which is the generalized expectation that outcomes and contingent on one's own behavior. The dimension has also been described as a perception of *general self-efficacy and control* over events in one's own life. This explanation of culture shock suggests that those who come from cultures or societies where instrumentalism (vs. fatalism) is encouraged, tend to adapt faster and more successfully (Ross *et al.*, 1983). The explanations should be able to account for the different distress rates of different immigrant groups. For instance, immigrants from a country whose religion is fatalistic should have more difficulty in adjusting than migrants from a country where personal responsibility is valued. However, there is ample evidence to suggest that this is not the case. For instance, Cochrane (1983) has shown that Indians adjust particularly well when immigrating to Britain yet supposedly come from a fatalistic culture. Another problem lies in self-selection. In order to voluntarily migrate (as opposed to being a refugee) one has to assume considerable personal responsibility and control over one's own affairs - financial, social and familial. It may be argued therefore that most people who migrate have, by definition, an internal locus of control and are therefore relatively homogeneous irrespective of their culture of origin.

c *Selective migration*
One of the oldest and most popular explanations for the different patterns of reaction to new environments by migrants is the neo-Darwinian idea of selective migration. It is an extension of the principle of natural selection, which states that all living organisms that cope best with the exigencies of the environment become the prevailing type. When people are selected for a new environment to which they are particularly suited, they will cope better than others who are not so matched (Cochrane, 1983).

There are a number of appealing features to this approach. First, it describes why different migrant groups to the same country at the same time may adapt differently because of different selective processes. Second, it tends to highlight which combination of general coping strategies is most appropriate to the particular requirements of a certain country. Hence, it can explain why people who were 'selected' by similar processes from the same country may adjust well in particular 'new' countries but not in others. However, this hypothesis has a number of limitations. First, considering the selective processes of the migrants themselves, it is not clear which barrier or obstacles select for adaptation and which do not. The sheer number of obstacles alone may predict a certain type of fitness or motivation but does not imply that those people necessarily adapt well. For instance, education, physical fitness, language ability and financial security may be important positive factors with regard to selection, while others such as religion may not. Rarely, if ever, do the optimally adaptive selectors exist in isolation from those factors that do not discriminate.

d *Expectations*
The more accurate, objective and comprehensive a sojourner/migrant's expectations of the visited country, culture, university, the more successful his/her adaptation.

Research findings suggest that high expectations that cannot and do not get fulfilled are related to poor adjustment and increased mental illness (Cochrane, 1983; Feather, 1982).

Expectancy-value theories have proved useful in predicting people's reactions to various types of adversity. Yet this theoretical approach is not without problems. First, it should be pointed out that the migrants have a wealth of expectations, some relating to social, economic, geographic and political aspects of life in their new country. They are bound to be wrong about some, expecting too much or too little. What is unclear is *which* expectations about *what* aspects of life in the new country are more important to adjustment than others. Second, the way in which unfulfilled expectations lead to poor adjustment is far from clear. For instance, do disappointed or unfulfilled expectations lead to anxiety, depression or anger? Third, from the above literature it would seem that having low expectations may be better for adjustment but worse for overall social mobility. Further, apart from refugees, few people would voluntarily migrate if their expectations were too low.

e   *Negative life-events*

For nearly twenty years psychologists, psychiatrists and sociologists have been collecting evidence on the relationships between recent stressful life-events and psychological and physical illness (Rahe *et al.*, 1964). The basic idea is that negative life-events, such as the death of a spouse, divorce or losing one's job, make people ill; the more negative in terms of intensity, duration, and consequences of the events, the more likely that one will become ill. Some research has also shown that *any change* in one's daily routine, not necessarily a negative one, has similar deleterious effects, although these findings have been questioned. Negative life-events have been associated with responses as varied as depression, neurosis, tuberculosis, coronary heart disease, skin diseases, hernias and cancer (Dohrenwend & Dohrenwend, 1974). Although the mechanism by which negative life-events influence health and illness is by no means clear, most studies have demonstrated a significant relationship between the two. Monroe (1982) has listed three reasons for the growth in this research area: first, it allows one to examine the attractive but elusive link between psychosocial processes and physical/psychological functioning; second, its conceptual basis is congruent with other areas of research; and third, the clinical implications seem clear and straightforward.

What is perhaps most surprising is how little the life-event literature appears to have filtered into the migration and the mental-health literature. Though it may not serve to account for a great deal of variance, the range, intensity and perceived threat of migrant's life-changes may go some way towards explaining the nature of the link between mental health and migration.

f   *Social support networks: reduction in social support*

There is rapidly growing, already considerable body of literature in clinical, community, medical and applied psychology regarding the supportive functions of interpersonal relationships (Sarason *et al.*, 1983). In the main these findings suggest that social support is directly related to increased speed and quality of adaptation as well as breaking the clear links between stress and illness.

Thus the various types of support provided by interpersonal relationships (emotional, financial, informational) play a crucial role in determining a person's general adaptive functioning and sense of well-being. It has been shown that the social networks of neurotics differ significantly from those of normal people and that persons with a well-developed primary group are substantially protected against neurotic symptoms (Brown *et al.*, 1975). Because migration often involves the leaving behind of family, friends and acquaintances, such as work colleagues and neighbors, sources of social support are reduced and there is, according to the theory, a consequent increase in physical and mental illness. Supportive relationships with family and friends are no longer available to the same extent to migrants and sojourners. Hence, the stresses associated with migration are not buffered against in the usual way.

g *Value differences*

The differences in values that exist between many cultures have also been used to account for the misunderstandings, distress and difficulties experienced by cross-cultural travelers. Ever since the work of Merton (1938) on the relationship between social structure and anomie, sociologists and psychologists have seen a link between deviance, delinquency and mental disorder, and a conflict in cultural values. There is a rich, interdisciplinary literature on the definition and consequences of values. Hofstede's (1984) work on four underlying value dimensions of cultures has done for cross-cultural psychology what trait theory has done for personality – namely provided a descriptive map whereby cultures can be compared.

To understand the consequences of value differences for migrants it is important to take three variables into consideration: the quality and quantity of differences in salient values between the hosts' and migrants' societies; the tolerance for varying cultural value systems within the same society; and the individuals' cognitive complexity, ability and motivation to change their cultural value system. Certain values, like stoicism and self-help, are perhaps more adaptive than others (Hofstede, 1984). It may, however, be that the values relate more to the reporting or not reporting of illness and unhappiness than to how people cope with stress. Value systems, then, may be useful predictors of both how much strain travelers feel and how they cope with the strain.

h *Social skills*

It was Argyle and Kendon (1967) who first suggested that it may be useful to construe the behavior of people interacting with each other, as a mutually organized, skilled performance. Inter-personal difficulties occur when this performance breaks down, falter, or indeed cannot be successfully initiated in the first place.

Socially inadequate individuals are people who have failed to learn a wide range of inter-personal skills, due to poor child-parent and peer group relationships, and because of other forms of social and physical deprivation. Such individuals are incompetent in, or incapable of, certain verbal exchanges; they are unable to accurately interpret or perform non-verbal signals; they may not have mastered the social conventions of the society at large, and may also be unaware of many of the rules of social behavior pertaining to their own particular sub-group. Thus it could be said that socially inadequate individuals are often like *strangers in their own land and culture*. Some of the specific behaviors which the socially incompetent perform unsatisfactorily include expressing attitudes, feelings and emotions; adopting the appropriate proxemic posture; understanding the gaze patterns of the people they are interacting with; carrying out ritualized routines such as greetings, leave-taking, self-disclosure, making or refusing requests; and asserting themselves. All of these elements of social interaction have been shown to vary across cultures.

Turning this argument around, it follows that people who are new to a culture or sub-culture will not have been socialized in the rules and routines of behavior pertaining to that society, and will therefore, at least initially, be socially unskilled in their new environment. The social skills model as it is being extended here has clear implications for the understanding and management of cross-cultural incompetence. The theoretical guidelines for remedial action are quite clear. First, it is necessary to identify the *specific* social situations, which trouble that particular sojourner, and then give the individual *specific* training in those skills that are lacking. Social skills training nearly always involves four key elements: instruction, modeling, practice and feedback. It has been shown to produce dramatic and rapid behavior change though there are doubts about the generalizability of training over different situations and time (Furnham, 1985).

Training intercultural skills

Few people would disagree with the idea that men or women working in culturally different environments require some sort of orientation program. Many techniques are available which differ according to theoretical orientation, length or training, type of training, etc. For instance, Brislin (1979) has listed five such programs; self-awareness training (in which people learn about the cultural bases of their own behavior); cognitive training (where people are presented with various facts about other cultures); attribution training (where people are learning the explanation of behavior from the point of view of people in other cultures); behavior modification (where people are asked to analyze the aspects of their culture that they find rewarding or punishing), and experiential learning (where people actively participate in realistic simulations). These techniques do overlap and are not mutually exclusive.

Furnham and Bochner (1986) have examined some of these in greater detail.

a   *Information giving*
The most common type of cross-cultural orientation usually involves providing prospective sojourners with specific information about their new culture. However, the effectiveness of such illustrative program is limited, because firstly the facts are often too general to have any clear specific application in particular, notably business circumstances; secondly the facts emphasis the exotic, yet, tend to ignore the mundane but more commonly occurring happenings; thirdly such programs give the false impression that a culture can be learned in a few easy lessons, whereas all that they convey is a superficial, incoherent and often misleading picture which glosses over the culture's hidden agenda; and finally, even if the facts are recommended they do not necessarily lead to action, or the correct action. If the cognitive information training is to be of any practical use it must be combined with some form of practical experiential learning in the appropriate setting.

b   *Cultural sensitization*
Programs based on this approach set out to provide trainees with information about other cultures, as well as to heighten their awareness about the cultural basis of their own behavior, and how the practices of their society differ from those of the host country. The aim is therefore to *compare* and *contrast* the two or more cultures, look at various behaviors from the perspective of each society, and thus develop a sensitivity to, and awareness of, cultural relativity. This view holds that human values, beliefs and behaviors are absolute and universal, and that what a particular individual believes to be true and good will depend on the norms prevailing in that person's society; norms that other societies may reject. Such programs often operate at two levels: the aim to achieve self-awareness about the model values and attitudes that are typically held by members of one's society; and to gain insight into one's own personal traits, attitudes and prejudices.

c   *Isomorphic attributions*
Many researchers have pointed out that a potential obstacle to effective cross-cultural communication is the inability of the participants to understand the causes of each other's behavior, i.e., to make correct attributions about the other's actions. Effective intercultural relations require isomorphic attributions, which means that observers offer the same cause of reason for actors' (others) behaviors as they would for themselves. The likelihood of making isomorphic attributions decreases as the divergence between the subjective cultures of the participants increases, and explains why intercultural relations are often characterized by mutual hostility, misunderstanding and poor effect.

One solution is to train individuals to understand the subjective culture of the other group, which in practice means teaching them how to make 'correct' behavioral attributions. A great deal depends on which particular critical incidents are selected to form the basic curriculum. Inevitably, exotic, strange and hence less common events tend to be given greater prominence than the less interesting but more frequently encountered day-to-day problems that make up the bread-and-butter content of inter-cultural contacts.

d *Learning by doing*

The limitations of information-based orientation programs led to various attempts to expose trainees to supervised real or stimulated second culture experience. Behaviorally based culture training programs rely on role-playing encounters between trainees and persons pretending to come from some other cultures, or if other-culture professional personnel are available, with such persons.

The vast majority of sojourners, or those who come into contact with members of other cultures in their own societies, receive no systematic culture training whatsoever. The little 'training' that does occur is done informally by experienced migrants who pass on useful information to the new visitors. In theory, experienced sojourners should have that rare capacity, but in practice some may have highly specialized, distorted, or even prejudiced views of one or both of their cultures, and perpetuate these distortions in the informal training they impart to highly impressionable newcomers.

e *Intercultural (social) skills training*

Although there are a number of different approaches to social skills training they share various elements in common. The first is an *assessment* or 'diagnosis' or particular problem (e.g., assertiveness) areas of situations (e.g., chairing meetings) that the person has or is likely to encounter. The second stage is an *analysis* or *discussion* of the elements in these problem areas possibly followed by a modeling exercise where a trainer enacts the role. This in turn is followed by a *role-play* by the trainee with critical *feedback* in length following each practice. The number, range and variety of contexts in which the role-plays are enacted add to the generalizability of the training. Trainees are also encouraged to do homework exercise between role-play and feedback sessions.

Conclusion

The world-wide growth in overseas students, traveling businessmen, refugees and migrants in the late twentieth century has been remarkable. Despite being bright, healthy and adaptable, many of these sojourning students and migrating people suffer homesickness and culture shock. For the last 30 years, social scientists have attempted to understand acculturation stress and adaptation, culture shock and homesickness. Because culture shock is a more encompassing concept, it is used more widely than homesickness. Some of these ideas have naturally filtered into the popular consciousness and everyday language. Researchers have spent a great deal of

32

time attempting to clarify concepts, build models or theories of adaptation, and evaluate training methods. Whilst there remains a plethora of clearly related terms, the evidence for what the major causes of adaptation and lack of adaptation are remain in dispute. Various factors have clearly been shown to be predictive of adaptation, but others less so. The research in this area is difficult but important. The costs to individuals alone merit the highest standards of theorizing and empirical research.

References

Adler, P. (1975). The transition experience: An alternative view of culture shock. *Journal of Humanistic Psychology, 15,* 13-23.

Anderson, L. (1994). A new look at an old construct: Cross-cultural adaptation. *International Journal of Intercultural Relations, 18,* 293-328.

Argyle, M., & Kendon, A. (1967). The experimental analysis of social performance. In: L. Berkowitz (Ed.), *Advances in experimental social psychology* (Vol. 3., pp. 55-98). New York: Academic Press.

Armes, K., & Ward, C. (1989). Cross-cultural transitions and sojourner adjustment in Singapore. *Journal of Social Psychology, 12,* 273-275.

Babiker, I., Cox, J., & Miller, P. (1980). The measurement of culture distance and its relationship to medical consultations, symptomatology and examination performance of overseas students at Edinburgh University. *Social Psychiatry, 15,* 109-116.

Ball-Rokeach, S. (1973). From pervasive ambiguity to a definition of the situation. *Sociometry, 36,* 133-145.

Berry, J., Kin, V., Minde, T., & Mok, D. (1987). Comparative studies of ac022l stress. *International Migration Review, 21,* 490-511.

Bochner, S. (Ed.) (1982). *Cultures in contact.* Oxford: Pergamon.

Bock, P. (Ed.) (1970). *Culture shock: a reader in modern psychology.* New York: A. A. Knopf.

Brewin, C., Furnham, A., & Howe, M. (1989). Demographic and psychological determinants of homesickness and confiding among students. *British Journal of Psychology, 80,* 467-477.

Brislin, R. (1979). Orientation programmes for cross-cultural preparation. In: A. Marsella, R. Thorp, & T. Cibrowski (Eds.), *Perspectives on cross-cultural psychology* (pp. 287-305). New York: Academic Press.

Brown, G., Bhrolcham, M., & Harris, T. (1975). Social class and psychiatric disturbance among women in an urban population. *Sociology, 9,* 225-254.

Byrnes, F. (1966). *Americans in technical assistance: A study of attitudes and responses to their role abroad.* New York: Praeger.

Church, A. (1982). Sojourner adjustment. *Psychological Bulletin, 91,* 540-72.

Cleveland, H., Margone, C., & Adams, J. (1963). *The overseas Americans.* New York: McGraw-Hill.

Cochrane, R. (1983). *The social creation of mental illness.* London: Longman.

Collett, P. (1982). Meetings and misunderstandings. In: S. Bochner (Ed.), *Cultures in contact* (pp. 81-89). Oxford: Pergamon.

Crano, S., & Crano, W. (1993). A measure of adjustment strain in international students. *Journal of Cross-Cultural Psychology, 24,* 267-283.

David, K. (1971). Culture shock and the development of self-awareness. *Journal of Contemporary Psychotherapy, 4,* 44-48.

Dohrenwend, B. P, & Dohrenwend, B. S. (1974). *Stressful life events: Their nature and effects.* New York: Wiley.

De Verthelyi, R. (1995). International students' spouses: Invisible sojourners in the culture shock literature. *International Journal of Intercultural Relations, 19,* 387-411.

Feather, N. (Ed.) (1982). *Expectations and actions: Expectancy-value models in psychology.* Hillsdale, NJ: Erlbaum.

Fisher, S., Murray, K., & Frazer, N. (1985). Homesickness, health and efficacy in first year students. *Journal of Environmental Psychology, 5,* 181-195.

Fisher, S., & Hood, B. (1987). The stress of the transition to university: A longitudinal study of psychological disturbance, absent-mindedness and vulnerability to homesickness. *British Journal of Psychology, 78,* 425-441.

Furnham, A. (1985). Social skills training: A European perspective. In: L. L'Abate & M. Milan (Eds.), *Handbook of social skills training and research* (pp. 555-580). New York: Wiley.

Furnham, A., & Bochner, S. (1986). *Culture shock.* London: Methuen.

Furnham, A., & Tresize, L. (1983). The mental health of foreign students. *Social Science & Medicine, 17,* 365-370.

Furnham, A., & Erdmann, S. (1995). Psychological and socio-cultural variables as predictors of adjustment in cross-cultural transitions. *Psychologia, 38,* 238-251.

Furukawa, T., & Shibayama, T. (1993). Predicting maladjustment of exchange students in different cultures: A prospective study. *Social Psychology and Psychiatric Epidemiology, 28,* 142-146.

Furukawa, T., & Shibayama (1994). Factors influencing adjustment of high school students in an international exchange program. *Journal of Nervous and Mental Diseases, 182,* 709-714.

Guthrie, G. (1975). A behavioural analysis of culture learning. In: R. Brislin, S. Bochner, & W. Lonner (Eds.), *Cross-cultural perspectives on learning.* New York: Wiley.

Hall, E. (1959). *The silent language.* Garden City, NY: Doubleday.

Harris, R. (1995). Overseas students in the United Kingdom university system. *Higher Education, 29,* 77-92.

Hofstede, G. (1984). *Culture's consequences: International differences in work-related values.* Beverley Hill, CA: Sage.

Holmes, T., & Rahe, R. (1967). The social readjustment rating scale. *Journal of Psychosomatic Research, 11,* 213-218.

James, W., & Hastings, J. (1993). Cross-cultural counseling: A systematic approach to understanding the issues. *International Journal for the Advancement of Counseling, 16,* 319-322.

Jenkins, H. (Ed.). (1983). *Educating students from other nations.* San Francisco, CA: Jossey-Bass.

Kagan, H., & Cohen, J. (1990). Cultural adjustment of international students. *Psychological Science, 1,* 133-137.

Lundstedt, A. (1963). An introduction to some evolving problems in cross-cultural research. *Journal of Social Issues, 19,* 3-19.

May, R. (1970). The nature of anxiety and its relation to fear. In: A. Elbing (Ed.), *Behavioural decisions in organisation* (pp. 46-64). New York: Scott, Foresman & Co.

Merton, R. (1938). Social structure and anomie. *American Sociological Review, 3,* 672-682.

Monroe, S. (1982). Life events and disorder: event-symptoms associations and the course of disorders. *Journal of Abnormal Psychology, 91,* 14-24.

Munoz, L. (1980). Exile as bereavement: Socio-psychological manifestations of Chilean exiles in Great Britain. *British Journal of Medical Psychology, 53,* 227-232.

Nash, D. (1967). The fate of Americans in Spanish setting: A study of adaptation. *Human Organization, 26,* whole no. 3.

Neto, F. (1995). Predictors of satisfaction with life among second generation migrants. *Social Indicators Research, 35,* 93-116.

34

Oberg, J. (1960). Culture shock: Adjustment to new cultural environments. *Practical Anthropology, 7,* 177-182.

Ptak, C., Cooper, J., & Brislin, R. (1995). Cross-cultural training programmes: Advice and insights from experienced travelers. *International Journal of Intercultural Relations, 19,* 425-453.

Rahe, R., Meyer, M., Smith, M., Kyar, G., & Holmes, T. (1964). Social stress and illness onset. *Journal of Psychosomatic Research, 8,* 35-44.

Rogler, L., Cortes, D., & Malgady, R. (1991). Acculturation and mental health status among Hispanics. *American Psychologist, 46,* 585-597.

Ross, C., Mirowsky, J., & Cockesham, W. (1983). Social class, American culture and fatalism: Their effects on psychological distress. *American Journal of Community Psychology, 11,* 383-398.

Sandhu, D. (1994). An examination of the psychological needs of the international students: Implications for counseling and psychotherapy. *International Journal for the Advancement of Counseling, 17,* 229-239.

Sam, D. (1995). Acculturation attitudes among young immigrants as a function of perceived parental attitudes to culture change. *Journal of Early Adolescence, 15,* 238-251.

Sam, D., & Berry, J. (1995). Acculturation stress among young immigrants in Norway. *Scandinavian Journal of Psychology, 36,* 10-24.

Sarason, I., Levine, H., Basham, R., & Sarason, B. (1983). Assessing social support: The social support questionnaire. *Journal of Personality and Social Psychology, 44,* 127-139.

Searle, W., & Ward, C. (1990). The prediction of psychological and sociocultural adjustment during cross-cultural transition. *International Journal of Intercultural Relations, 14,* 449-464.

Seeman, M. (1959). On the meaning of alienation. *American Sociologist Review, 24,* 783-791.

Smalley, W. (1963). Culture shock, language shock and the shock or self-discovery. *Practical Anthropology, 10,* 49-56.

Smart, J., & Smart, D. (1995). Acculturative stress: The experience of the Hispanic immigrant. *The Counseling Psychologist, 23,* 25-42.

Stone-Feinstein, B. E., & Ward, C. (1990). Loneliness and psychological adjustment of sojourners: New perspectives on culture shock. In: D. Keats, D. Munro, & L. Mann (Eds.), *Heterogeneity in cross-cultural psychology* (pp. 537-547). Lisse, The Netherlands: Swets & Zeitlinger.

Tornbiorn, I. (1982). *Living abroad: Personal adjustment and personnel policy in an overseas setting.* Chichester: Wiley.

Ward, C., & Kennedy, A. (1993a). Psychological and socio-cultural adjustment during cross-cultural transitions. *International Journal of Psychology, 28,* 129-147.

Ward, C., & Kennedy, A. (1993b). Where's the culture in cross-cultural transition? *Journal of Cross-Cultural Psychology, 24,* 221-249.

Ward, C., & Searle, W. (1991). The impact of value discrepancy and cultural identity on psychological and socio-cultural adjustment of sojourners. *International Journal of Intercultural Relations.*

Zwingmann, C., & Gunn, A. (1963). *Uprooting and health: Psycho-social problems of students from abroad.* Geneva, Switzerland: WHO.

3 The Psychological Context of Homesickness

MIRANDA A.L. VAN TILBURG

Introduction

Homesickness is a common experience. Everybody has an intuitive idea about homesickness is and how it is experienced. Many of us can even draw from personal experiences. Throughout history it has also been subject of many poets and writers. The first written accounts of homesickness can be found in the Bible, Psalm 137: "By the rivers of Babylon there we sat down, yeah wept when we remembered Zion" and in Homer's description of Ulysses who was weeping and rolling on the floor when he was thinking of home. From the 17th century onward systematic (case) studies of homesickness have been reported, although they are sparse. For instance, one case described by the 17th-century Swiss physician Johannes Hofer (cited in Rosen, 1975) is of a young man who was lying on his death-bed when homesickness was diagnosed. When he was sent home his condition improved immediately. Another illustration is the case, described by Jaspers (1909), of a 16-year-old maid who starts fires in four places in order to destroy the house. As a consequence she would be useless to the lady of the house and be sent home.

These personal accounts, in either prose or case studies, probably do not do justice to the very different manifestations of homesickness. However, insight into the psychological context of homesickness is very important for the generation of hypotheses. Furthermore, it is helpful in distinguishing homesickness from other more or less related concepts like nostalgia, depression and separation anxiety. The current scientific literature is rather slim and scattered. Therefore, in this chapter I will integrate these findings and discuss the nature of homesickness and the corresponding reactions. However, first homesickness will be differentiated from related concepts like nostalgia and grief.

How does homesickness relate to other concepts?

Homesickness is an emotion which is felt after leaving house and home and is characterized by negative emotions, ruminative cognitions about home, and somatic symptoms. The question is how this feeling can conceptually be distinguished from related emotions and syndromes like nostalgia, separation anxiety, school phobia, grief, depression, adjustment disorder, agoraphobia, depletion anxiety, claustrophobia, and topophilia. In this section homesickness will be compared with each of these concepts and resemblances and differences will be highlighted.

Nostalgia

Nostalgia is a literal translation of the German 'Heimweh' into Greek and was first introduced by Hofer (cited in Werman, 1977). The two terms are often used interchangeably and some authors regard homesickness and nostalgia as the same phenomenon (Rosen, 1975; Zwingmann, 1973a,b). However, in a strict sense they are conceptually different (Werman, 1977). Nostalgia is a yearning or longing for bygone days. In the Oxford Dictionary (1989) it is defined as 'a sentimental longing for things that are in the past.' Homesickness, on the other hand, is defined as 'sadness because one is away from home' (*Oxford Advanced Learner's Dictionary*, 1989). And returning to this home is at least theoretically possible. In addition, homesickness is associated with sadness and negative mood, while the affective coloration of nostalgia can best be described as bittersweet, including both joy and sadness (Werman, 1977).

Separation anxiety and school phobia

In DSM-IV (*American Psychiatric Association*, 1994) separation anxiety and school phobia are described as youth disorders. Separation anxiety is defined as an excessive anxiety concerning separation from attachment figures. School phobia refers to a fear and avoidance of school. In DSM-IV homesickness is included as one possible manifestation of separation anxiety. Thus, in homesickness, separation anxiety and school phobia the child is extremely upset after separation and longs for his or her mother. Therefore, it is very difficult to make a differentiated diagnosis. The concepts can be distinguished on the basis of the kind of separation situation that evokes the feelings of fear and avoidance. The phobic child is fearful of and avoids *school* alone. The separation-anxious child is fearful of and avoids a host of situations related to *separation from an attachment figure*. The homesick child is characterized by fear and avoidance of situations related to *separation from home*. The problem is that, practically, separation from home and from attachment figure often goes together.

Baier and Welch (1992) performed a conceptual analysis in order to distinguish homesickness from related concepts such as separation-anxiety and school phobia. These authors state that separation anxiety is a more serious condition than homesickness: "… homesickness could be present with any one of the DSM-III-R criteria for separation anxiety enumerated under 'A. Excessive anxiety …,' but three additional criteria would be necessary for a diagnosis of separation anxiety" (p. 58). Furthermore, school phobia is differentiated from homesickness in that school phobia is an emotionally paralyzing condition while homesickness is not, according to these authors.

Grief

Grief is the emotional pain or anguish experienced after the loss of a loved one. Bowlby (1980) indicated that after a loss of an attachment figure the person moves through four phases: (1) numbing, unbelief and outbursts of intense distress; (2) yearning and searching for the lost person; (3) disorganization and despair; and (4) reorganization. Moving from home similarly implies multiple losses of persons and objects like a house, places of emotional significance, possessions, friends and family, jobs, roles, etc. Thus, homesickness can be conceived of as a grief-like reaction to losing one's home. Especially Bowlby's (1980) second phase, yearning and searching, bears many resemblances to homesickness.

Fisher (1989) concludes that grief and homesickness are similar in that they are both very specific manifestations of distress associated with a known cause, i.e., a loss. The only way the two concepts can be distinguished is on the basis of the nature of the loss and the associated cognitions. Grief is felt after the loss of a beloved *person*. Missing the deceased person and longing for reunion with this person are associated cognitions. Homesickness, on the other hand, is experienced after leaving home, which is why cognitions are centered on missing home and longing for reunion with home. Leaving home is, however, a reversible loss. Home does not cease to exist and can be contacted, either symbolically or by visits.

Depression

The essential feature of a major depressive episode in DSM-IV (American Psychiatric Association, 1994) is either a depressive mood or the loss of interest in nearly all activities. Other criteria are: weight loss or decrease or increase in appetite, insomnia or hypersomnia, psychomotor agitation or retardation, fatigue, feelings of worthlessness or excessive guilt, diminished ability to think or concentrate, recurrent thoughts of death or suicide. All these symptoms have been observed in the homesick as well. Therefore, homesickness is often considered to be a reactive depression to leaving home (e.g., Baier & Welch, 1992; Eurelings-Bontekoe *et al.*, 1994; Fisher, 1989). Characteristic of the homesick, as opposed to the depressed, are the ruminative and obsessive thoughts about home and the desire to return home. As there are no generally accepted criteria for the diagnosis of homesickness, many homesick adults are being diagnosed as depressed. Whether therapy for depression is also helpful for the homesick has not been systematically evaluated until now.

Adjustment disorder

Homesickness is related to adjustment disorder. According to the DSM-IV (American Psychiatric Association, 1994) criteria, adjustment disorder is a maladaptive response to an identifiable psychosocial stressor occurring within three months and remitting within six months of the termination of the stressor. The reaction must be in excess of a normal and expectable reaction to the stressor(s) and/or it has to impair school or work performances and hinder social activities or interpersonal relationships. Six subtypes have been distinguished which characterize the predominant symptoms. Severe homesickness may be seen as a particular form of two of these subtypes, namely *adjustment disorder with depressed mood* or *adjustment disorder with physical complaints*, when two other conditions are fulfilled, namely being away from home (the stressor) and thinking a lot about home. But if homesickness is not severe enough to hamper daily activities like work and social activities then, according to DSM-IV criteria, homesickness has to be viewed as a *normal* reaction to being away from home. Homesickness can both be labeled as an *acute adjustment disorder* (remittance of symptoms within six months), in the case of persons whose homesickness feelings disappear or persons who return within six months, and as *chronic adjustment disorder* (persistence of symptoms for six months or longer) in cases of severe homesickness.

Agoraphobia

Homesickness also shares some characteristic features with agoraphobia. Agoraphobics fear being in places or situations from which escape might be difficult (or embarrassing), or in which help might not be available, in the event of sudden incapacitation or panic attack. (DSM-IV, APA, 1994). In DSM-IV, a distinction is made between agoraphobia with and without a history of panic disorder. Common agoraphobic situations include being outside home and traveling, which are also common homesick situations. In addition, Fyer (1987) classifies the multiple fears and avoidance behaviors of agoraphobics in: fear of leaving home, fear of being alone, and fear of being away from home. Anxiousness and distress in these situations can either be labeled as agoraphobia or as homesickness. Homesick women have been reported to develop fear-of-fear like cognitions, characteristic for panic disorder with or without agoraphobia (Van Tilburg *et al.*, 1996). However, the homesick do not fear incapacitating or embarrassing symptoms like loss of bladder control, becoming dizzy, fainting, etc., rather they fear the homesickness itself (Van Tilburg *et al.*, 1996). Furthermore, agoraphobia is rare in children (Tearnan *et al.*, 1984), while homesickness is quite common in children. In addition, the homesick have not been reported to fear being alone. Thus, although agoraphobia and homesickness have much in common they are conceptually distinct syndromes.

Depletion anxiety

Verwoerdt (1976, 1980) distinguished three types of anxiety in the elderly: (1) primary anxiety, in response to an overwhelming influx of stimuli; (2) secondary or depletion anxiety, referring to the anticipation of loss of external supplies; and (3) tertiary anxiety, signaling unacceptable impulses or fantasies. Secondary or depletion anxiety is developmentally related to separation anxiety according to Verwoerdt. The anxiety arises due to anticipation of loss of external supplies or object loss and the possibility of isolation and loneliness. This depressive, helpless kind of anxiety is often precipitated or exacerbated by a loss or an environmental change. Thus, homesickness can be conceived of as a special case of depletion anxiety due to the anticipation of losing home. However, depletion anxiety has only been described in the elderly, while homesickness is a psychological state experienced in all age groups.

Claustrophobia

Claustrophobia is an abnormal fear of being in an enclosed space (*Oxford Advanced Learner's Dictionary*, 1989). Claustrophobia is classified under specific phobia, situational type in DSM-IV (American Psychiatric Association, 1994). The diagnosis of a specific phobia is appropriate when there is avoidance, fear, anxious anticipation of encountering the phobic stimulus, interference with daily routines and recognition that the phobia is excessive or unreasonable. Our unpublished data show that claustrophobia coincides with homesickness. Not only do many homesick women report being claustrophobic, the intensity of the claustrophobic feelings seem to vary with the intensity of the feelings of homesickness also. In the homesick the enclosed spaces are feared because escape is difficult or impossible. They express the need to be able to go home whenever they want to. This need is expressed for example by fearing an unknown room when doors en windows are closed because this will hamper their return home. Typically claustrophobic experiences are not reported at home; as the fear is not related to the small space but rather to the inability to go home. Thus, it is as if home has to be near and accessible for the homesick all the time even when being away from home for only a few minutes. Characteristic claustrophobic situations in the homesick are public transport, unknown rooms, crowds, and elevators.

Topophilia

Tuan (1974) described the topophilic sentiment in his book *Topophilia: A study of environmental perception attitudes and values*. Topophilia refers to the affective ties of human beings with their material environment. According to this author the environment can become a carrier of emotionally charged events or the environment can be perceived of. as a symbol. In these cases the topophilic sentiment will be very strong and we are attached to a place. Attachments to surrounding develop naturally. Tuan states: "Beyond clothing, a person invests bits of his emotional life in his home, and beyond the home in his neighborhood. To be forcibly evicted from one's home and neighborhood is to be stripped of a sheathing, which in its familiarity protects the human being from the bewilderments of the outside world" (p. 99). Thus, the topophilic sentiment can be an origin of feelings of homesickness. Homesickness is evoked when people leave the surroundings which they are extremely attached to.

The homesickness experience

If homesickness is conceptually distinct from related emotions and syndromes, the question arises what is homesickness? This is a question we asked 229 homesick women who completed a questionnaire designed to explore several dimensions of the homesickness experience, namely, antecedents, reactions, symptoms, coping and control processes, and causes (derived from Aebischer and Wallbott, 1986). The questionnaire was partly based upon Wallbott and Scherer's (1986) questionnaire for studying emotional experiences. The subjects completed the questionnaire referring to the last time they were in a homesickness situation. The discussion of the results will be guided by a model of the emotion process as developed by Scherer (1986). This model consists of four interrelated aspects: (1) the antecedent situation, (2) the person, (3) the response and reactions, and (4) social regulation and control. In addition to the results of the present study I will draw on knowledge from the literature.

The antecedent situation

Homesickness is considered to be a reaction to having left one's home. Thus, the antecedent situation is the transition from an old familiar environment to a new situation/environment. Which of these two situations, the new or the old, causes the homesickness feelings? Fisher (1989) suggests that both difficulties in separating from the old environment and difficulties in adapting to the new environment can elicit homesickness feelings. However, data from the current study suggests that difficulties with the new environment might not be a major cause or even sufficient condition for the development of homesickness. In contrast, it appears to be the separation from the old environment that elicits the homesickness. For example, our data indicate that homesickness is a *direct* reaction to the separation from home. Most subjects in our study felt homesick before they have had time to explore the new environment. In addition, quite a large number of these subjects were in pleasurable holiday situations with their families and still developed severe homesickness. Moreover, we have recently described a phenomenon we called 'anticipation homesickness' which is experienced before having left the old environment (Van Tilburg et al., 1996). The obsessive thoughts about and the focus on the old environment of the homesick inhibit and interfere with the exploration of and adaptation to the new environment.

As homesickness is a reaction to leaving a familiar environment, it is generally studied in those who have to leave their homes like, conscripts (Bergsma, 1963; Dijkstra & Hendrix, 1983; Eurelings-Bontekoe et al., 1994), migrant populations and refugees (e.g., Eisenbruch, 1990; Hertz, 1988; Hojat & Herman, 1985; Larbig et al., 1979; Schmitz, 1994), non-resident students, student nurses and boarding school children (Brewin *et al.*, 1989; Carden & Feicht, 1991; Fisher, 1989; Fisher *et al.*, 1984, 1985, 1986; Fisher & Hood, 1987, 1988; Miller & Harwell, 1983; Porritt & Taylor, 1981), and institutionalized people (Taylor, 1986).

One intriguing question concerns the most frequent types of antecedent situations in homesickness. Thijs (1992) asked a group of Dutch adults to describe the situations in which they had ever been homesick. Vacations, sleep overs and boarding school were mentioned most frequently. Furthermore, in our study among homesick adult women we also found moves and vacations to be the predominant homesickness eliciting situations. When moving or on a vacation, one does not have to leave behind those who are most close and intimate like partner and children. It was found that only 15% reported to be alone in the homesickness situation, indicating that separation from attachment figures does not play a causal role in homesickness. Separation can, however, aggravate the homesickness. Family can give support when in a stressful situation, thereby alleviating the homesickness a little bit. In addition, leaving one's family behind also implicates a greater change in habits and way of living, which can be an important facilitating factor in homesickness.

In the same study it was found that geographical distance does not play a role in the development of homesickness. For about 6% of the cases the old situation was within walking distance (≤ 5 kilometers). Eventually homesickness usually fades away. Yet, there is no guarantee for curing, because homesickness can last a life time. One woman in our study indicated to have been homesick for 58 years.

The person

People differ in their reaction to leaving home for longer or shorter time periods. Some people are thus more prone or vulnerable to developing homesickness than others. In two other chapters in this book the role of personality in homesickness is addressed. From the studies referred to in these chapters and from data of our own research group it emerged that rigidity is especially important for the development of homesickness. Rigidity implies strong attachment to regular life and an aversion of new situations. Rigid people thus have more difficulties in separating from an old environment and entering a new environment, which means that there is more of a risk for them to become homesick. For the interested reader I refer to the other chapters in this book. Here, I will focus on biographical variables.

Homesickness is generally thought of as being more common among children than adults. Baier and Welch (1992) even suggested that adults are not susceptible to homesickness at all. However, there is ample evidence of homesickness in adults, like conscripts (Bergsma, 1963; Dijkstra & Hendrix, 1983; Eurelings-Bontekoe *et al.*, 1994) and adult migrants and refugees (e.g., Eisenbruch, 1990; Hertz, 1988; Hojat & Herman, 1985; Larbig *et al.*, 1979; Schmitz, 1994). Unfortunately, no data are available concerning the difference of prevalence between children and adults.

Results on gender differences with respect to homesickness have been mixed. Fisher (1989) failed to find any sex differences. Brewin *et al.* (1989) reported sex differences in coping with homesickness and Gruijters (1992) in the prevalence of homesickness. This issue requires more investigation, taking into account differences in sampling and measurement methods, and differences in culture.

Cultural differences have not been studied systematically. Hojat and Herman (1985) found no cultural differences between Iranian and Filipino physicians in the US in the prevalence of homesickness. In contrast, Carden and Feicht (1991) reported greater prevalence figures of homesickness among Turkish than among American first-year students attending universities in their own country.

Early childhood experiences may also play a role in homesickness. Eurelings-Bontekoe *et al.* (1994) found youth histories to be an important predictor of adult homesickness. Homesick conscripts were characterized by a history of homesickness experiences, problems with separating from parents, fewer and shorter vacations without parents or alone, and avoidance of dating and going out.

A final issue is the role of family background. There is now some evidence from the current data and data of others (for instance, see the chapters by Eurelings-Bontekoe and Hannigan) that attachment might play an important role in the development of homesickness. Insecure attachment to care-givers can make one more vulnerable to homesickness. Insecurely attached persons experience great anxiety when separated from their attachment figure and long desperately for reunification with the attachment figure. This anxiety can be expressed in terms of feeling homesick because one longs to return home in order to reunite with the left-behind attachment figure. In addition, the image of the attachment figure as inconsistently responsive can be transferred to the home environment, thereby establishing an insecure attachment to the home environment resulting in intense longing for home and anxiety when separated from home. Until now, the exact relation between insecure attachment and homesickness is still unclear, however. In DSM-IV (American Psychiatric Association, 1994) homesickness is incorporated in the description of separation anxiety, a youth disorder related to attachment problems.

Reactions

Both the antecedent situation and the person determine the intensity and nature of the emotional reaction to leaving home. A reaction pattern includes cognitions, physiological symptoms, behavioral tendencies, and subjective feelings. These will be discussed separately.

Cognitions

At the cognitive level missing home, obsess ional thoughts about home, aversion to and negative thoughts about the new environment and absent-mindedness are reported (for an overview of the literature see Van Tilburg *et al.*, 1996). Attention is not primarily directed at problems at home, but rather at idealizing home. These cognitions distinguish homesickness from related concepts like nostalgia and depression.

Physiological symptoms

Various aches and vague complaints are associated with homesickness (Van Tilburg *et al.*, 1996). The most frequently reported physical symptoms are: stomach and intestinal complaints, sleep disturbances, appetite loss, headache, fatigue and a 'funny feeling' in the legs. We found crying to be one of the most common reactions to homesickness in our group of adult females, which is remarkable because it has never been reported in previous studies on homesickness. Furthermore, not only minor aches were reported as a manifestation of homesickness but also some more severe clinical pictures, for instance binge eating, suicide attempts, tightness of the chest, heart complaints, etc. This indicates that homesickness is linked with psychobiological reactions which can have rather severe and even hazardous health consequences.

Behavioral characteristics

The homesick are generally described as apathetic, listless, lacking initiative, and having little interest in their current environment (Van Tilburg *et al.*, 1996). These observations led some researchers and clinicians to believe homesickness is a reactive depression (e.g., Baier & Welch, 1992; Eurelings-Bontekoe *et al.*, 1994; Fisher, 1989).

Emotional manifestations

Homesickness is generally characterized by a depressive mood. Moreover, feelings of insecurity, loss of control, nervousness, and loneliness are frequently reported (Van Tilburg *et al.*, 1996). Our data indicate that almost 50% of those in chronic homesickness situations (e.g., after a move) reported being frustrated, while this feeling did not play a significant role in short-term homesick situations (e.g., a vacation). As most of these subjects felt that the only solution to their homesickness is returning home, those in unchangeable situations like in a move feel frustrated not being able to do anything about their homesickness.

Social regulation and control

There is evidence that homesickness is socially sanctioned and therefore not expressed easily. Baier and Welch (1992) observed that homesickness is sometimes experienced with embarrassment or denial. Feelings of homesickness are frequently not acknowledged nor processed intrapersonally and homesick children are generally encouraged to suppress their feelings. Fisher (1989) found that homesick students were rated as less successful, less intelligent, and less socially desirable by their fellow students. Fisher observed in her study that sufferers of homesickness think it is childish or silly to be homesick. In our study the same pattern emerged. About 50 to 60% of homesick adult women did not express their feelings to others. Furthermore, sufferers thought of themselves as childish, a mommy's boy, not grown up, etc. One woman said: "I thought I had grown over it ... I thought I was more mature now and could handle it." Being homesick generally lowers the self-esteem significantly. As a consequence expression of homesickness was inhibited and in some cases subjects even denied their feelings to others and themselves. In addition, data from our study revealed that homesickness is typically not anticipated even though most of the subjects have had homesickness experiences before. One may wonder whether most persons, due to the fact that it is conceived as something immature, think that their vulnerability of homesickness disappears with time. People again and again try to leave their house for a short or longer period of time, although homesickness strikes almost every time.

Conclusion

Homesickness is a reaction to leaving one's home and house and occurs often during vacations and after a move. There are indications that the separation from the old environment causes the homesickness feelings, but it is not known what factors are most important. Separating from persons in the old environment does not always play a significant role.

Rigid people are most vulnerable to become homesick as they have difficulties altering their routines and way of living. Homesickness generally starts from a young age onwards and continues into adulthood. There are some indications that insecure attachment is related to feelings of homesickness.

Homesickness can be an extremely intense and overwhelming emotion. Merely missing home or having a dim desire to return home does not make one homesick. Homesick persons feel miserable and depressed. They are apathetic and listless. Various minor and major pains and aches are felt, mostly stomach and intestinal complaints, appetite loss, sleep disturbances, crying, and headaches. Attention is focused (almost) completely on the old environment and the possibility of return. Homesick persons miss home desperately, they have obsessional thoughts about home, idealize home and wish to return home. They continue to live mentally in their old environment. The new situation is avoided as much as possible and thought about negatively. Thus, homesickness hampers adaptation to the new situation.

As homesickness is seen as something childish, it is socially sanctionized even among children. Therefore, the feelings of homesickness may be suppressed and denied. The response pattern of homesickness bears many resemblances to other syndromes and emotions. However, homesickness appears to be a distinct concept because it can be distinguished on the basis of the cognitive orientation of the homesick person. To quote Fisher (1989): "If, for example, a person who was bereaved was in one room and a person who was homesick in another, and the job of the investigator was to decide which person was homesick and which was bereaved by asking only one question, that question should concern the focus of cognitive activity and not the nature of the distress symptoms" (p. 22). This statement is applicable to all other of the discussed concepts related to homesickness, not only grief.

As homesickness is a conceptually distinct manifestation of distress with a known cause it is important to acknowledge it as such. At this moment there are no diagnostic criteria for homesickness or valid measurement tools that can truly separate the homesickness reaction pattern from other emotions. Therefore, it is of utmost importance to develop diagnostic criteria for clinicians and valid measurement tools for researchers. Up to that moment homesick persons run the risk of being diagnosed with another syndrome, receiving therapy which might not be helpful and in some cases even counterproductive.

References

Aebischer, V., & Wallbott, H. G. (1986). Measuring emotional experiences: Questionnaire design and procedure, and the nature of the sample. In: K. R. Scherer, H. G. Wallbott, & A. B. Summerfield (Eds.), *Experiencing emotion: A cross-cultural study* (pp. 28-38). Cambridge: Cambridge University Press.

American Psychiatric Association (1994). *Diagnostic and statistical manual of mental disorders (4th ed.)*. Washington, DC: Author.

Baier, M., & Welch, M. (1992). An analysis of the concept of homesickness. *Archives of Psychiatric Nursing, 6*, 54-60.

Bergsma, J. (1963). *Militair heimwee* [Homesickness in the army]. Unpublished Ph.D. thesis. Groningen, The Netherlands: Groningen University.

Bowlby, J. (1980). *Attachment and Loss. Volume III: Loss sadness and depression.* New York: Basic Books.

Brewin, C. R., Furnham, A., & Howes, M. (1989). Demographic and psychological determinants of homesickness and confiding among students. *British Journal of Psychology, 80,* 467-477.

Carden, A. I., & Feicht, R. (1991). Homesickness among American and Turkish college students. *Journal of Cross-Cultural Psychology, 22,* 418-428.

Dijkstra, S. J., & Hendrix, M. J. J. L. (1983). Heimwee, een verkenning [Homesickness, an exploration]. *De Psycholoog, 18,* 3-10.

Eisenbruch, M. (1990). Cultural bereavement and homesickness. In: S. Fisher & C. L. Cooper (Eds.), *On the move: The psychology of transition and change* (pp. 191-206). Chichester, UK: Wiley.

Eurelings-Bontekoe, E. H. M., Vingerhoets, A. J. J. M., & Fontijn, T. (1994). Personality and behavioral antecedents of homesickness. *Personality and Individual Differences, 16,* 229-235.

Fisher, S. (1989). *Homesickness, cognition, and health.* London: Erlbaum.

Fisher, S., Frazer, N., & Murray, K. (1984). The transition from home to boarding school: A diary-style analysis of the problems and worries of boarding school pupils. *Journal of Environmental Psychology, 4,* 211-221.

Fisher, S., Frazer, N., & Murray, K. (1986). Homesickness and health in boarding school children. *Journal of Environmental Psychology, 6,* 35-37.

Fisher, S., & Hood, B. (1987). The stress of the transition to the university: A longitudinal study of psychological disturbance, absent-mindedness and vulnerability to homesickness. *British Journal of Psychology, 78,* 425-441.

Fisher, S., & Hood, B. (1988). Vulnerability factors in the transition to university: Self reported mobility history and sex differences as factors in psychological disturbance. *British Journal of Psychology, 79,* 309-320.

Fisher, S., Murray, K., & Frazer, N. (1985). Homesickness, health, and efficiency in first year students. *Journal of Environmental Psychology, 5,* 181-195.

Fyer, A. J. (1987). Agoraphobia. *Modern Problems of Pharmaco-psychiatry, 22,* 91-126.

Gruijters, I. (1992). *Heimwee en situatiekenmerken* [Homesickness and situation characteristics]. Unpublished M.A. thesis. Tilburg, The Netherlands: Tilburg University.

Hertz, D. G. (1988). Identity - lost and found: Patterns of migration and psychological and psychosocial adjustment of migrants. *Acta Psychiatrica Scandinavica, 78 (344, Suppl.),* 159-165.

Hojat, M., & Herman, M. W. (1985). Adjustment and psychological problems of Iranian and Filipino physicians in the US. *Journal of Clinical Psychology, 41,* 131-136.

Jaspers, K. (1909). *Heimweh und Verbrechen* [Homesickness and crime]. Unpublished doctoral dissertation. University of Heidelberg, Leipzig, Germany.

Larbig, W., Xenakis, C., & Onishi, M. S. (1979). Psychosomatische Symptome und funktionelle Beschwerden bei Arbeitnehmern im Ausland - Japaner und Griechen in Deutschland, Deutsche im Ausland [Psychosomatic and functional symptoms of Japanese and Greeks in Germany, and Germans in foreign countries]. *Zeitschrift für Psychosomatische Medizin und Psychoanalyse, 25,* 49-63.

Miller, D. F., & Harwell, D. J. (1983). International students at an American university: Health problems and status. *The Journal of School Health, 1,* 45-49.

Oxford Advanced Learner's Dictionary (1989). Oxford, UK: Oxford University Press.

Porritt, D., & Taylor, D. (1981). An exploration of homesickness among student nurses. *Australian and New Zealand Journal of Psychiatry, 15,* 57-62.

Rosen, G. (1975). Nostalgia: A 'forgotten' psychological disorder. *Psychological Medicine, 5,* 340-354.

Scherer, K. R. (1986). Studying emotion empirically: Issues and a paradigm for research. In: K. R. Scherer, H. G. Wallbott, & A. B. Summerfield (Eds.), *Experiencing emotion: A cross-cultural study* (pp. 3-27). Cambridge, UK: Cambridge University Press.

Schmitz, P. G. (1994). Acculturation and adaptation processes among immigrants in Germany. In: M. Bouvy, F. J. R. Van de Vijver, P. Boski, & P. Schmitz (Eds.), *Journeys into cross-cultural psychology: Selected papers from the Eleventh International Conference of the International Association for Cross-Cultural Psychology* (pp. 142-157). Lisse, the Netherlands: Swets & Zeitlinger.

Taylor, R. E. (1986). Homesickness, melancholy and blind rehabilitation. *Journal of Visual Impairment & Blindness, 80,* 800-802.

Tearnan, B. H., Telch, M. J., & Keefe, P. (1984). Etiology and onset of agoraphobia: A critical review. *Comprehensive Psychiatry, 25,* 51-62.

Thijs, H. (1992). *Heimwee en andere emoties* [Homesickness and other emotions]. Unpublished M.A. thesis. Tilburg, The Netherlands: Tilburg University.

Tuan, Y. (1974). *Topophilia: A study of environment perception, attitudes, and values.* Englewood, NJ: Prentice Hall.

Van Tilburg, M. A. L., Vingerhoets, A. J. J. M., Kirschbaum, C., & Van Heck, G. L. (1996). Mood changes in homesick persons during a holiday trip: A multiple case study. *Psychotherapy and Psychosomatics, 65,* 91-96.

Van Tilburg, M. A. L., Vingerhoets, A. J. J. M., & Van Heck, G. L. (1996). Homesickness: A review of the literature. *Psychological Medicine, 26,* 899-912.

Verwoerdt, A. (1976). *Clinical gerospsychiatry.* Baltimore, MD: Waverly Press.

Verwoerdt, A. (1980). Anxiety, dissociative and personality disorders in the elderly. In: E. W. Busse & D. G. Blazer (Eds.), *Handbook of geriatric psychiatry* (pp. 368-380). New York: Van Nostrand Reinhold.

Wallbott, H. G., & Scherer, K. R. (1986). How universal and specific is emotional experience? Evidence from 27 countries on five continents. *Social Science Information, 25,* 763-795.

Werman, D. S. (1977). Normal and pathological nostalgia. *Journal of the American Psychoanalytical Association, 25,* 387-398.

Zwingmann, C. (1973a). The nostalgic phenomenon and its exploitation. In: C. Zwingmann & M. Pfister-Ammende (Eds.), *Uprooting and after* (pp. 19-47). New York: Springer-Verlag.

Zwingmann, C. (1973b). Nostalgic behavior. In: C. Zwingmann & M. Pfister-Ammende (Eds.), *Uprooting and after* (pp. 143-151). New York: Springer-Verlag.

4 Geographical Moves and Psychological Adjustment

SHIRLEY FISHER

Background

Research on geographical moves has been evident since the turn of the century when large population movements occurred for various reasons. Immigration between countries was stimulated by changes in agricultural and industrial conditions and generally the populations involved sought to better their predicaments. Research carried out on these populations however, indicated that geographical transitions were stressful and likely to increase the risk of changes in mental or physical health. What was never clear was whether there is self-selection into moves, which favors all those relatively at risk for ill health. Studies identified the vulnerability of those who chose to move either within or between countries. In the case of migrants for example, Odegaard (1932) reported greater rates of hospital admissions for mental disorder amongst Norwegian migrants to Minnesota in the U.S.A. than for either the natives of either Norway or Minnesota.

General effects of relocation evident from statistics provide unclear indications of underlying mechanisms. Also, there were some contradictions. For example, Kleiner and Parker (1963) demonstrated the greater prevalence of psychoneurotic and neurotic symptoms in native born individuals migrating within the U.S.A. Circumstantial factors such as educational backgrounds, achievement level and the degree of planning for moves appears to be involved.

Moves and mental health

Clearly, research, which identifies the effects of moves in specific contexts, is more likely to provide specific details on the personal reaction of people to moves. Faris and Dunham (1939) provided an attempt to identify specific effects. Using home ownership as an index of personal stability and rental status as an index of mobility, they reported significant negative correlations between mobility and ill health. However, the causal direction is complex, lack of ability to cope with new conditions may create poverty and social drift down to social disorganization and resulting mental ill health.

Physical ill health, cardiovascular disease, gastric disorders and infectious illness such as tuberculosis, have been identified as more prevalent in migrant populations (see Medalie & Kahn, 1973; Cruze-Coke et al., 1964; Wolff, 1953; Christenson & Hinkle, 1961). However, self-selection of those who move cannot be precluded.

GEOGRAPHICAL TRANSITIONS

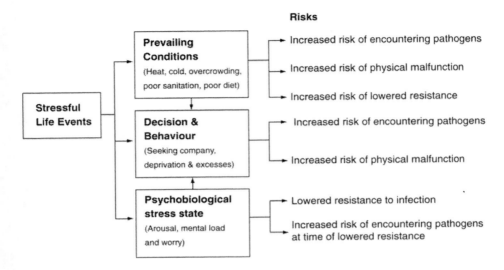

Figure 4.1.   Conceptual model of factors increasing the risk of disease following a stressful
life event, e.g., migration, relocation, bereavement, marital separation, and
divorce (Fisher, 1988, with kind permission of John Wiley & Sons).

Figure 4.1 illustrates some possible reasons for the vulnerability of migrant groups.
First, there may be adverse dietary changes, changes in exercise facilities, difficult
conditions of travel. There may also be encounters with pathogenic factors and lack
of ability to maintain adequate hygiene. An additional unknown factor is the strain
due to insecurity, fear of the unknown and the possibility of adverse difficulties
ahead. Finally, the possibility of stress caused specifically by change is likely to be
influential. Hormones associated with prolonged stress have been shown to suppress
the immune system (see Amkraut & Solomon, 1975), because stress hormones
mediate the response to environmental and social factors, there is the likelihood of
ideal conditions for the development of disease.

Specific effects of relocation

In order to identify the effects of geographical transition on mental and physical
health, examination of psychological changes following the move is needed.
Unfortunately, there have been few studies of this nature. However, one useful study
was carried out by Fried (1962) who examined the reaction of slum dwellers to
enforced moves into better housing within the city of Chicago. The moves to better
housing should have been perceived positively. However, pre- and post-relocation

interviews showed that psychological reactions were intense, overwhelming, prolonged, and characterized by grief for home: "I felt as if the heart was taken out of me." Depressive mood and a sense of helplessness were major features of the observed reaction following the move.

Fried's study also emphasized the central importance of objects and places as critical factors. The role of situational and personal factors was emphasized. Status, defined by occupational, educational, and income factors was positively associated with successful adjustment; 72% of the higher-income group adjusted successfully to the move as compared with 22% of their lower-income counterparts. Equally, planning for the move was a critical factor. 52% who reported planning for the move were subsequently found to have adjusted well, as compared with 24% of those who did not. This may indicate self-selection factors. However, Fried developed the idea of 'preparedness for transition' as a critical determinant of the success of adaptation. 'Mastery' defined in terms of the determination to struggle and persist against all envisaged problems was seen as a sign of 'inner preparedness' for the impending move.

Theoretical bases of the effects of moves

There are four main theories that provide possible understanding of the factors, which are likely to be counterproductive, or which may create short or long term stress.

Attachment and loss

On first consideration, the most appropriate theoretical format for understanding the effects of leaving home is in terms of attachment and loss. The death of a loved person such as a parent or spouse is a major significant stressful experience for most of those who experience it.

Studies by Bowlby (1969) have probed the basis of the reaction to loss of immediate contact between mother and child and indicate that the maintenance of a close bond between child and parents creates a sense of security and is itself sought at time of stress. The infant reacts with alarm characterized by protest, searching, and distress when there is no visual contact with the mother.

Weiss (1975, 1982) investigated attachment behavior in adults and indicated that adult relationships may have similar properties to the mother-infant bond. Care relationships are likely to evolve in most adult close bonds. Weiss notes the similarity of the response to loss at all ages and sees this as suggesting the operation of a single perceptual-emotional system.

Bowlby (1980), concerned with loss in children and adults, identified four phases of loss. The first is a phase of numbing that may be accompanied by outbursts of panic or anger. There is then a 'yearning phase' characterized by searching for the lost person. A phase of disorganization, chaos and despair may then be followed by a final phase of attempted reorganization. Parkes (1972) elaborated four elements of a theory of bereavement on such basic principles. The effects are argued to be so profoundly disturbing for the victims, that the possibility that loss creates a form of mental illness is viable.

Interruption and discontinuity

An alternative explanation of the adverse effects of leaving home is that it creates interruption or discontinuity in existing life-styles and routines. Discontinuity may in fact be an important common denominator of many life events. Loss of a close person may mean that the bereaved is faced with a discontinuity in life-style which itself may have implications for psychological and physical health. The change is not permanent but may nevertheless represent a break in the normal continuities of lifestyle and behavior.

Laboratory studies involving experimental interruption of tasks (Mandler, 1975) have provided evidence to suggest that increased arousal is manifest as anxiety in some cases. Mandler and Watson (1966) found that interruption of an on-going laboratory task resulted in increased intensity of persistence towards completion of the interrupted sequences and increased vigor with which the sequence is pursued. Perhaps systems and plans, which previously dominate behavior, continue to dominate, and drive inappropriate thoughts or activities in the new environment. Thus, the domination and persistence of old plans might be partly responsible for adverse reactions to leaving home. Nostalgia (derived from 'nosos' meaning past and 'algia' meaning pain) implies that the past can carry poignant emotions.

The capacity of previous plans to dominate attention may have origins in survival and natural selection. Fisher (1984) argued that reflective activity involving past plans might be a prerequisite for the development of future plans. Acquired resources from previous experience may then be integrated. The sense of separation and loss, triggered by the dominance of old plans in memory may create inappropriate emotions. Thus, 'home addiction' may create emotional pain as an epiphenomenon, with the capacity to prevent a person from taking on new commitments because of anticipated emotional pain. People who do not take up jobs and opportunities may be disadvantaged by fear of leaving home.

The control model

The concept of control or power and mastery of the environment provides a different explanation, with more emphasis on the new environment as a determinant of distress.

Increasingly there has been research interest in the notion that when personal control over a situation is possible because of instrumentality or skill, threat is reduced (Fisher, 1984). Some backing for these ideas has come from the animal studies where being given the means to escape shock creates less extensive ulceration or weight loss than being helpless (see Mowrer & Viek, 1948; Weiss, 1968, 1970).

Studies with human beings are rather less convincing. When faced with a choice of accepting self-delivered or machine-delivered shock, about two thirds of a sample show a preference for control. However, there is the possibility that there may be different 'agendas' operating. Those who appear to opt for low control may be operating different plans.

Fisher (1986) developed the control theory of the response to change and transition arguing that many major life events including a move away from home, result in a period of reduction of personal control. New aspects of life have to be learned and new skills acquired. Previous patterns of behavior may be inadequate for the new situation, and may convey the feeling of being lost or disturbed.

Role change and self-consciousness

A different conceptualization, but one which also emphasizes the importance of the new environment as a causal factor in distress, is that transition produces a change in perceived role; one set of commitments ends and another new set is initiated. An individual takes on new roles and there has to be an adjustment to self-image. It has been shown that the amount of self-focus increases with the strangeness of the new environment (Wickland, 1975).

Thus a new environment will involve a period of adjustment to new roles and will create periods of raised anxiety. It is argued by Hormuth (1984) that lack of discrepancy between desired and actual self-perception will create instability. Oatley and Bolton (1985) identified a general theory in which life events as provoking agents create increased risk of depression because they propose threats to 'self-hood' and require new roles and new attitudes.

The sense of the role of the self (student, mother, housewife, banker, doctor) depends on evidence made available by daily interactions in social contexts. Others who respect the role and interact meaningfully with it reinforce one's role. The role will collapse or become threatened when this reciprocity is not maintained (see Ryle, 1982). Thus, following transition, strain may occur as part of adjustment to new roles. Seen in this context, relocation involves a change of social environment and involves the opportunity to take on new roles. At the same time contact with the old roles may be maintained. It would follow that there should be a period of self-awareness (Wickland, 1975). Self-focused attention could dominate resources and reduce capacity available for normal life experiences. During this period it might be expected that anxiety, self-preoccupation and absent-mindedness would occur.

The effects of conflict

One possibility, which must also be considered, is that to give up security and comfort associated with life at home in order to obtain new experiences, social, educational or financial improvements could create conflict. The new environment is less secure but more challenging.

Table 4.1. Features utilized in definitions of homesickness and non-homesick school
pupils

Feature categories from definitions provided	Frequency of reported features and percentage of subjects reporting each feature	
	Homesick (N=82) f (%)	Non-homesick (N=33) f (%)
'Missing parent family'; longing for people at home	54 (65.9)	25 (75.8)
'Missing home environment'; missing house, home, area, etc.	28 (34.1)	12 (36.4)
'Wanting to go home'; feeling a need to return home	21 (25.6)	10 (30.3)
'Missing friends'; longing for friends	12 (14.6)	1 (3.0)
'Feelings of loneliness'	10 (12.2)	1 (3.0)
'Crying'	3 (3.7)	3 (9.1)
'Unsettled'	4 (4.9)	1 (3.0)
'Hating the present place'	4 (4.9)	1 (3.0)
'Feeling unhappy'	4 (4.9)	1 (3.0)
'Not getting on with people'	3 (3.7)	0 (0.0)
'Dissatisfied with the present situation'	3 (3.7)	0 (0.0)
'Feeling depressed'	2 (2.4)	1 (3.0)
'Disorientation'; feeling lost in a new environment	2 (2.4)	0 (0.0)
'Regret that life had changed'; a feeling of regret	2 (2.4)	0 (0.0)
'Never been away from home before'	2 (2.4)	0 (0.0)
'Feeling ill'	2 (2.4)	0 (0.0)
'Unable to do anything'	2 (2.4)	0 (0.0)
'Feeling unloved'	0 (0.0)	2 (6.1)

Note. The following features were endorsed by only one person in the following groups. *Homesick:* 'problem at school'; 'missing someone close to talk to'; 'obsession with thoughts of home'; 'looking for familiar company and faces'; 'feeling isolated'. *Non-homesick:* 'feeling uneasy'; 'unable to cope'; 'feeling full and weary'; ''thinking home is better than here'. In Fisher *et al.* (1986).

The conflict might be particularly evident for university students where obtaining a college place is a privilege. The conflict between wanting to persist with such an educational opportunity and not wanting to leave home could be important (see Fisher *et al.*, 1984).

Cameron and Margaret (1951) gave central importance to conflict as a causal factor in psychopathology. They noted the prevalence of conflict in clinical groups and identified different conflict typologies based on approach and avoidance elements. Homesickness has the capacity to create an approach-avoidance conflict: the need to go home competes with the desire for a new future with opportunity, etc.

General features of homesickness

Research by Fisher *et al.* (1985) established that a pre-requisite for research on self-reports of homesickness, required that the term should be understood in the same way across homesick and non-homesick groups. Self-definition of states may be liable to error and misinterpretation. *Table 4.1* illustrates that personal statements as to the meaning of homesickness, for homesick and non-homesick groups are correlated. Results showed that the non-homesick do not differ in their listing of causes and symptoms. Neither are there any gender or age differences in homesickness reporting levels.

Homesickness, psychological disturbance, and health

Studies of university students reporting homesickness (Fisher *et al.*, 1985; Fisher & Hood, 1987) have indicated that they are distinguished from their non-homesick counterparts by raised levels of psychoneurotic scores on non-clinical scales such as the Middlesex Hospital Questionnaire ('MHQ'; Crown & Crisp, 1966) and raised absent-mindedness scores on the Cognitive Failures Questionnaire ('CFC'; Broadbent *et al.*, 1982; see *Table 4.2*). Taken collectively, the practical implication is that the new student resident is distressed and likely to behave non-effectively in the new environment. The evidence from the above studies also indicates poorer adaptation to university life as assessed by the College Adaptation Questionnaire ('CAQ'; Crombag, 1968).

Personal and circumstantial factors in homesickness reporting

The evidence suggests that there are no gender or age differences in home-sickness reporting but that being given decisional control over the move is an important positive circumstantial factor (Fisher *et al.*, 1985). Most primary or secondary pupils reported little control over the transition to a new residential school.

Table 4.2. Cognitive failure, mental health, and adjustment profiles before and after the transition in homesick and non-homesick residents[a]

	Not homesick (n=42)		Homesick (n=22)	
	χ	SD	X	SD
At Home				
MHQ1	22.81	(8.6)	29.0[c]	(12.5)
Obsessional (personality)	2.61	(2.2)	3.72[b]	(2.7)
Somatic	3.21	(2.5)	4.54[b]	(2.7)
Depression	1.89	(1.6)	3.82[c]	(2.8)
CFQ1	32.65	(10.7)	36.0	(12.3)
Sixth Week at University				
MHQ2	23.00	(11.5)	33.04[c]	(14.1)
Anxiety	3.78	(3.1)	6.48[c]	(3.7)
Somatic	2.63	(2.1)	5.17[d]	(2.9)
Depression	2.56	(2.3)	4.48[c]	(3.2)
Obsessional (symptoms)	2.54	(1.6)	3.35[b]	(2.1)
CFQ2	38.21	(11.9)	42.78	(13.5)
CAQ	100.69	(17.7)	84.31[d]	(18.2)
DRI	4.00	(3.2)	8.50[d]	(4.2)

a As designed by 'not homesick' versus three other categories of 'homesick' on self-rating scale (from Fisher & Hood, 1987).
b $p < 0.05$
c $p < 0.01$
d $p < 0.001$

For the young therefore, the stress of moves may be profound in impact. Yet in the UK, children as young as seven years may be sent away to board at school.

Part of the circumstances likely to influence the effect of the transition includes the attractiveness of the new environment. There was no significant effect of extraversion or of self-esteem.

Fisher (1990) reported that the amount of geographical distance traveled to a new residence was a factor of importance. The greater the distance involved, the worse the homesickness effects were found to be. The average distance within the UK for homesick students to travel was 364 miles on average for those who reported homesick, and 203 miles for those who reported no homesickness effects. However, the frequency of homesickness bouts was not distinguished by differences in distance, and no particular home locations were identified for the homesick students. There was no evidence that they were from either rural or urban based settings and no evidence of ethnic influence. Home background and life history did not appear to have a strong effect on homesickness reporting.

In a comparison where subjects wore a voice key to record speed of response, they were asked to report first thought of a *positive* aspect of university life, or in another condition a *negative* aspect. The homesick were faster to report positive aspects of home life quickly and negative aspects of home life slowly, as compared with the non-homesick. This suggests that there is a hedonic set in the way the homesick perceive their environment. It was found that the responses were different from the responses of the depressed, who were fast to produce negative thoughts of both home and university.

A multifactor model of homesickness

Taking into account the previous findings, it might be useful to consider a multi-causal influence, which maintains adverse cognitive material in focus following a major move or environmental change, and features distress in a limited capacity system. The cognitive material is driven by a number of possible conditions, such as loss of home contact, change of role, or interruption. These may function together or separately to maintain the 'past' as a feature of current cognition. The presence of these thoughts in cognition sustains the emotions, which are negative, perhaps as an epiphenomenon.

Figure 4.2 illustrates the possibility that for moves which involve geographical change or leaving home, the individual continues with a mental 'present' which is actually the past. This may have evolutionary advantage in creating a situation where the best of previous plans and experiences can be carried over to new experiences to help develop new plans. The environment may then gradually begin to introduce on the dominant material in cognition gradually changing the focus of daily thought. If successful, a change for the focuses of the future could be implemented bringing forward the best of the old to contribute to the new. The psychological and social environment could help to create the capacity for change across time. Maximum exposure to the new environment for maximum time would thus seem to be the best method of behavior. However, the mediating effects of distress might need to be offset. Seeking distraction or companionship during the early part of the transition could help.

One issue of interest however, is that about 30% of students arrive non-homesick and build up homesickness as a state as time progresses. 'Job strain' or dislike of the new environment is a possible alternative explanation. Thus, homesickness may be a reaction to unpleasant or difficult environments. University students may be particularly affected by situations if the new educational environment is not congenial. Therefore, creating pleasant congenial environments may be a critical method of enhancing the positive role that the present environment can achieve.

1. DEMAND STRENGTH MODEL

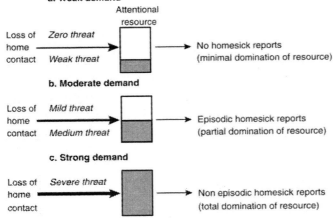

a. Weak demand

Attentional resource

Loss of home contact → Zero threat / Weak threat → No homesick reports (minimal domination of resource)

b. Moderate demand

Loss of home contact → Mild threat / Medium threat → Episodic homesick reports (partial domination of resource)

c. Strong demand

Loss of home contact → Severe threat → Non episodic homesick reports (total domination of resource)

2. COMPETING DEMANDS MODEL

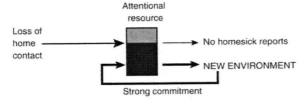

a. Commitment to new environment dominates resource

Attentional resource

Loss of home contact → No homesick reports

NEW ENVIRONMENT

Strong commitment

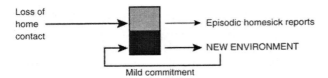

b. Mild commitment to new environment partially dominates resource

Loss of home contact → Episodic homesick reports

NEW ENVIRONMENT

Mild commitment

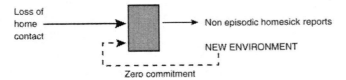

c. Zero commitment to new environment (no demand on resource)

Loss of home contact → Non episodic homesick reports

NEW ENVIRONMENT

Zero commitment

Figure 4.2.   Attentional demand models of homesick reporting

Desertion in the trenches in war may be an example of homesickness response, rather than being cowardly.

The belief that intense focus on the past debilitates the future may be false if the new environment provides the tool by which cognitive focus on the old environment is weakened.

A critical factor is the issue of why the effect of a move maintains negative and painful cognitive material in focus. Moves may create forms of threat and have urgent tenure in a limited capacity mental system. The new environment may then gradually attenuate the negative cognitive material, replacing it with plans more useful for the future.

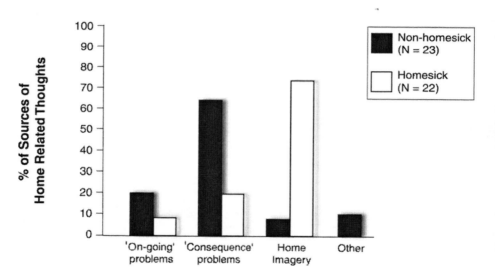

Figure 4.3.   Self-reported classes of home ruminations in students

The cognitive nature of responses to leaving home

The form of material in cognition may differ for the homesick and non-homesick. *Figure 4.3* illustrates that in self-reported home-related thoughts, the homesick report home imagery ('imagining being in my room, taking the dog out,' etc.). By comparison, the thought content of the non-homesick with regard to home tends to focus more on practical issues, e.g., 'what will happen if the dog is pining'; 'what happens if the car will not start and my mother is on her own,' etc. Thus, home imagery dominates the cognition of the homesick whereas the non-homesick focus on problems at home or problems related to leaving home (e.g., finance, etc.).

60

Thus, it is possible that the form of cognitive activity is different for the homesick and involves cognitive components of distress. By comparison, the non-homesick focus on the practical issues of being away from home.

The job strain model

There is a possibility that the intrusive material so evident in the homesick is reinforced by job strain. It was found that 35% of students do not arrive with feelings of distress and homesickness but become affected by it as the term progresses. Thus, the possibility that homesickness is created entirely by the new environment must be considered.

Conclusion

Homesickness understood to imply distress from leaving home, has a number of features, which imply causal processes. First there is the possibility that there is a direct effect of the separation from emotional ties due to a move. Secondly, there is the possibility of distress caused by unpleasant environments or job conditions. Prevalence of unpleasant work environments, different relations with people at work, etc. may all create a sense of distress and isolation. Ultimately, some explanation is needed in terms of a cognitive capacity model. Where home thoughts dominate capacity, other competing pleasant material may not obtain access, and thus homesickness is propagated.

References

Amkraut, A., & Solomon, G. F. (1975). From the symbolic stimulus to the pathophysiologic response immune mechanisms. *International Journal of Psychiatry in Medicine, 5,* 541-563.

Bowlby, J. (1969). *Attachment and loss. Vol. 1: Attachment.* New York: Basic Books.

Bowlby, J. (1980). *Attachment and loss. Vol. 3: Loss, sadness and depression.* New York: Basic Books.

Broadbent, D. E., Cooper, P. F., Fitzgerald, P., & Parkes, K. R. (1982). The Cognitive Failures Questionnaire (CFQ) and its correlates. *British Journal of Clinical Psychology, 21,* 1-16.

Cameron, N. A., & Margaret, A. (1951). *Behaviour Pathology.* New York: Houghton.

Christenson, W. W., & Hinkle, L. E. (1961). Differences in illnesses and prognostic signs in two groups of young men. *Journal of the American Medical Association, 177,* 247-253.

Crombag, H. F. M. (1968). *Studie motivatie en studie attitude [Study motivation and study attitude].* Groningen: Walters.

Crown, S., & Crisp, A. H. (1966). A short clinical diagnostic self-rating for psycho-neurotic patients. *British Journal of Psychiatry, 112,* 917-923.

Cruze-Coke, R., Etcheverry, R., & Nagel, R. (1964). Influences of migration on blood pressure of Easter Islanders. *Lancet, March 28,* 697-699.

61

Faris, R. E. L., & Dunham, H. W. (1939). *Mental disorders in urban areas: An ecological study of schizophrenia and other psychoses*. Chicago: Chicago University Press.

Fisher, S. (1984). *Stress and the perception of control*. London: Lawrence Erlbaum Associates Ltd.

Fisher, S. (1986). *Stress and strategy*. London: Lawrence Erlbaum Associates Ltd.

Fisher, S., & Hood, B. (1987). The stress of the transition to university: A longitudinal study of vulnerability to psychological disturbance and homesickness. *British Journal of Psychology, 78,* 425-441.

Fisher, S., Frazer, N., & Murray, K. (1984). The transition from home to boarding school: A diary study of spontaneously reported problems and worries in boarding school children. *Journal of Environmental Psychology, 4,* 211-221.

Fisher, S., Murray, K., & Frazer, N. (1985). Homesickness and health in first-year students. *Journal of Environmental Psychology, 5,* 181-195.

Fried, M. (1962). Grieving for a lost home. In: L. J. Duhl (Ed.), *The environment of the metropolis*. New York: Basic Books.

Hormuth, S. (1984). Transitions in commitments to roles and self-concept change: Relocation as a paradigm. In: V. L. Allen & E. Van de Vliert (Eds.), *Role transitions: explorations and explanations*. New York: Plenum.

Kleiner, R. J., & Parker, S. (1963). Goal-striving and psychosomatic symptoms in a migrant and non-migrant population. In: M. B. Kantor (Ed.), *Mobility and mental health*. Springfield, Ill: Charles C. Thomson.

Mandler, G. (1975). *Mind and emotion*. New York: John Wiley & Sons.

Mandler, G., & Watson, D. L. (1966). Anxiety and the interruption of behaviour. In: C. D. Spielberger (Ed.), *Anxiety and behaviour*. New York: Academic Press.

Medalie, J. H., & Kahn, H. A. (1973). Myocardial infraction over a five-year period: Prevalence, incidence and mortality experience. *Journal of Chronic Diseases, 26,* 63-84.

Mowrer, O. H., & Viek, P. (1948). An experimental analogue of fear from a sense of helplessness. *Journal of Abnormal Social Psychology, 43,* 193-200.

Oatley, K., & Bolton, W. (1985). A social cognitive theory of depression in relation to life events. *Psychological Review, 92, 3,* 372-388.

Odegaard, O. (1932). Emigration and insanity: A study of mental disease among the Norwegian born population of Minnesota. *Acta Psychiatrica et Neurologica,* Supplement 1-4.

Parkes, C. M. (1972). *Bereavement*. New York: International University Press.

Ryle, A. (1982). *Psychotherapy: A cognitive integration of theory and practice*. London: Academic Press.

Weiss, J. M. (1968). Effects of coping responses on stress. *Journal of Comparative and Physiological Psychology, 65,* 251-266.

Weiss, J. M. (1970). Somatic effects of predictable and unpredictable shock. *Psychosomatic Medicine, 32,* 397-408.

Weiss, R. (1975). *Marital separation*. New York: Basic Books.

Weiss, R. (1982). Attachment in adult life. In: C. M. Parkes & J. Sevenson-Hinde (Eds.), *The place of attachment and loss in human behaviour*. London: Tavistock Press.

Wickland, R. A. (1975). Objective self-awareness. In: L. Berkowitz (Ed.), *Advances in experimental social psychology, 8* (pp. 233-275). New York: Academic Press.

Wolff, H. G. (1953). *Stress and disease*. Springfield, Ill: Charles C. Thomas.

5 Homesickness and Acculturation Stress in the International Student

Terence P. Hannigan

Introduction

This chapter provides a review of factors that are related to homesickness and acculturation stress, as well as personal observations of the author who has worked with international students for fourteen years. In this role, a common task is preparing students who are about to study beyond the boundaries of their country for the many positive and negative experiences they will have during their sojourn. One of these negative experiences is homesickness, a term which is defined as, "longing for home and family while absent from them" (Mish *et al.*, 1986). Church (1982) cites a list of problems encountered by international students, starting with the most important and most frequently mentioned: "language difficulties, financial problems, adjusting to a new educational system, homesickness, adjusting to social customs and norms, and for some students, racial discrimination" (p. 544). It is important to note that homesickness is near the top of the list of student sojourners' complaints.

In the psychological literature, it is difficult to find references to homesickness. More frequent are references to loneliness, of which a cause is moving to a new location. Loneliness is too broad a term, however, since its causes are many, not just the result of relocation. More acceptable terms include culture shock or acculturation stress; it appears that homesickness is a symptom of these phenomena.

As for acculturation, theorists and researchers are not in agreement on a standard definition. Harriman (1969) defines it as "… The process of a newly arrived immigrant in learning the customs of the adopted country; the imposition of a foreign culture upon the subject group." Hannigan (1990) comments that along with *assimilation* it is, "… used to describe changes that occur as the result of living in a new cultural environment" (p. 92). It would follow that *acculturation stress* refers to the psychological and physical discomfort experienced as a result of adjusting to a new cultural environment. Indeed, most international students experience this discomfort and most will acknowledge a critical incident in which they felt frustrated, disoriented and that it would have been best to return home and forget about their dreams to learn a second language and skills that might have been difficult to acquire in their homeland. Alexander *et al.* (1981) describe the plight of the international student as being isolated from the host culture and having lost social anchorage in the home culture. Some students note that, although there is some correlation between social isolation and homesickness, it is not uncommon for a student to have developed a network of host country contacts and still experience homesickness. Often the contact with the social network in the host country distracts the student sojourner, yet after social contacts, the international student becomes acutely aware of the longing for home and family. For instance, students report strong bouts of homesickness after a particularly good experience at a party or other activities with host nationals. However, once they separate from this support group, they become acutely aware of missing home, family and the support of host nationals as well. International students have also reported a dread of approaching weekends or holidays when their established role as student is minimized, since school is closed and contact with peers may be limited until Monday morning. They are less distracted at these times and experience their separateness from the host culture in a more profound way, thus nurturing the feeling of how comforting it would be to be among friends and family.

My own critical incident as an international student occurred at the Eiffel Tower as I ascended the elevator on an August afternoon after a flight from New York to Paris. I had only a few hours in Paris before I continued on to Madrid to begin my studies there, and a visit to this Parisian landmark was an attempt to distract myself so that I would not realize a new day had dawned and I was three thousand miles from friends and family. This was one of many times I would experience homesickness in the following months and I probably can trace my current career to such feelings and the commitment to help other students manage homesickness during the critical first months or first year of their studies abroad.

Host country language proficiency and homesickness

Perhaps the most salient variable in predicting which students are at high risk for homesickness is how well they speak the language of the country in which they will be studying. In the academic setting, the ability to communicate in the host language becomes a major measure of success and mobility. In some institutions there is a laissez-faire attitude toward international students. It is their responsibility to navigate the reading assignments, lectures and examinations. Those who do not have the necessary linguistic skills simply fail, and continue to fail until they master the lingua franca. In most U.S institutions of higher learning, there is a gatekeeping system in which students are barred from taking courses until they demonstrate English language mastery. English as a Second Language-program is the only enrolment option. This often is expensive and yields little or no academic progress toward graduation. From either student development perspective, the international student faces the shame of not being linguistically prepared for the task at hand and this is a source of acculturation stress.

Little or no host language mastery further isolates the newcomer. There is substantial research supporting this relationship for the international student as well as the Peace Corps Volunteer (Deutsch & Won, 1963; Harris, 1973; Oberg, 1960; Pruitt, 1978a; Sewell & Davidsen, 1956). Poyrazli (2003) also provides support for

English language proficiency predicting psychosocial adjustment among International students studying in the U.S.A. Guzman and Burke (2003) developed a taxonomy of international student performance that cites writing and using the local language as one of eight performance dimensions that predict cross-cultural adjustment of International students enrolled in a Mexican institution of higher learning. Evidence of the importance of host country language proficiency is an important factor both within and beyond the class room walls. Compatriots must be depended on in the new environment or isolation becomes more acute. Studying in a foreign country with a different language limits the monolingual student sojourner to interactions with persons from the homeland, and in the best of circumstances, to those individuals from other countries with a common linguistic tradition. However, without knowledge of the host country language, there is a strong likelihood that the student sojourner will experience homesickness since the host culture will appear to be particularly foreign. In essence, the lack of the host language locks international students out of many interactions, infantilizes them and sets the stage for homesickness. Some, but few, can find a way around the linguistic barrier in the task of establishing friendships which is an important component in overcoming homesickness.

For example, if they are musicians or outstanding athletes to the point where they can offer their skills in the concert hall or on the soccer field of their chosen university, they can integrate into the host culture more easily. In such cases they are valued for these special skills and may be able to settle into the support system of fellow musicians or athletes. This will very likely provide the learning environment for developing host language conversational ability and will help them feel successful in their new environment – an important inoculation against homesickness. Research supports the hypothesis that the more integrated into the host culture that international students are, the less likely they are to suffer from homesickness (Pruitt, 1978a, b; Winkelman, 1994).

Employment and homesickness

It is common on U.S. campuses for students to work part time while they are enrolled. During the summer months, many U.S.A. students work full time in order to earn the money to cover some part of the expenses of the academic year. In other countries, this secondary role of student as wage earner may be less common. As the work ethic is at the foundation of U.S. values, this system of working while studying fits with this mainstream American ethic. Interestingly enough, the majority of students who enter the U.S. on student visas are restricted from working. Therefore, they are out of step with their American counterparts because they frequently cannot work legally. Also, the transition to the primary role of overseas student has restricted many of their familial roles (son/daughter, brother/ sister, in some cases spouse and/or parent) and, because of employment restrictions, they cannot legally assume the role of part-time worker. While U.S. students are busy with their jobs, international students have fewer opportunities to integrate into this aspect of the host culture. Again, they are isolated and left with the task of finding meaningful activities to fill their schedules. Without employment as a means of integrating the international students, they have more time to focus on their homesickness. The difficulty in securing a job also means the loss of a valuable opportunity to interact with host country nationals and further develop host country language skills.

Developmental factors and homesickness

Most international students are in their late adolescence or early adult years. From a developmental standpoint, such individuals are dealing with the issue of personal and career identity. Chickering and Reisser (1993) comment that, "Establishing identity certainly involves growing awareness of competencies, emotions and values, confidence in standing alone and bonding with others, and moving beyond intolerance toward openness and self-esteem" (p. 173). For students who choose to study in a different culture, they carry the above developmental baggage along with the task of working through these issues in a less familiar environment, away from the support network of the home culture. Indeed, the issue of acculturation stress and homesickness is compounded in many cases by the critical period in the life cycle in which many students cross borders to study. This is very likely a major factor in why homesickness is common among international students.

Cultural and individual differences as they relate to homesickness

As mentioned earlier, linguistic difference is a major factor in homesickness. However, other cultural differences also can add to homesickness due to isolation. Students who appear foreign or different in most cases will have more obstacles to overcome. Church (1982) points out that for international students in the U.S.A.: Canadians and West Europeans are consistently found to be more socially involved with host nationals and report fewer adjustment problems; students from the Far East are least involved socially and report the greatest number of adjustment difficulties. Indians, Black Africans, Latin Americans and Middle Easterners appear to fall in-between these two extremes (p. 547). These above-mentioned difficulties are very likely due to the differences in skin color, dress, diet, religious observance and/or accent. These factors may mark the international student as an outsider, either a foreigner or as mistakenly identified as someone from a minority group in the host culture.

Earlier it was noted that university students are struggling with standing alone and bonding with others. The task of standing alone often is directly related to separating from family and adjusting to making decisions more independently, and it is even more demanding for the university students who are overseas. A new way for researchers and practitioners to view homesickness and acculturation stress is through an attachment theory perspective. This theory may be a useful model in understanding who experiences homesickness and acculturation stress and why. Furthermore, attachment theory suggests that differences in how parents relate to their children during infancy and early childhood may provide a psychological advantage or liability to an individual's ability to comfortably deal with an unfamiliar environment.

Attachment theory characterizes three types of child-parent bond:

1. *Secure attachment* in which the individual is confident that the parent figure will be available, responsive and helpful in a difficult situation
2. *Anxious resistant attachment* is characterized by uncertainty about the parent's availability, responsiveness, and helpfulness. There is a tendency toward separation anxiety, clinging and worry about venturing out beyond the familiar setting. This is a result of inconsistency on the part of the parent, and/or threats of abandonment or separation.
3. *Anxious avoidant attachment* in which the individual has no confidence that support will be available when needed. Such individuals may respond by becoming emotionally self-sufficient and appear to be narcissistic.

In his book, *A secure base, parent-child attachment and healthy human development*, Bowlby (1988) states that this theory "... was formulated to explain certain patterns of behavior, characteristic not only of infants and young children but also adults and adolescents ..." (p. 119). Bowlby believes that the secure attachment type will have an easier time of moving out and exploring in increasingly wider circles (e.g., study overseas) as the individual matures. The individual who is classified as the secure attachment type should demonstrate less difficulty with homesickness. The concept of the secure base remains indispensable for high level functioning and mental health of the individual. Individuals who fall into the anxious resistant type would have more difficulties with the challenge of studying in a foreign culture. The anxious avoidant type would tend to depend on him or herself rather than developing a social network to meet emotional needs in the host culture.

Some research has been done on separation anxiety among college students using attachment theory (Hoffman, 1984; Kenny, 1990; Lopez *et al.*, 1988; Rice *et al.*, 1990). This research involved university students studying in their home country, albeit, away from their homes and families. Attachment theory could also be applied to university students who study abroad, serving as a tool for predicting risk for acculturation stress and homesickness.

Gender also is important in understanding the dynamics of how individuals manifest homesickness and acculturation stress. There is some evidence that women are more at risk for homesickness and this may be related to the tendency for women socialized in traditional cultures to be dependent, passive and family oriented (Pruitt, 1978b; Zwingmann & Gunn, 1983), whereas the traditional male role is to be strong and independent. For those who work with university students, especially those from overseas, it is important to recognize that both men and women suffer from this problem but may manifest it in different ways. Lopez *et al.* (1986) examined psychological separation and adjustment on a U.S.A. college campus. They have presented findings that suggest different dynamics at work for men and women in the process of adjusting to a new environment such as a university campus. As psychological separation from parents increased, as measured by the Psychological Separation Inventory (PSI, Hoffman, 1984), women reported less depression than men, but were less adjusted to college. By contrast, men did not demonstrate such a clear relationship between separation and how it relates to depression and college adjustment. It was also noted that, "… parent-young adult conflict during the college years facilitates men's adjustment while it undermines women's emotional health and further complicates their appropriate separation" (p. 55). Carden (1991) points out that there are cultural as well as sex differences in the level of comfort in self-disclosing about one's homesickness; she also demonstrated that both Turkish and American female students suffering from homesickness tended to be less self-reliant than their peers who were not homesick.

Other factors related to homesickness and acculturation

Stress
Student sojourners who arrive with realistic expectations and accurate information about the host culture will fare better in their new environment (Hawes & Kealey, 1981; Pruitt, 1978b; Winkelman, 1995). Chiu (1995) presents a different perspective on expectations: the level of anticipatory fear of International students, and she argues that moderate levels of anticipatory fear are related to better adjustment outcomes. Those students with unrealistically low expectations for problems in the sojourn benefited most from a stress inoculation treatment (SIT) that included three psycho-educational workshops, stress management strategies and visualization of possible problems in the new cultural environment. The high fear group seemed to be most at risk in that they benefited less (from SIT) than the low fear group yet they had higher levels of anxiety. The moderate level group had the least benefit from the SIT and it appears that they were already engaging in adapting to stressors in the new environment in an effective manner. Chiu (1995) points out that evaluating students' levels of anticipatory fear is key to effectively planning interventions for students who will study overseas.

Another factor which also helps the sojourner deal with transition in the host culture is flexibility (Gullahorn & Gullahorn, 1963; Hanvey, 1976; Ruben & Kealey, 1979; Torbiorn, 1982) and this can be thought of as a safety net for those areas where cultural information has not been provided and where expectations are not realistic. In such situations, the flexible student can more effectively respond to unexpected factors in the host culture.

Pruitt (1978a, 1978b) reports that maintenance of religious commitment was the best predictor of adjustment among African students studying in U.S.A. colleges and universities. This should not be surprising in that it is an example of the successful transplant of one aspect of one's home culture to the host culture. Such a strategy provides student sojourners with some degree of control in their new environment in that they maintain a comfortable and familiar aspect of the home culture in the new environment.

Recommendations for working with homesick students

This section will provide some practical suggestions in assisting the international student suffering from acculturation stress and homesickness. In terms of orientation, it is important to provide sojourners with accurate and up-to-date information about the study experience before they depart for their destination. Another tool that may assist students at this pre-departure stage is the Cross-Cultural Adaptation Inventory (Kelley & Meyers, 1995) to raise awareness of their levels of flexibility/openness, emotional resilience, perceptual acuity and personal autonomy, factors which are important in the cross-cultural adjustment process.

Upon arrival, workshops are important for providing more detailed information and to help groups of recently arrived students develop a group identity and a sense that they are not alone, nor unique in their adjustment difficulties.

Those working with international students should also provide opportunities for each newcomer to meet individually with helping professionals. Such a strategy will provide individuals with a chance to raise concerns about homesickness and other difficulties without an audience to observe their difficulties. Providing both individual and group support covers the different needs of students regardless of their communication preferences and cultural values. Students at risk for homesickness may need assistance in developing skills in self-reliance. This may be as fundamental as an exercise in developing a list of things to do over a weekend or in having students exchange phone numbers so that they can contact each other during the first few weeks of the sojourn. Walton (1990) also stresses the importance of incorporating healthy behaviors into the routine in the new culture including proper eating, exercise, rest, recreation, meditation or relaxation techniques.

Newcomers should also be made aware of what hobbies and interests can be pursued in the new culture and sojourners should be encouraged to do this since it will add a degree of stability to a life in transition. An example of this is continued commitment to religious beliefs, as recommended by Pruitt (1978a, 1978b). The sojourner should also be encouraged to seek out experiences which replace activities typical of his/her homeland but which are not available in the host culture. For example, surfing may replace downhill skiing for the Scandinavian sojourner studying in warmer, coastal areas.

Another important programmatic strategy is a language interchange program between the host country nationals interested in learning more about the language and culture of the student sojourner and the student sojourner. Each takes the opportunity to help the other with the new language. All of these suggestions provide an arsenal of interventions that can help integrate the newcomer and provide opportunities that will keep newcomers from having large amounts of time to contemplate how far they are from friends and family.

Conclusion

Acculturation stress and homesickness among international students are more frequent among those with limited host country language ability; primarily because this affects the amount of interaction the student sojourner can have with host country nationals. This underscores the importance of providing language training opportunities and structured situations in which the newcomer will be able to interact with host nationals on an ongoing basis. Another source of interaction is employment for the newcomer. This assists newcomers in experiencing themselves as useful and productive at a time when they may be disoriented and feel that they are inadequate in their new and unfamiliar setting. Other situations (music, sports, etc.) in which the sojourner is integrated into the host culture during the early, critical stage of the sojourn are helpful. Generally speaking, the student who is most different from the norms of the host culture will experience more acculturation stress, particularly if their difference is in language, physical appearance, dress, religion, customs and values. In terms of gender, women tend to report more problems than men during the transition; however, it should not be assumed that men are having an easier time in the acculturation process, but rather that they may feel it is less appropriate to discuss their difficulties with separation from the home culture. Carden (1991) points out that it may be counterproductive to attempt to prevent and cure homesickness. She states that moving through the homesickness experience may be an important process for the student sojourner. Chiu (1995) also refers to the 'work of worrying' that is important in the process of working through acculturation stress and homesickness. Based on this idea of the value of some stress, it follows that, rather than eliminating these uncomfortable feelings, those working with International students should provide opportunities for newcomers to integrate into the new culture rather than attempting to eliminate the symptoms of cross-cultural transition.

References

Alexander A. A., Klein, M. H., Fikre, W., & Miller, M. H. (1981). Psychotherapy and the foreign student. In: P. Pedersen, J. G. Draguns, W. J. Lonner, & J. E. Trimble (Eds.), *Counseling across cultures*. Honolulu, HI: University of Hawaii Press.

Bowlby, J. (1988). *A secure base: Parent-child attachment and healthy human development*. New York: Basic Books, Inc.

Carden, A. I. (1991). Homesickness among American college and Turkish college students. *Journal of Cross-Cultural Psychology, 22*, 418-428.

Chickering, A. W., & Reisser, L. (1993). *Education and identity* (Rev. ed.). San Francisco, CA: Jossey-Bass Publishers.

Chiu, M. L. (1995). The influence of anticipatory fear on foreign student adjustment: An exploratory study. *International Journal of Intercultural Relations, 19*, 1-44.

Church, A. (1982). Sojourner adjustment. *Psychological Bulletin, 91*, 540-572.

Deutsch, S. E., & Won, G. Y. M. (1963). Some factors in the adjustment of foreign nationals in the United States. *Journal of Social Issues, 19*, 115-122.

Gullahorn, J., & Gullahorn, J. (1963). An extension of the U-curve hypothesis. *Journal of Social Issues, 19*, 33-47.

Guzman, E., & Burke, M. J. (2003). Development and test of an international student performance taxonomy. *International Journal of Intercultural Relations, 27*, 659-681.

Hannigan, T. P. (1990). Traits, attitudes and skills that are related to intercultural effectiveness and their implications for cross-cultural training: A review of the literature. *International Journal of Intercultural Relations, 14*, 89-111.

Hanvey, R. G. (1976). Cross-cultural awareness. In: E. C. Smith & L. F. Luce (Eds.), *Toward internationalism: Readings in cross-cultural communication* (pp. 44-56). Rowley, MA: Newbury House Publishers.

Harriman, P. L. (Ed.). (1969). *Handbook of psychological terms*. Totowa, NJ: Littlefield, Adams & Co.

Harris Jr., J. G. (1973). A science of the South Pacific: Analysis of the character structure of the Peace Corps volunteer. *American Psychologist, 28*, 232-247.

Hawes, F., & Kealey, D. (1981). An empirical study of Canadian technical assistance: Adaptation and effectiveness on overseas assignment. *International Journal of Intercultural Relations, 4*, 239-258.

Hoffman, J. A. (1984). Psychological separation of late adolescents from their parents. *Journal of Counseling Psychology, 31*, 170-178.

Kelley, C., & Meyers, J. (1995). *The Cross-Cultural Adaptability Inventory Manual*. Minneapolis, MN: National Computer Systems.

Kenny, M. E. (1990). College seniors' perceptions of parental attachments: The value and stability of family ties. *Journal of College Student Development, 31*, 39-46.

Lopez, F. G., Campbell, V. L., & Watkins, C. E. (1986). Depression, psychological separation and college adjustment: An investigation of sex differences. *Journal of Counseling Psychology, 33*, 52-56.

Lopez, F. G., Campbell, V. L., & Watkins, E. C. (1988). Family structure, psychological separation and college adjustment: A canonical analysis and cross-validation. *Journal of Counseling Psychology, 35*, 402-409.

Mish, F. C., et al. (Eds.). (1986). *Webster's ninth new collegiate dictionary*. Springfield, MA: Merriam-Webster, Inc.

Oberg, K. (1960). Culture shock: Adjustment to new cultural environments. *Practical Anthropology, 7*, 177-182.

Poyrazli, S. (2003). Ethnic identity and psychosocial adjustment among international students. *Psychological Reports, 92,* 512-514.

Pruitt, F. J. (1978a). The adaptation of African students to American society. *International Journal of Intercultural Relations, 2,* 90-117.

Pruitt, F. J. (1978b). The adaptation of foreign students on American campuses. *Journal of the National Association for Women Deans, Administrators and Counselors, 41,* 144-147.

Rice, K. G., Cole, D. A., & Lapsley, D. K. (1990). Separation-individuation, family cohesion, and adjustment to college: Measurement validation and test of a theoretical model. *Journal of Counseling Psychology, 37,* 195-202.

Ruben, B. D., & Kealey, D. J. (1979). Behavioral assessment of communication competency and the prediction of cross-cultural adaptation. *International Journal of Intercultural Relations, 3,* 15-47.

Sewell, W. H., & Davidsen, O. M. (1956). The adjustment of Scandinavian students. *Journal of Social Issues, 12,* 9-19.

Torbiorn, I. (1982). *Living abroad: Personal adjustment and personnel policy in the overseas setting.* New York: Wiley.

Walton, S. J. (1990). Stress management training for overseas effectiveness. *International Journal of Intercultural Relations, 14,* 507-527.

Winkelman, M. (1994). Cultural shock and adaptation. *Journal of Counseling and Development, 73,* 121-126.

Zwingmann, C. A. A., & Gunn, A. D. G. (1983). *Uprooting and health: Psychosocial problems of students from abroad.* Geneva: World Health Organization, Division of Mental Health.

6 Psychological and Psychosocial Adjustment of Migrants: Families in a Changing Environment[1].

DAN G. HERTZ

Preface and rational

The actuality and topicality of this paper has been facilitated by the many and often unexpected events and political changes which are taking place at the present time in different parts of the world. The author does not intend to enumerate all of them; however the aftermath of 'glasnost and perestroyka,' the unification of Europe in 1992-1994 and the impending changes in South East Asia in 1997 are quoted as examples. The question to be asked is not whether these changes affect the physical and mental health of the world population, but rather to what extent are behavioral scientists, researchers, clinicians and medical specialists ready to meet the changes of this new historical 'migration of nations' (*Völkerwanderung*) and its consequences on the health of individuals and families.

This chapter emphasizes the complexity of contemporary migration research. In a selected review different choices for investigation are presented, namely the biological, psychological and social aspects. The presentation, however, focuses mainly on two specific topics: (a) the process of adjustment of migrant families, and (b) coping of aging migrants with traumatic stressors experienced in the past.

Introduction

Voluntary and forced migration is one of the most permanent themes of human history, which did not lose its actuality with the passing of time. On the contrary, it has become in the twentieth century a major and increasingly demanding central issue facing many governments all over the world.

Some areas of the world have larger populations than they are able to support properly without depriving them of the basic needs of human existence. At the same time, however, many other nations continue to make active efforts to bring people to their area. Their action can be motivated by ideological, political, religious or economic considerations, or, as it often happens, by the combination of some or all the factors mentioned.

---

1   An earlier version of this paper appeared in: *Family issues: an interdisciplinary view on family stresses and their consequences* (1994) Dan G. Hertz MD (Editor), Gefen Publishing House, Scientific Publication Division, New York, Jerusalem (Copyright Dan G. Hertz).

People, who are forced or who wish to settle in another part of their country or in another area of the world, present problems, which have attracted growing attention, both nationally and internationally (Cohen, 1981). These problems have become of major interest for psychologically oriented studies of culture-change, which deal with correlations between sociocultural factors and different areas of physical and mental health (Fabrega, 1969; Born, 1970; Brody, 1970).

The change of environment as a result of migration frequently confronts individuals and families with demands they are not ready or able to meet. Previous studies of migrants tried to correlate sociocultural factors with physical and emotional health. These studies reflect a wide range of methods and approaches, including ethno-psychiatric and sociological studies, epidemiological and clinical investigations of individuals and groups exposed to environmental changes (Weinberg, 1961; Sanua, 1970; Kagan & Levi, 1971).

In recent years increased emphasis has been put on the biological aspects of migration defining the consequences of migration. This approach describes human migration as the mechanism that injects DNA from one gene pool to another, and also as the mechanism that inserts similar kind of individuals into diverse environments (Mascie-Taylor & Lasker, 1988).

Although migration is a world-wide phenomenon, its complex influence on the health of the migrant and his family has not yet been explored. Controversies exist whether the process of migration impairs the health of migrants (Dutt & Baker, 1978; Hertz 1980). The available literature shows a divided opinion. The issue becomes even more complicated when one attempts to study emotional reactions and their psycho-physiological consequences in migrant populations. Sex and age differences in these groups only add further challenge to the problem (Nathanson, 1977; Mechanic, 1978).

Coping with environmental stimuli

It is important to stress the impact of changing physical and social environment on migrant individuals and families. There is an inborn tendency in man to search for the environment, which provides him with the proper level of stimulation. Man will usually avoid environments, which either fail to offer the necessary stimulus or exceed his individual tolerance. When the individual is overloaded by stimuli, he will necessarily develop coping methods and defenses. The efforts involved in achieving these coping mechanisms might lead to the occurrence of physical or mental pathology, or both.

Excessive environmental stimuli may cause excessive arousal of the cortical and autonomous nervous system, increasing the susceptibility to physical and emotional disorders (Ex, 1966; Lipowski, 1973). The same principle has been described in a theoretical model showing that a person's physiological and psychological reactions are closely related to the combined effect of psychobiological factors based on genetic and early environmental influences and of psychosocial stimuli.

Once the intensity and duration of the stimuli have become extreme, the total organic system may be affected eventually causing increased morbidity. The above theoretical formulation is easily applicable to the environmental changes caused by migration (Kagan *et al.*, 1971).

Definitions

Migration is often defined as the more or less permanent movement of persons or groups over a significant distance. However, the definition becomes more complex when it intends to classify an individual or a family as a migrant, e.g., in terms of place of birth or place of socialization (age at the time of arrival or recency of arrival). Distinction must also be made between migrations and moving: "All migrants are persons who have moved but not all movers are migrants" (Hertz, 1981a,b,c).

There seems to be a definite effect, which can be found in people, and families who have made a major environmental change when compared to those who have not. These effects are greatly dependent on the form and nature of migration. Kirk (1947) has differentiated between *internal migration*, within the same country, *international migration* within one continent, and *overseas migration*. According to the motivation and emotional atmosphere of the migration, one can also define *voluntary, forced, ideological* and *political* migration. According to the legal aspects one has also to differentiate between *legal* and *illegal* migration (Hertz, 1981a,b, 1984; Hertz & Freyberger, 1982).

From the variety of factors mentioned in different research publications, there is a consensus to focus attention on (individual) factors, which may affect the fate of migrant person and/or of the migrant family. It has still to be remembered that the decision of migration does not necessarily depend on the migrant alone but also on the law which determined who is going to migrate (emigrate and/or immigrate) and where to.

Among the individual factors, specific variables play specific roles, such as age, sex, ethnic origin, socio-economic status, personal, family and medical background, in addition to manifest and hidden motives affecting the decision to make the move from one country to another (Murphy, 1961).

Social scientists claim that migration should be understood as a process of *desocialisation*. Therefore, the adaptation to the new environment has been considered as a result of *resocialization*. To achieve this, the recipient community must be prepared to show its tolerance towards the new immigrants (individual and family) to learn by trial and error new clues of behavior, before expecting that they will be able to assume their new role and social identity in terms of the new environment (Shuval, 1963; Weintraub, 1971).

Erikson (1956, 1960) emphasized the relation between identity and uprooted ness. He claimed that during different crisis situations a new and often transitory identity develops. He stressed mainly the importance of intrapsychic mechanisms, which are involved in the maintenance of the individual sense of identity. In our opinion however, the role of social determinants must be equally taken into consideration; such as, motivation for the migration; the process of separation from the earlier environment; stages of absorption and reinvolvement in the new environment (Hertz, 1980).

Migration and health

Human migration is often motivated by biological necessity, physical deprivation or suffering, but also by realistic and symbolic needs in man. Persecution, ideological disputes and substandard living conditions have contributed separately and together, to bring about human changes of place.

Many conditions of the lives of those who migrate may affect health. Climatic factors, temperature, humidity, altitude, amount of solar radiation, air pollution and intercurrent disease can all influence directly and indirectly the individual through air, food and skin, and possibly in other ways (Hull, 1979). The lifestyles of migrants, such as food preparation, sanitary habits and occupation, may be inappropriate, maladaptive or even pathogenic in new settings (Hertz et al., 1982).

As a social phenomenon, migration is not well understood and its influence on health is ambiguous. However, it does provide special situations in which to develop and test hypotheses having to do with the relative and/or collective influence of heredity and environment, the impact of the change factor itself and the differing impact of the environment, depending on the time of life the change took place.

The study of migrant human populations is intrinsically challenging because of the increase in the world-wide migration rates. At the same time, it also emerges as a methodology for studying the causes of biological variation among human populations (Mascie-Taylor et al., 1988).

While the social and demographical causes and consequences of migration have been extensively studied, the sequelae of migration to health have been poorly explored. Such studies as have been completed are almost always concerned with migrants who move from poor or peasant living conditions into modern urban situations. These studies, not surprisingly often show an overall improvement of health. At the same time selected disease frequencies may rise and evidence of increased psychological stress is often reported. Although such selected migration has led to health improvement, it has been argued that theoretically the process of migration as such should not necessarily improve health (Hertz, 1980; Hertz et al., 1986). Instead, a general health decline may occur with the specific nature of the health alteration determined by the overall natural and cultural environmental change related to the migration (Dohrenwend & Dohrenwend, 1975; Kuo, 1976). Migration, in and of itself, does not precipitate the development of illness. Migration, however, does involve changes in environment, which require adjustment on the part of the migrant. These adjustments may be reflected in improved or worsened health.

By viewing the relationship between migration and health there are four major theoretical formulations, namely the theories of social isolation, cultural shock, goal-striving stress and cultural changing, which can be identified as the most stress producing life changes experienced by the migrant (Kuo, 1976). According to the theory of *social isolation* often experience strong feelings of loneliness, alienation, desocialization, low self-esteem and inability to sustain social relationships.

Although the second theory contends that the immigrant's most severe adjustment problem is caused by *cultural shock* the concepts have never been adequately defined. For instance, Handlin (1951) stated that migrants experience shock because of severe feelings of personal inefficacy, lack of norms and role instability.

On the other hand Eisenstadt (1954) suggested that migrants are affected by the experience of living in an unstructured, incompletely defined social field. The only consensus between the different definitions is that "the shorter the immigration period, the greater the shock." Thus making the distress more intense, but that as the immigrants become acculturated, the intensity toward development of illness will be gradually reduced.

The third theory of *goal striving stress*, describes a unique aspect of the immigrant's adjustment problem, that of unfulfilled aspirations. It has been established that among foreign immigrants from less urbanized and industrialized societies, the first generation will experience lower goal-striving stress than their descendants.

The fourth and last theory emphasizes the disrupting effect of the cultural change on the psychological orientation of the new migrant undergoing acculturation. Proponents of this theory claim that the adoption of new cultural values involves a fundamental disruption and shift in the cognitive, affective and valuative modes of behavior in the migrant's native culture. Thus, the cultural change theory, which states that "the more intense the pressure of acculturation, the greater the psychological distress will be", directly conflicts with the hypothesis of the cultural shock (Wolstenholme & O'Connor, 1966; Westermeyer, 1989).

The problem of acculturation

It has been proposed by the author that migrants, individuals and families, experience a period of grief after migration but gradually recover from it and eventually adjust to the new environment (Hertz, 1981, 1982a, 1984, 1985, 1986). The migrant's difficulties derive from the process of acculturation (Herskovits, 1958; Redfield *et al.*, 1967; Berry *et al.*, 1987). Our latest definition of this term emphasizes biological aspects as well as environmental changes. Acculturation is defined as "the total adaptive and coping process affecting not only the cultural patterning and value system, but also the psychological structure and psychophysiological functions of individuals and families. This occurs as adaptation is made to changed conditions created by the impact of people and their environment upon each other" (Hertz, 1981b, 1985, 1988).

Difficulties in the process of acculturation contribute to the development of culture shock. It usually derives in migrant populations from intrapsychic and interpersonal sources. The intrapsychic factors are often connected with the failure of proper verbal and non-verbal communication with the environment. In the past relatively little attention was given to the non-verbal system of *kinesics* (communication by movement, gestures and expressions). Misunderstanding in the non-verbal sphere tends to create unexplained emotional reactions no less than verbal communications. It stands to reason that the difficulties in communication increase when accompanied by the lack of ability for verbal communication. Limitation of language reinforces the sense of emotional and social isolation. However, non-verbal misunderstandings often have a longer lasting effect than verbal ones (Hartog, 1971).

When the migrant person, family and/or group are confronted with cultural misunderstanding or does not estimate properly the new environment, interpersonal conflicts will be easily reinforced. The faulty application of certain social habits, taboos and costumes may often precipitate the intensity of such conflicts (e.g., taking the initiative in social contacts, handshaking, touching, etc.). Preconceived ideas, eventually prejudices originating from the cultural background of the migrant group may interfere with the process of acculturation.

Especially the feeling that another cultural, racial or religious group cannot understand the migrants, may be misinterpreted as an expression of condescending view and discrediting attitude of the new environment. It may add to the consequent loss of self-esteem in the migrant group (Hertz, 1993b).

Positive adjustment following migration

Positive adjustment can be described by three consecutive stages:
1. Pre-immigration
2. Coping stage of migration
3. Settlement

All three of these stages comprise a combination of positive and negative emotional factors. The correlation between the two, in other words the proper utilization of the positive elements and the control of the negative ones, can be used as an indicator in the prediction of immigrant adjustment and mental health (Hertz 1980, 1988, 1993a, b).

1. *Pre-immigration*

The individual and/or the family need motivation for the change. They use rationalization and justification for making the move. Positive expectation from the outcome of migration creates the proper emotional atmosphere for getting ready for the move. However, if denial of future difficulties and over-idealization of the new environment distorts reality testing, the outcome may become high risk for future maladjustment.

2. *Coping stage of immigration*

This period has to be divided into three consecutive stages of development: (1) impact level, (2) rebound level and (3) coping level. The impact level is experienced at the moment of arrival to the destined new environment. It is characterized by elation, relief and feeling of fulfillment. This level is relatively quickly followed by a rebound reaction, after having encountered the reality of the new environment. It manifests itself by expression of disappointment, which is often followed by anger and aggressive behavior or depression and/or dysthymic mood. It can be considered the psychological and societal equivalent of the physiological 'fight or flight' reaction. The clinical manifestations in this sub-stage can be either an expression of acting out of anger or complete withdrawal and avoidance of involvement with the new environment.

The coping level comprises the process of learning and mastery. Modes of communication will be improved with the environment, which is also reinforced by learning the language. This stage also comprises the development of familiarity with the support system of the social network and also learning the potential and readiness of the new environment for offering understanding and help. Strengthening emotional ties through adjustment of children and relatives enhances the development of the feeling of trust and increased sense of security.

3. *Settlement stage*

The process of positive adjustment reaches a climax in this stage. Readiness of the immigrant and his/her family to accept compromises with the new environment plays a major role. Once the family feels it is understood by its surroundings, it will also be more prepared to understand and accept the demand of the outside world towards them. Progressive identification with the aims and goals of the community will slowly bring about the sense of belonging.

Family adjustment (confrontation with cultural changes)

There is no unified theory about the coping mechanism of families with changing socio-cultural environment. Eisenstadt (1954) has described five different types of family constellations with various results in attempting to cope with migration stress. His definitions make a basic distinction between isolated and cohesive families.

Surprisingly, not all the isolated families are prone to have adjustment difficulties. Even socially isolated families are able to overcome adjustment problems, depending on their ability to mobilize inner resources.

Only a combination of apathy and isolation will lead to absolute social breakdown in the family's functioning. Stable and active isolated families show reasonable prognosis for positive adjustment. The best outcome was found in those active families, which belong to a cohesive ethnic group. Such an individual and social constellation will reinforce the collective ability of the migrant family to undertake active steps for self-transformation in a new social milieu. Families belonging to this category will enjoy not only intra-familial support but also the cohesive influence of the ethnic group.

The study of traditionally oriented, patriarchal families and westernized immigrant families during and after the first year of arrival show striking differences between the factors to be used as predictors for successful adjustment (Hertz, 1981a,b, 1993a).

The integration of the traditionally oriented, patriarchally functioning families is mainly determined by the ability to deal adequately with the changes connected with the process of migration. Both generations, fathers/mothers and sons/daughters, are confronted with sets of demands emanating partly from the new situation, partly from each other. In this process, the parents' (fathers') readiness to accept changes in the family's function has to be complimented by the children's (sons/daughters) proneness to maintain to some extent the family traditions.

Once the two conflicting parties, the old and new generations, reach a mutually acceptable compromise, the family will succeed to maintain undisturbed intrapsychic and interpersonal functions. However, if the understanding between parents and children fails to materialize, it will result in a breakdown of functioning, expressed by individual and family psychopathology.

The parent in the traditional patriarchal system is confronted with new situations, where decisions to be made are contested and shared by other members of the family. This is expressed not only in the growing influence and participation of the wife in making decisions for the family but also in general liberalization of the family atmosphere.

Changes in the status of women (working outside the family home) and a different educational system add to development of new family constellations (Hertz et al., 1986; Dumon, 1989). The danger exists for the father to be overruled and opposed by other family members who become better educated than the parents. The former belief that the father is absolute and infallible authority in the family is often challenged by his unsuccessful struggle against new bureaucratic rules and demands which he never experienced before. If the father can mobilize family support for the newly presented situation, the result will become 'closing the ranks' and the development of increased solidarity within the family.

The parental generation has to overcome the painful loss of authority, which might be compensated by stronger and warmer family relations. Usually, the individual frustration of the 'pater familias' following the loss of status, deprives him of the ability to balance it by eventual reinforcement of family ties. Family and clan solidarity may grow stronger, but the father will never again become the central authority figure. He will also be forced to come to terms with the separation of his sons from the family home.

Children in the traditional family need to prove their willingness in continuing to accept parental authority. The earlier accepted ways of communication, such as requesting permission and consulting father before decisions will be made, is expected to be continued. Similarly, remaining 'in the family orbit,' accepting parental participation in the selection of their marital partners, will also decrease intergenerational conflicts precipitated by the process of immigration and might enhance better adjustment for the immigrant family as a social unit.

The westernized families present a completely different set of factors in the adjustment process. Western families usually allow more freedom for individual family members. Their symptoms of maladaptation originate from different sources than those of the traditional families. The Western families usually strive for acceptance by the environment, express their wish, and quest for security by their inclination for rapid mastery of the new setting. Maladjusted westernized immigrant families present the following major emotional issues:

1. Feeling of emotional isolation
2. Suffering from lack of satisfactory social contacts
3. Concern about insecurity in the future

Moral dependence on the social environment, lack of regular independent income and frustration to master the new social situation are considered as additional precipitating factors for adjustment difficulties.

Problems originating from the encounter with an entirely new (earlier not experienced) societal and economic system may add to the development of a temporary crisis situation. Families immigrating from countries which lack democratic rule and where restrictive migration laws were practiced, often complain about the feeling of reaching a 'point of no return,' meaning the loss of option to make free decision about eventual remigration to their country of origin. This may add to the difficulties experienced after immigration. Nostalgic longing and homesickness perturbs those immigrants when they realize that they have been deprived from the choice to renegotiate their earlier choice, to return 'home,' even if in reality they would hardly consider it. The above experiences have been often found in migrants and refugees from Eastern European and other totalitarian regimes (Hertz, 1980, 1993a,b).

Historical aspects of nostalgia and homesickness

Through the ages, the typical response of humans separated from their homes, families and native cultural environment has been described as 'nostalgia' or 'homesickness.' Nostalgia is defined by the Concise Oxford Dictionary as 'sentimental yearning for the past.' The expression originates from the Greek nostos, 'to return home' and algos, 'pain' (Rosen, 1975, Hertz, 1986, 1990, 1993a). This condition was first described by Hofer in Basel in 1685, but the manifestations of separation from the home and environment have been a topic of classical literature as far back as the Bible.

Homer described Ulysses as weeping and rolling on the floor when he thought of his home. The same indications of homesickness are reflected in Psalms 137: "By the waters of Babylon we sat down, yeah, wept when we remembered Zion." Studying accounts of nostalgia in 18th and 19th century medical literature, Jaspers (1909) reported a variety of symptoms related to migration, including persistent thoughts of home, melancholia, insomnia, loss of appetite, weakness, anxiety, palpitations, diffuse pain, tension and even stupor.

Modern psychology has delineated two further aspects of migration and separation from home. The first relates to the fact that in many languages, people speak of their home country in parental terms. Germany is usually referred to as the 'Vaterland' (Fatherland). The French use the expression, 'La Patrie,' combining masculine and feminine elements. The Irish refer to Ireland as a mother and also with some sexual overtones, as a beautiful woman. The Hebrew 'Moledet' also has feminine connotations associated with birth.

The second recent development in the study of migration equates the migrants' feelings of separation and loss with grief. Over thirty years ago, Engel (1962) pointed out that not enough attention has been paid to the medical implications of grief. At that time, the prevailing view considered grief a purely subjective psychological experience, which did not involve somatic changes.

In previous publications this author theorized that the migrant could experience a period of grief after migration, but would gradually recover from it and eventually adjust to the conditions of his new environment. However, he might retain ambivalent feelings towards his homeland. At the same time, it was also assumed that although health care may actually improve as a consequence of migration, existentially present stress factors could either precipitate stress manifestations or cause a shift from one type of illness to another.

The move from one environment to another can be considered a crisis situation because the consequences of the environmental change are experienced by the migrant individual/family as localized, time-related and focused life events. The stresses following migration can affect coping patterns and mechanisms, which then will become maladaptive. Psychological symptoms and psychophysiological reactions may arise and previously existing ones may be aggravated, and possibly lead to disability.

Nostalgia, homesickness and pathogenesis

There appears to be little published work on homesickness as a clinical entity (Rosen, 1975; Werman, 1977; Hertz, 1985, 1986), although the literature on crises related to loss and separation is extensive. The scant work dealing specifically with nostalgia does not offer a unified view. Opinions greatly differ revealing an apparent dichotomy between psychological and psychodynamic explanations on one hand and psychophysiological (psychosomatic) interpretations on the other.

Retrospective clinical studies show a marked tendency toward somatic over-concern and a greater number of somatic complaints in several refugee groups. Recent publications report a variety of clinical pictures as manifestations of homesickness. Barros-Ferreira (1976) described an atypical clinical condition in Portuguese immigrants ('bastard hysterical syndrome') which is characterized by fatigue, anxiety, sense of suffocation, dyspnoea, coughing, chills, abdominal and gastric pain, headaches, paresthesia, backache, vomiting, diarrhea, cardiac pains, palpitations, dizziness and collapse. The symptoms were usually attributed to such precipitating causes as familial death, trauma without importance, work conflict, etc. The most frequent cause however was 'the strange climate' with reference to the foreign emotional environment. The symptomatology was explained mainly by the migrants' attempts to substitute the attention of a physician or social services, or of the employer, for that of his absent family.

Larbig et al. (1979) studied Greek, Japanese and German workers in foreign countries, investigating the development, frequency and characteristic symptomatology of psychosomatic and functional disorders. Social changes were defined as pathogenic stressors, which were followed by psychopathological consequences on human behavior (Larbig, 1981). According to his definition, homesickness is a "cognitive affective phenomenon with intense wish for geographic and chronological changes".

Aging migrants

As mentioned above, we have studied the reactions of aging migrants in order to define how these people dealt with their past, and what role if any, their memories played in preserving or breaking down their usual coping mechanisms. In these studies, methodological considerations required that the various stressors related to environmental changes be identified generally as physical, psychological, and psychosocial stressors. In the research population a group of aging Holocaust survivors was also included. A summary of the findings in aging migrants in general reflect that some of the conclusions could be applied as well to Holocaust survivors (Hertz, 1994).

The major common characteristics of migrants and survivors were the following:
1. Sudden (traumatic) separation from home and family.
2. Exposure to various extreme stress situations.
3. Partial or total loss of family ties (significant figures).
4. Establishment of a 'new life' in a new place.
5. Development of a 'new life cycle'.
6. Coping and adjustment (A. escape into activity, B. retreat into illness).
7. Onset of aging. Increased emergence of memories (Reminiscences, nostalgic longings).

To cope with these experiences, both groups mobilized a wide range of psychological defenses. With advancing age, a variety of physical and mental symptoms appear in different constellations of psychophysiological and emotional responses, which were often over-shadowed by reminiscences, reappearance of memory traces and nostalgic longings.

The reader must be reminded that a distinction has to be made between *memory* and *reminiscence*. The two concepts definitely do not overlap. According to Castelnuovo-Tedesco (1978), memory encompasses much more than simple reminiscence. It includes the processes by which memories are established, organized and retrieved; the problems of memory distortion and also its restoration. Similarly, different definitions of reminiscence have been offered. Castelnuovo-Tedesco (1978), describes reminiscence with positive overtones as "the act or habit of thinking about, or relating past experiences, especially those considered personally most significant." Another definition however stresses the normative aspects but also includes eventual psychopathology: "Reminiscence is a normal, universal process of life review in the elderly prompted in part by the realization of approaching death. The person reviews past life and conflicts and possibilities for their resolution. Depression, anxiety, regret and despair may be present" (APA Psychiatric Glossary, 1984).

As mentioned before, separation from family and home environment (a characteristic of the migrants' emotional experience) was described as accompanied usually by a feeling of loss, similar to grief. This definition included the expectation that a certain period of mourning, limited in time, will be terminated through a gradual recovery. This assumption however, did not always hold true. Many Holocaust survivors, who were exposed to brutal force and abrupt separation from their family (which was followed by loss of family ties forever) reported the experience of 'permanently engraved' memories. Those experiences are often and easily recalled and followed by reliving the experience accompanied by the same emotions they felt when the original trauma took place (Hertz et al., 1982).

In earlier studies we stressed the close relationship between nostalgia and the tendency for regression, which provides an escape of the displaced migrant into the remembered gratification of an earlier stage of development. The hypothesis is put forward that nostalgia should be considered more a *symptom* than a disease.

The English expression, 'home-sickness' implies rather a disease entity and therefore it can be misleading. A better understanding and more effective clinical approach is obtained if nostalgic manifestations are considered symptoms which may be the sole indicators of a temporary stress situation in many cases. In others, however, they become the precursor of a developing illness.

Nostalgia encompasses a variety of multidimensional factors:

1. It may be manifested as an *intense, almost unbearable longing for home,* mixed with and based on the pleasure felt as a child.
2. The intense longing for a particular time or place is often *mistakenly interpreted as a rejection of the time and place* where the migrant currently is.
3. The appearance and manifestation of nostalgia is further clinical proof that our environment, like our inner world, *is made up of significant psychic objects,* (not only physical objects). *Any kind of object loss may become a potential stress* especially when it occurs during a vulnerable developmental stage, like aging. Actual loss can negatively influence total adjustment. Under such conditions nostalgic manifestations are likely to appear.
4. Apparently, the physiological manifestations accompanying nostalgic symptoms and longings are controlled by the *limbic and reticular activating systems (RAS).* Psychophysiological (psychosomatic) symptoms appear to be possible *substitutes for inhibited verbal-motor response* to psychosocial stress through increased autonomous, visceral or endocrine activity (eventually eliciting even sensory manifestations).
5. Nostalgic reactions may occur in *groups* as well as in *individuals.* Group nostalgia appears to have fewer psychophysiological consequences due, at least in part, to the influence of the group as a support system.
6. Prolonged deprivation may result in regressive behavior. *Continuous nostalgic manifestations* might therefore indicate *biological and social maladaptation.*

Nostalgic reactions in the aged are partially related to organic changes in the central nervous system. It has been recognized that the decreased ability of the aged person to perceive and store new stimuli reinforces the tendency to recall past events with nostalgic overtones (Hertz, 1985, 1986).

With the age, the ego progressively loses its previous well-functioning defenses and tries to compensate for the threat 'from within.' The vacuum caused by partial memory failure might be successfully filled in by nostalgic thoughts which provide some gratification through the idealization of the past but at the same time also confront the aging person with the irreversible fact that the past (and the loved ones belonging to the past) are gone forever. Thus a bitter-sweet feeling expresses the ambivalence arising from unfulfilled wishes and the conflict between escape into the past and acceptance of the present.

Reminiscing and dealing with nostalgic reactions are important in general for successful adaptation to old age. It is even more so in older migrants and displaced persons (refugees) who have been exposed to a conglomeration of traumatic experiences and separation in earlier stages of their life. Their reminiscence and nostalgia embrace issues of time, loss, mourning, and also maintenance of identity. Theoretically these phenomena offer further evidence of the role and place of internal representation in the organization of the mind.

They also demonstrate that the mind is 'peopled.' Figures of the past are more than abstract remnants of another time; they become also part of current realities. When memory summons them to life, they become three-dimensional with all the concomitant emotional intensity (Castelnuovo-Tedesco, 1978; Hertz, 1990).

The eventual role of sensory stimuli in the reminiscences and nostalgic feelings of aging migrants must be emphasized. Smell and taste may elicit vivid reminiscences. It has been observed in migrants and Holocaust survivors that olfactory sensory stimuli are related to specific sensory events experienced during episodes of starvation. It seems that corresponding reminiscences are replicated through sensory pathways, and can activate intense memories related to threat, persecution and death. These sensory experiences are often followed by recollections of painful memory traces. The accompanying affective response may reflect both excitement and pleasure. However, the examination of the associative consequences reveals that the pleasure expressed by the aging migrants on such occasion relates to the perception of their 'survival' and not to the experience itself.

Conclusions

In this chapter an attempt was made to present theoretical considerations and clinical characteristics of adjustment of migrant families exposed to intense environmental stressors (separation, migration, acculturation). The reader must be reminded that due to the very wide scope of the problem (and to avoid superficiality) the author had to focus his presentation only to some arbitrarily selected issues.

Introducing the concept of crisis in the understanding of the acculturation process of migrant families, the necessity of accepting the developmental approach in dealing with the stress of migration is repeatedly emphasized.

It seems that no migration can be carried out without emotional and often physical stress and traumata, which expose the migrant/immigrant family to somewhat predictable but frequently unexpected additional stress factors. This process can be compared with the natural development and course of different grief reactions. Our approach advocates that a natural course of reactions must be experienced before reaching the state of emotional and social stability following migration. To support the theoretical considerations, the course of positive family adjustment was described in detail. Differences between adjustment reactions of traditional and westernized families were also pointed out.

The above-mentioned condition exists also in families that have been confronted with stressful and life threatening situations (like major natural and man-made catastrophes; floods, earthquakes; persecution and war). In this context, correspondence between stress of migration and earlier experienced traumatic stressors of other sources in aging migrants, have been put forward.

The process of acculturation of migrant families can be better understood when approached with a multi-determined bio-psycho-social concept. This dynamic process reflects the continuous interaction between individual, family and socio-cultural environment.

As migration presents the best *in vivo* situation for testing hypotheses concerned with the etiology and pathogenesis of many conditions, further research may help to solve basic and still controversial issues having to do with the relative contribution of genetic and other host factors versus environmental factors (Wessen, 1971; Hull, 1979) One can even hope that better understanding of the health response to migration may also bring to find new ways to extend the limits of the human adaptive capacity.

References

The American Psychiatric Association's Psychiatric Glossary (1984). Washington, DC: American Psychiatric Press, Inc.

Barros-Ferreira, M. (1976). Hysterie et fait psychosomatique chez l'immigrant portugais. *Acta Psychiatrica Belgica, 76*, 551-578.

Berry, J. W., Kim, V., & Minde, T. (1987). Comparative studies of acculturative stress. *International Migration Review, 21*, 491-511.

Born, D. O. (1970). Psychological adaptation and development under acculturative stress. *Social Science & Medicine, 3*, 529-543.

Brody, E. G. (Ed.) (1970). *Behavior in new environments*. Beverly Hills, CA: Sage Publications.

Castelnuovo-Tedesco, P. (1978). The mind as a stage: Some comments on reminiscense and internal objects. *International Journal of Psychoanalysis, 59*, 15-25.

Cohen, J. D. (1981). Psychological adaptation and dysfunction among refugees. *International Migration Review, 15,* 255-275.

Dohrenwend, B. S., & Dohrenwend B. P. (Eds.) (1975). *Stressful life events: Their nature and effects.* New York: Wiley.

Dumon, W. A. (1989). Family and migration. *International Migration Review, 27*, 251-270.

Dutt, J. S., & Baker, P. T. (1978). Environment, migration and health in Southern Peru. *Social Science & Medicine, 12*, 29-38.

Eisenstadt, S. N. (1954). *The absorption of immigrants.* London: Routledge & Kegan Paul.

Engel, G. L. (1962). Is grief a disease? *Psychosomatic Medicine, 23*, 18-22.

Erikson, E. H. (1956). The problem of ego identity. *Journal of American Psychoanalytical Association, 4*, 56-121.

Erikson, E. H. (1960). Identity and uprootedness in our time. In: *Uprooting and resettlement.* London: World Federation of Mental Health.

Ex, J. (1966). *Adjustment after migration.* The Hague, The Netherlands: Martinus Nijhoff.

Fabrega, H. Jr. (1969). Social psychiatric aspects of acculturation and migration: a general statement. *Comprehensive Psychiatry, 10,* 314-326.

Handlin, O. (1951). *The uprooted.* New York: Grossett & Dunlop.

Hartog, J. (1971). Transcultural aspects of community psychiatry. *Mental Hygiene, 55*, 35-44.

Herskovits, N. J. (1958). *Acculturation: The study of culture contact.* Gloucester, MA: Peter Smith.

88

Hertz, D. G. (1980). Remigration: psychological problems of the returning resident. In: W. M. Pfeiffer & W. Schoene (Eds.), *Psychopathologie im Kulturvergleich* (pp. 282-293). Stuttgart, Germany: Ferdinand Enke Verlag.

Hertz, D. G. (1981a). The stress of migration: Adjustment reactions of migrants and their families. In: L. Eitinger & D. Schwarz (Eds.) (pp. 70-83). Bern, Switzerland: Hans Huber Publishers.

Hertz, D. G. (1981b). Arrival and departure: Theoretical considerations and clinical observations on migrants and immigrants. *Psychiatric Journal of Ottawa, 6*, 234-238.

Hertz, D. G. (1981c). Le problem de la migration et de l'acculturation en Israel [The problem of migration and acculturation in Israel]. *Evolution Psychiatrique, 46*, 349-356.

Hertz, D. G. (1982). Psychosomatic and psychosocial implications of environmental changes on migrants. *Israelian Journal of Psychiatry and Related Sciences, 19*, 329-338.

Hertz, D. G. (1984). Psychological and psychiatric aspects of remigration. *Israelian Journal of Psychiatry and Related Sciences, 21*, 57-68.

Hertz, D. G. (1985). Homesickness and psychosomatic illness. In: P. Pichot, P. Berner, R. Wolf, & K. Thau (Eds.), *Psychotherapy and Psychosomatic Medicine* (pp. 387-402). New York: Plenum Press.

Hertz, D. G. (1986). Nostalgia rediscovered: A psychophysiological reappraisal of symptom formation in homesickness. In: J. H. Lacey & D. A. Sturgeon (Eds.), *Psychosomatic Research* (pp. 340-343). London: John Libbey.

Hertz, D. G. (1988). Identity – lost and found: Patterns of migration and psychological and psychosocial adjustment of migrants. *Acta Psychiatrica Scandinavia Suppl., 78: S 344*, 159-166.

Hertz, D. G. (1990). Trauma and nostalgia: New aspects on the coping of aging Holocaust survivors. *Israelian Journal of Psychiatry and Related Sciences, 27*, 189-198.

Hertz, D. G. (1993a). Coping with environmental and psychosocial changes: Theoretical considerations and clinical applications. In: B. Strauss, C. Bahne Bahnson, & H. Speidel (Eds.), *New Societies – New Models in Medicine* (pp. 17-26). New York: Schattauer.

Hertz, D. G. (1993b). Bio-psychosocial consequences of migration stress: A multidimensional approach. *Israelian Journal of Psychiatry and Related Sciences, 30*, 204-212.

Hertz, D. G. (1994). The stress of migration: Adjustment problems of migrant and displaced families. In: D. G. Hertz (Ed.), *Family Issues: An interdisciplinary view on family stresses and their consequences.* Jerusalem, Israel: Gefen Publishing House.

Hertz, D. G., & Freyberger, H. (1982). Factors influencing the evaluation of psychological and psychosomatic reactions in survivors of the Nazi persecution. *Journal of Psychosomatic Research, 26*, 83-89.

Hertz, D. G., & Molinski, H. (1986). *Psychosomatik der Frau* (3rd rev. ed.). Heidelberg, Berlin/New York: Springer Verlag.

Hull, D. (1979). Migration, adaptation and illness: A review. *Social Sciences & Medicine, 13A*, 25-36.

Jaspers, K. (1909). Heimweh und Verbrechen [Homesickness and crime]. *Archiv für Kriminal-anthropologie und Kriminalistik, 35*, 1-116

Kagan, A., & Levi, L. (1971). Adaptation of the psychosocial environment to man's abilities and needs. In: *Society, Stress and Disease* (pp. 99-404). London: Oxford University Press.

Kirk, D. (1947). European migrations: prewar trends and future prospects. In L. J. Reed (Ed.), *Postwar problems of migration*. New York: Milbank Memorial Fund.

Kuo, W. (1976). Theories of migration and mental health: An empirical testing on Chinese-Americans. *Social Sciences & Medicine, 10*, 297-306.

Larbig, W., Xenakis, Ch., & Onishi, M. (1979). Psychosomatische Symptome and funktionelle Beschwerden bei Arbeitsnehmern im Ausland. *Zeitschrift für Psychosomatische Medizine und Psychoanalyses, 25,* 49-63.

Larbig, W. (1981). Homesickness as a disease factor. *Mediziniscvhe Klinik, 75,* 36-39.

Lipowski, Z. J. (1973). Psychosomatic medicine in a changing society: Some current trends in theory and research. *Comprehensive Psychiatry, 14,* 203-215.

Mascie-Taylor, C. G. N., & Lasker, G. W. (Eds.) (1988). *Biological aspects of human migration.* Cambridge, UK: Cambridge University Press.

Mechanic, D. (1978). Sex, illness, illness behavior and the use of health services. *Social Sciences & Medicine, 12B,* 207-214.

Murphy, H. B. M. (1961). Social change and mental health. In: *Causes of mental disorders: A review of epidemiological knowledge.* New York: Milbank Memorial Fund.

Nathanson, C. A. (1977). Sex, illness and medical care. *Social Sciences & Medicine, 11,* 13-25.

Redfield, R., Linton, R., & Herskovits, M. J. (1967). Memorandum for the study of acculturation. In: *Beyond the frontier: Social process and cultural change.* Garden City, NY: Natural History Press.

Rosen, G. (1975). Nostalgia: A 'forgotten' psychological disorder. *Psychological Medicine, 5,* 340-354.

Sanua, V. D. (1970). Immigration, migration and mental illness. In: E. B. Brody (Ed.), *Behavior in new environments* (chapter 13). Beverly Hills, CA: Sage Publication.

Shuval, J. (1963). *Immigrants: On the threshold.* New York: Prentice Hall, Atherton Press.

Weinberg, A. A. (1961). *Migration and belonging: A study of mental health and personal adjustment in Israel.* The Hague, The Netherlands: Martinus Nijhoff.

Weintraub, D. (1971). *Immigration and social change.* Jerusalem, Israel: Israel University Press.

Werman, D. S. (1977). Normal and pathological nostalgia. *Journal of the American Psychoanalytical Association, 25,* 387-398.

Wessen, A. F. (1971). The role of migrant studies in epidemiological research. *Israelian Journal of Medical Sciences, 7,* 1584-1591.

Westermeyer, J. (1989). *Psychiatric care of migrants: A clinical guide.* Washington D.C.: American Psychiatric Press.

Wolstenholme, G. E. W., & O'Connor, M. (1966). *Immigration: Medical and social aspects.* London: Churchill.

7 Individual Differences in Acculturative Stress Reactions: Determinants of Homesickness and Psychosocial Maladjustment

PAUL G. SCHMITZ

Cultural adaptation and stress

Previous research findings (Berry, 1976, 1988; Berry *et al.*, 1976; 1987; Schmitz, 1992b, 1994a; Zheng & Berry, 1991) have shown that the immigrants may experience their efforts to acculturate as stressful. An immigrant is confronted with a variety of problems, such as maintenance or change of his own cultural identity, and dealing with conflicts between different systems of values, beliefs and behavior, namely those of the mainstream society, those of his own ethnic group, and those belonging to his own personal sphere. In addition, an immigrant has to solve problems such as housing, finding adequate nutrition, often acquiring a new language, realizing his or her traditional religious practices, finding a job, dealing with immigration and other public authorities of the host society, adjusting to a different educational system, initiating new social contacts, etc. In particular the first months of an immigrant's life in a new society, while he is trying to find his way to acculturate, are experienced as stressful because adequate acculturation strategies have not yet been developed.

Stress reactions of immigrants differ in quality and intensity. The following types of typical acculturative stress reactions are distinguished in the literature (Berry *et al.*, 1987; Schmitz 1994a, 1995): (1) feelings of distress; (2) homesickness; (3) depressive reactions, going along with alienation and hopelessness; (4) psychosomatic complaints, vulnerability to diseases; and (5) psychosocial maladjustment, psychopathic behavior.

In this chapter the following types of reactions to acculturative stress will be discussed in more detail: homesickness, depression, and psychopathic behavior. The investigation of homesickness as an indicator of reactions to acculturative stress is of great scientific and clinical interest, since this reaction is more frequently found among immigrants and more closely related to acculturation processes than the other stress reactions.

According to Berry and coworkers (1987) extent and phenotype of acculturative stress reactions vary with the degree of stress experienced by an immigrant, the number of stressors, and the extent of acculturation experience. The relationship between these components is influenced by a number of factors which can be regarded as moderator variables, such as mode of acculturation, phase of acculturation, nature of larger society, characteristics of acculturating group and, finally, characteristics of acculturating individual.

In the next paragraphs the following moderator variables will be discussed in order to show their relevance with regard to the explanation of individual differences in acculturative stress reactions:
1. personality traits of the acculturating individual,
2. styles of acculturation,
3. phases of acculturation, and
4. characteristics of the acculturating group the immigrant belongs to.

Influence of personality traits

Empirical findings show that, independent of the specific acculturation strategy a person prefers, excessive and exaggerated efforts to acculturate are often accompanied by psychological distress (Schmitz 1992c, 1994a,b). A high degree of distress experienced by an immigrant over a longer period of time may result in impairment of his or her psychological and physical health. Especially, if personality traits which usually make an effective adjustment more difficult are very marked, e.g., high scores on personality traits, such as neuroticism, psychoticism, closed-mindedness, and rigidity, and if adequate coping strategies are not available to the immigrant. On the other hand, acculturative stress experienced by a person does not necessarily lead to decreased psychological and physical health, if task-oriented instead of emotion- or avoidance-oriented coping styles are applied (Endler & Parker, 1990) and if coping modes are flexibly used with regard to specific stressful situations (cf. Schmitz, 1992a).

Table 7.1 represents the correlations found between personality features, cognitive structure, and coping strategies, on the one hand, and stress reactions, such as feelings of homesickness, depressive reactions, and psychopathic behavior, on the other. The personality traits have been measured by questionnaires (cf. EPQ: Eysenck & Eysenck, 1985; CISS: Endler & Parker, 1990; D-Scale: Rokeach, 1960; ZKPQ: Zuckerman *et al.*, 1991) and the stress reaction variables were assessed by rating scales. The data were collected among immigrants, respectively migrants (N=180) from Southern-European, North African, and North-West European countries who had been living less than one year in Germany.

Table 7.1 illustrates different correlation patterns for the three different stress reaction types, homesickness, depression, and psychopathic behavior. Homesickness and depression are positively related to those traits describing emotional instability and feelings of uncertainty, such as Eysenck's neuroticism, Zuckerman's anxiety, Rokeach's closed mindedness, and Endler's emotion- and avoidance-orientation. These relationships nicely fit data collected in interviews.

Table 7.1   Correlations between personality features and stress-reactions

	Homesick-ness	Depression Alienation Hopelessness	Psychopathic behavior
Eysenck's Basic Dimensions (N=180)			
Neuroticism	.43***	.56***	-.05
Extraversion	.52***	.49***	.02
Psychoticism	-.10	-.02	.48***
Zuckermann's 'Big Five' (N=132)			
Impulsivity/ Sensation Seeking	-.61***	.01	.51***
Sociability	.58***	.51***	-.07
Anxiety	.32***	.42***	-.23**
Hostility/Aggression	.20*	-.02	.47***
Activity	-.14	.01	.29***
Rocheach's Cognitive Structure (N=85)			
Closed Mindedness	.57***	.51***	.44***
Endler's Coping Styles (N=62)			
Task Orientation	-.06	-.34**	.10
Emotion Orientation	.38*	.41***	-.19
Avoidance Orientation	.32*	.11	.03
Social Support	.42**	.33**	-.23
Distancing	.20	-.10	.34**

* $p < 0.05$; ** $p < 0.01$; *** $p < 0.001$, assessed by rating scales.

The findings may be interpreted in the following way: if migrants and immigrants experience new situations as threatening and if they feel overwhelmed by the demands of these situations, they are more likely to suffer from homesickness and depression than during the other phases of acculturation. They often react to this acculturative stress by showing a relatively high level of anxiety. In their attempts to cope with anxiety they often become cognitively more closed-minded. Closed-mindedness is referred to by Rokeach (1960) as a network of defenses that forms a cognitive system, shielding a vulnerable mind. As a consequence coping strategies applied are less task-oriented and more emotion- and avoidance-oriented.

Some facets of homesickness can probably be interpreted as avoidance-orientation. This raises the question why some persons react by developing homesickness, while others become depressed. The explanation can probably be found in differences in the individuals' personality structure. As the data illustrate, homesickness and depression differ in their relationship with Zuckerman's complex dimension impulsivity/sensation seeking. Homesickness is significantly negatively associated with this dimension, whereas depression is not. But it seems that the sensation-seeking component of this dimension has to be considered as the most relevant element. Interview data show a similar tendency: sensation seekers suffer less from feelings of homesickness, they are even interested in experiencing new and complex situations and they prefer thrill and adventure (Zuckerman, 1979, 1991). Psychopathic behavior (aggressiveness, norm violence, drug and alcohol abuse, etc.), another potential form of reaction to acculturative stress occasionally also found among immigrants, is positively associated with personality traits, such as psychoticism, hostility, and aggression, as well as with distancing, a component of Endler's avoidance-orientation. Persons practicing distancing as their favorite coping strategy often consume alcohol and drugs or look for different kinds of distractions (Endler & Parker, 1990).

To summarize the main findings from interviews and questionnaires applied with (im)migrants: basic personality dimensions, as defined in Eysenck's as well as in Zuckerman's personality model can be considered as relevant variables to explain individual differences in acculturative stress reactions, such as homesickness, depression, and psychopathic behavior. The highly consistent findings of questionnaire studies focusing on different personality models generally support our expectations. The data obtained from immigrant samples also correspond to those reported by Dutch researchers who collected data with several non-immigrant samples (Eurelings-Bontekoe et al., 1994; 1996; Van Tilburg et al., 1996; Vingerhoets et al., 1995).

Modes of acculturation and adaptation

Another important issue when exploring manifestations of acculturative stress, concerns the possible moderator variables, in particular acculturation style.

Acculturation refers to a process, which groups or individuals undergo when they are confronted with changes in their cultural surrounding (cf. Berry et al., 1992). It refers both to process and outcome. Acculturation is not a simple reaction to changes in the cultural context, but rather an active dealing with challenges experienced by immigrants when being confronted with cultural changes. Process and outcome of acculturation can be described as different adaptational strategies, which may be preferred by a society and its members.

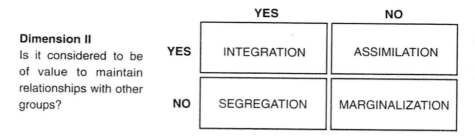

Figure 7.1.   Model of acculturation styles (modified from Berry *et al.*, 1992).

Berry (1988) presents a fourfold model of acculturation, which serves as a heuristically useful basis for categorizing and describing different types of acculturation attitudes and behavior strategies of persons belonging to minority groups as well as to those who are members of the mainstream society (Schmitz 1987, 1988b). It relates to two dimensions: the first one refers to cultural maintenance or change and the second to group relationship. The central issue of the former dimension (I) can be expressed as follows: "Are the own cultural identity and life style of value to be retained or should they be given up in order to become part of the dominant society?" The latter dimension (II) relates to the question whether there are interactions and positive relations with members of the main-stream society, which are considered to be of value and are to be maintained. Each dimension can be regarded as a continuum where individual acculturation attitudes and behavior can be positioned. That means that individuals can be categorized on the basis of their answers to both questions. In Berry's model both dimensions are combined, resulting in four types of acculturation. These four types are referred to as 'integration,' 'assimilation,' 'separation' or 'segregation' and 'marginalization.' If a person answers both questions affirmatively, the style is labeled 'integration.' Integration is defined by Berry *et al.* (1992) as maintenance of the cultural integrity of an individual or a group as well as the movement by a person or a group to become an integral part of a larger societal framework. 'Assimilation' implies the abandonment of the own cultural identity and life-style and the maintenance of positive interactions with persons of the mainstream society at the same time. 'Separation' or 'segregation' signifies the maintenance of own cultural identity with no or little interest in building up positive relations with members of the host society. The fourth option is called 'marginalization.' This option is defined as giving up own cultural identity and not being interested in positive relations with members of the host society.

The individual's well-being and health behavior are determined by the amount of acculturation stress, experienced personally by the migrant or immigrant, and the situation-specific application of particular acculturation strategies. Concerning the long-term outcome of each acculturation mode, integration and assimilation can be considered as effective strategies in most cases. Both strategies lead to an arrangement with the mainstream society and clarify the relationship with the own ethnic group. If integration is preferred, a compromise between values, norms and life styles of the host society and the own ethnic group has to be achieved. If assimilation is chosen, the immigrant attempts to assimilate himself to the mainstream society on the one hand and to give up the ties with the own ethnic group on the other hand. Finally, in case segregation is chosen, the relationship with the mainstream society is mostly perceived as negative and remains unclear (Berry & Kim, 1988; Berry et al., 1992; Schmitz, 1992c). A possible conflict between the needs and expectations of members of the mainstream society and those of the immigrant himself often remains unresolved for a longer time, and this situation may be experienced as a chronic stressor, possibly resulting in health problems (Berry, 1988). The worst consequences have been found among immigrants practicing marginalization. However, since it is very difficult to motivate marginalizers to participate in scientific research, only few findings on this issue have been reported in the literature (cf. Berry et al., 1992).

Table 7.2.   Correlations between acculturation styles and stress-reactions

	Homesickness Alienation Hopelessness	Depression	Psychopathic Behavior
Integration	.23***	-.39***	-.43***
Assimilation	-.35***	-.42***	-.45***
Segregation	.38***	.39***	.42***

*** $p < 0.001$.

Table 7.2 summarizes the findings concerning the relationship between acculturation styles and stress reactions (Schmitz, 1995). Integration is negatively associated with depressive reactions and psychopathic behavior, but shows a weak positive correlation with homesickness. As postulated in Berry's model of acculturation, immigrants preferring integration are interested in maintaining elements of their own traditional cultural identity as well as in adopting elements of the new culture at the same time. As the interview data reveal, the tendency to maintain elements of the old cultural identity is related to nostalgia, often defined as longing for something in the past. Nostalgia obviously shows in some cases a relationship with mild manifestations of homesickness. These findings regarding the relationship between integration, nostalgia, and homesickness obtained in interviews probably explain the weak positive correlation we find between integration and homesickness.

Assimilation is negatively associated with each of the three stress reactions. Most researchers consider integration and assimilation, defined in Berry's model as giving up the own traditional cultural identity and taking completely over the culture of the host-society, as relatively effective strategies of acculturation (cf. Berry *et al.*, 1992). If an immigrant can successfully realize assimilation, norm and value conflicts are minimized. Moreover, the process of assimilation needs time and energy so that there is often not enough time left to pursue feelings of nostalgia and homesickness. With regard to the negative correlations usually found between assimilation and psychopathic behavior, we speculate as follows: behaving in a psychopathic way impedes the process of assimilation and has to be considered as counterproductive with regard to a successful cultural adaptation. Immigrants preferring assimilation thus show a higher degree of sociability and agreeableness, are more socially active, less aggressive, more tolerant, and more socially adjusted. This particular personality structure is supposed to make a successful assimilation easier. This may also explain why depression, alienation and pathological forms of homesickness are not frequently found among assimilators.

Segregation shows positive relationships with each of the stress reactions. Interviews with immigrants revealed that persons preferring segregation are not highly motivated to have close relationships with members of the host society and that they are not strongly interested in the host culture. In addition, they do not consider themselves as persons who like to seek new cultural experiences. With regard to their personality structure, persons preferring segregation have low scores on the sensation-seeking dimension (Schmitz, 1994b). They prefer to join members of the own ethnic group. This type of affiliation helps them to avoid anxiety and to reduce insecurity during the process of acculturation. Their coping style is more avoidance- than task-oriented (Schmitz, 1992b). Due to their specific personality structure, they have difficulties in initiating new social contacts and in maintaining them. Even worse, they are often rejected by members of the host society, isolate themselves and feel a strong need for warmth and security which they expect to find in their own ethnic group. Joining their own ethnic group and maintaining the old traditional culture gives them the security they badly need. If such contact is not possible for shorter or longer terms, severe forms of homesickness can emerge and a state of depression may ensue, in particular if returning to the own cultural roots appears not realizable and alternative forms of cultural adaptation, such as assimilation or integration, cannot be achieved.

Phases of acculturation and stress reactions

When we intend to understand individual differences in reactions to acculturative stress, we also have to take into consideration the phases of acculturation. Immigrants usually pass through the following five phases of acculturation: (1) pre-contact, (2) initial contact, (3) conflict, (4) crisis, and (5) adaptation (Berry & Kim, 1988). The duration of each phase varies from one person to the other. The phases of acculturation also differ remarkably in terms of the amount of behavioral adaptations requested from an immigrant. During the phases of pre-contact and initial contact the necessary behavioral adaptations are limited, whereas they are increasingly needed during the later phases of the acculturation process. Behavioral adjustments are often accompanied by feelings of uncertainty and anxiety, in particular during the phases of conflict and crisis. In the phase of conflict immigrants often feel overwhelmed by the experience of discrepancies between demands of their own traditional system of values and norms and that of the host society, whereas a feasible way to solve this conflict is not yet seen. This often results in passivity and lethargy. During the following phase of crisis, an immigrant becomes more active and attempts to test different acculturative strategies, such as integration, assimilation, separation, and marginalization in order to find a personally adequate coping strategy. This phase of active coping with one's personal situation is still accompanied by a relatively high degree of uncertainty and is therefore experienced by immigrants as highly stressful. Once having reached the phase of adaptation and having selected a successful acculturation strategy, the amount of acculturation stress and acculturative stress reactions, such as psychosomatic complaints, homesickness and depressive reactions, may decrease.

In the following, the discussion will be confined to the relationship between homesickness and phase of acculturation: It is hypothesized that during the phases of conflict and active coping (crisis) the intensity of the homesickness will be higher than during the other phases of acculturation. To test this hypothesis, immigrants were asked to rate the degree of homesickness they were experiencing on a 9-point rating scale. In a series of analyses of variance (ANOVA), the influences of the factor phase of acculturation together with other relevant factors (types of migrant groups, regional origin of migrants, and gender) on homesickness were examined. The most important results are presented in the *Figures 7.2-7.4*.

Figure 7.2 shows the effects of the factors phase and migration (seasonal migrants, N=40; immigrants (persons planning to stay for ever or for a longer time in the host country), N = 40; and refugees, N=40) on self-reported homesickness. *Figure 7.3* displays the effects of the factors phase and region of origin of migrants (North-African, N=40; South-European, N=40; and Northwest-European countries, N=40) on homesickness. *Figure 7.4*, finally, presents the homesickness scores obtained from migrants, which were divided equally into subgroups according to phase and gender (males, N=40; females, N=40).

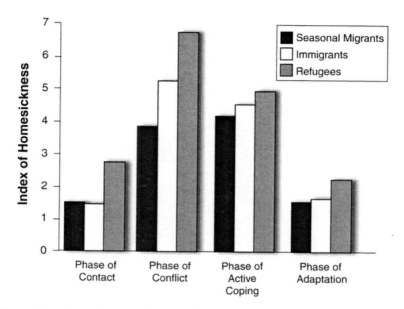

Figure 7.2. The influence of phase of acculturation and type of immigration on homesickness.

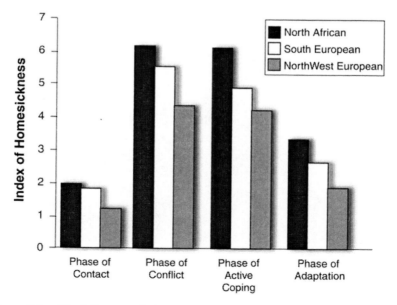

Figure 7.3. The influence of phase of acculturation and geographical origin of migrants on homesickness

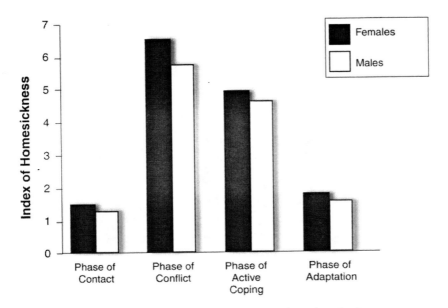

Figure 7.4. The influence of phase of acculturation and gender of migrants on homesickness

In the following, we will first discuss the influence of the factor phase and subsequently (in the next paragraph) reveal the characteristics of the acculturating group. The ANOVA results with type of migrants, geographical origin, and gender as between subject factory showed that the intensity of homesickness differs from one phase to the other: the highest scores were found for the phase of conflict, followed by the phase of active coping (crisis) and adaptation, the lowest values were obtained when migrants were in the phase of contact.

The indices of homesickness differed significantly ($p < .05$) for all phases in the analysis in which the type of migration was controlled (cf. *Table 7.2*). In the other analyses (control for geographical origin, cf. *Table 7.3*, and control for gender, cf. *Table 7.4*) the phases of conflict and active coping do not differ significantly ($p < .10$) from each other, but the homesickness scores are significantly higher ($p < .05$) for both the phase of conflict and the phase of active coping (crisis) than for the phases of contact and adaptation. Corresponding findings were obtained for psychosomatic complaints, depressive reactions, psychopathic behavior, and feelings of well-being (inverted order) (Schmitz, 1995). These results thus show that 'phase of acculturation' has to be taken into consideration, when attempting to explain individual differences in the various acculturative stress reactions.

Characteristics of the acculturating group

Finally, the focus is on the role of characteristics of the acculturating group. In the previous paragraph, where we considered the influence of the phase of acculturation, we had already touched characteristics of the acculturating group, more specifically the type of migration (cf. *Figure 7.2*), geographical origin of migrants (cf. *Figure 7.3*), and gender (cf. *Figure 7.4*). These factors will be discussed below in more detail.

Migrants differ with respect to control over the decision to move and permanence of the move. There is a tendency to stay temporarily among seasonal migrants while immigrants strive for permanent residence in the host country. Refugees differ from these groups in terms of freedom of choice: their migration has been involuntary and they often do not know if and when they are able to return to their own country. It can be postulated that each of these groups will give preference to a particular acculturation style and will differ in the amount of acculturation stress and kind of stress reactions. *Figure 7.2* shows that there are striking differences in the intensity of homesickness between the different migrant groups. Consistent differences were found with regard to all phases of acculturation. Most of the differences regarding homesickness were statistically significant ($p < .05$). The degree of homesickness was higher for refugees than for seasonal migrants and immigrants.

Migrant groups also differ in the extent to which their culture is similar or dissimilar to that of the host society. Relevant variables are for example: religion, language, life style habits, family structure, and value systems. Interview data showed that acculturation conflicts and, consequently, acculturative stress were more marked among immigrants belonging to groups whose culture of origin is more different from that of the host society than among immigrants whose culture is more similar to that of the host society. If immigrants were asked to rate the degree of similarity between their own culture and the culture of the host society, North-African migrants experienced less similarities between their culture and the culture of the host-society (Germany) than South-Europeans did, and the latter group observed more differences between their cultural backgrounds and that of the host society than migrants from North-West Europeans countries did (Schmitz, 1995). The ANOVA results support these findings: *Figure 7.3* illustrates, that during all phases of acculturation North-Africans showed a higher degree of homesickness than South-Europeans and members of the latter group reported a greater degree of homesickness than North Europeans. *Figure 7.4* presents gender differences with regard to homesickness: female migrants do not report statistically significant higher intensities of homesickness than males. With respect to the phase of acculturation, the findings were consistent with those presented in previous figures. Homesickness is significantly more intense ($p < .05$) during the phases of conflict and active coping than during the phases of contact and adaptation.

These empirical findings provide some evidence that cultural characteristics have to be considered as relevant moderator variables helping to explain individual differences in homesickness.

Summary

Research findings show that type and intensity of acculturative stress, indicated by characteristics, such as feelings of unwell-being, homesickness, depressive reactions, psychosomatics and psychopathic behavior, depend on a series of factors. At the societal level, relevant factors include the specific features of the host society, such as ideologies concerning acculturation (cf. Berry *et al.*, 1992), and characteristics of the acculturating group, e.g., status, support, type of migration. At the individual level, important variables are acculturation experiences in the past, phase of acculturation, and specific characteristics of the immigrant (age, gender, status, and personality traits). Relevant personality characteristics influencing the process of acculturative adaptation are basic personality dimensions, such as anxiety, aggression-hostility, sociability, sensation-seeking, cognitive styles (e.g., field-dependence), coping strategies in general, and acculturation attitudes and behavior in particular (cf. Schmitz, 1992c, 1994b). These characteristics may be considered as relevant variables moderating the relationship between the individual acculturation experience and acculturative stress (cf. Berry *et al.*, 1992; Schmitz, 1994b).

The particular relevance of these personality dimensions as moderators becomes obvious when we take into account the links between these personality traits and Berry's acculturation styles which in their turn have an influence on acculturation outcome (Schmitz, 1987, 1992b, 1992c, 1994a, 1994b). Our findings are not surprising, since personality and situational factors are known to determine social behavior in general (Eysenck & Eysenck, 1985; Schmitz, 1988a; Zuckerman 1981). Consequently, it is also not surprising that empirical data show that basic personality dimensions are specifically related to acculturative strategies, acculturative stress and acculturation outcome. The individual degree of homesickness thus can be considered to be the result of a complex interplay of personality characteristics, situational conditions, and socio-cultural factors.

References

Berry, J. W. (1976). *Human ecology and cognitive style: Comparative studies in cultural and psychological adaptation.* New York: Sage/Halsted.

Berry, J. W. (1988). Acculturation and psychological adaptation: A conceptual overview. In: J. W. Berry & R. C. Annis (Eds.), *Ethnic Psychology: Research and practice with immigrants, refugees, native peoples, ethnic groups a sojourners* (pp. 41-52). Amsterdam, The Netherlands: Swets & Zeitlinger.

Berry, J. W., & Kim, U. (1988). Acculturation and mental health. In: P. Dasen, J. W. Berry, & N. Sartorius (Eds.), *Cross-cultural psychology and health: Towards applications* (pp. 207- 236). London: Sage.

Berry, J. W., Kalin, R., & Taylor, D. M. (1977). *Multiculturalism and ethnic attitudes in Canada.* Ottawa, Canada: Government of Canada.

Berry, J. W., Kim, U., Minde, T., & Moke, D. (1987). Comparative studies of acculturative stress. *International Migration Review, 21,* 491-511.

Berry, J. W., Poortinga, Y. H., Segall, M. H., & Dasen, P. R. (1992). *Cross-cultural Psychology. Research and applications.* Cambridge: Cambridge University Press.

Endler, N. S., & Parker, J. D. (1990). The multidimensional assessment of coping: A critical evaluation. *Journal of Personality and Social Psychology, 58,* 844-854.

Eurelings-Bontekoe, E. H. M., Tolma, A., Verschuur, M. J., & Vingerhoets, A. J. J. M. (1996). Construction of a homesickness questionnaire using a female population with two types of self-reported homesickness. Preliminary results. *Personality and Individual Differences, 20,* 415-421.

Eurelings-Bontekoe, E. H. M., Vingerhoets, A. J. J. M., & Fontijn, T. (1994). Personality and behavioral antecedents of homesickness. *Personality and Individual Differences, 16,* 229- 235.

Eysenck, H. J., & Eysenck, M. W. (1985). *Personality and individual differences. A natural science approach.* New York: Plenum Press.

Rokeach, M. (1960). *The open and closed mind: Investigations into the nature of belief systems and personality systems.* New York: Basic Books.

Schmitz, P. G. (1987). *Acculturation attitudes and beliefs of immigrants.* Paper presented at the First Regional North American Conference of the IACCP, Kingston, Canada.

Schmitz, P. G. (1988a). *Personality, temperament, and social behaviour.* Paper presented at the Fourth European Conference on Personality, Stockholm, Sweden.

Schmitz, P. G. (1988b). *Reciprocal acculturation: Mutual influences.* Paper presented at the Ninth International Congress of the IACCP, Newcastle, Australia.

Schmitz, P. G. (1992a). Personality, stress-reactions, and diseases. *Personality and Individual Differences, 13,* 683-691.

Schmitz, P. G. (1992b). Acculturation styles and health. In: S. Iwawaki, Y. Kashima, & K. S. Leung (Eds.), *Innovations in cross-cultural psychology* (pp. 360-370). Amsterdam, The Netherlands: Swets & Zeitlinger.

Schmitz, P. G. (1992c). Immigrant mental and physical health. *Psychology and Developing Societies, 4,* 117-132.

Schmitz, P. G. (1994a). Acculturation and adaptation processes among immigrants in Germany. In: A. M. Bouvy, F. J. R. Van de Vijver, P. Boski, & P. G. Schmitz (Eds.), *Journeys into cross-cultural psychology* (pp. 142-157). Amsterdam, The Netherlands: Swets & Zeitlinger.

Schmitz, P. G. (1994b). Personalité et acculturation. *Les Cahiers Internationaux de Psychologie Sociale, 24,* 33-53.

Schmitz, P. G. (1995). The influence of personality on feelings of well-being: Immigrants' psychosocial adaptation. Paper presented at the 13th World Congress of the International College of Psychosomatic Medicine, September 1995, Jerusalem, Israel.

Van Tilburg, M. A. L., Vingerhoets, A. J. J. M., & Van Heck, G. L. (1996). Homesickness: A review of the literature. *Psychological Medicine, 26,* 899-912.

Vingerhoets, A. J. J. M., Van Tilburg, M. A. L., & Van Heck, G. L. (1995). Determinants of the intensity of self-reported homesickness. *Psychosomatic Medicine, 57,* 93-94.

Zheng, X., & Berry, J. W. (1991). Psychological adaptation of Chinese sojourners in Canada. *International Journal of Psychology, 26,* 451-470.

Zuckerman, M. (1979). *Sensation seeking: Beyond the optimal level of arousal.* Hillsdale, NJ: Erlbaum.

Zuckerman, M. (1991). *Psychobiology of personality.* Cambridge, UK: Cambridge University Press.

Zuckerman, M., Kuhlman, D. M., Thornquist, M., & Kiers, H. (1991). Five (or three) robust questionnaire scale factors of personality without culture. *Personality and Individual Differences, 12,* 929-941.

8 The Cry for the Lost Placenta: Cultural Bereavement and Cultural Survival among Cambodians who Resettled, were Repatriated, or Stayed at Home

MAURICE EISENBRUCH

Introduction

In this chapter I consider five themes fundamental to the plight of displaced persons world-wide: (1) cultural bonds to home and community; (2) the role of tradition in sustaining the cultural bonding and hence well-being of refugees; (3) the notion of cultural bereavement and how it may be worsened when culture is threatened; (4) how indigenous traditions need to be preserved in the face of intrusion of Western cultural paradigms; (5) the importance of cultural, as well as psychic, losses of displaced persons in their attempts to cope with movements from homeland, and with going home. These five themes will be illustrated by the case of Cambodian refugees.

> "In a new twist to the use of homesickness, a captured Khmer Rouge soldier reported that three Western hostages held in captivity by the Khmer Rouge were getting progressively thinner. In his opinion, their weight loss was caused by homesickness, despite their being well fed by the general who held them captive and who, eventually, murdered them" (Sokhet, 1994).

Cultural bonding to place of birth

The cry for the lost placenta

The instant that a Cambodian baby is born, it undergoes a separation from its previous life, and becomes locked in a bond with the place of birth when, according to tradition, its parents bury the placenta nearby, in the prescribed direction. The burial site (the placenta is sometimes burned) is covered with cactus or spiny plants, to protect it from interference by dogs or by spirits. The location is critical, according to the traditional healers, who explain that the placenta is the 'globe of the origin of the soul' of the child. People fear that a violation of this code may cause harm to the mother, or to the baby. A blood-hungry spirit may eat the placenta and attack the mother, who may develop a mental disorder for the rest of her life. If the placenta is safe, so is the child – provided it does not stray too far. If the placenta is disturbed, so is the child, who may develop an illness, known as ឆ្លង of the preceding mother' (Eisenbruch, 1992). The ritual of burying the placenta is widely practiced in Southeast-Asia (Laderman, 1983), and it gives expression to the local belief that a person is safe at home and enters a state of danger on journeying from it (see Ewing, 1960; Geertz, 1960; and Laderman, 1983). The placenta is sometimes regarded as 'the tree of life'.

The Hmong, for example, believe that when a person dies he must collect his placenta in order to enter the next life (Rice, 1994). After years in Australia, on giving birth in the hospital, Hmong refugees realize that they cannot bury the placenta near their home and want it buried, at any rate, in the hospital.

Loss of ties to home as a cause of disease
In the case of 'vanquished by the water-earth', the term for one sort of malaria, Cambodian traditional healers explain the disease by saying that the person out of his familiar village inadvertently upset the local guardian spirits in the new location and they attacked him to cause malaria. This belief reinforced the idea of danger inherent in journeying far from home. The traditional healers prevented the voyager from falling ill by keeping the old environment alive inside him. And should disease strike, they treated it by returning the familiar environment to the sufferer.

Given these strong ties to place of birth, it is hardly surprising that Cambodians have not been known as great travelers since the Angkorian era. The modern Khmer term for tourism, ទេសចរណ៍, is a loan-word from Sanskrit. Few felt the need to travel far beyond the village of birth or of the spouse, or to make a pilgrimage to Angkor Wat, and almost none journeyed outside Cambodia. Sometimes, when old people died and were cremated, their bones (not just the ashes) were brought back to the village of their birth – where their placental remains had, in a sense, been waiting for them all their lives; perhaps the dead took up residence in a favorite childhood tree to become a guardian spirit.

If, as I suggest, the placenta can be regarded as an anchor of the Cambodian version of home boundness, we may perhaps consider in that light the canvas of global forced migration of refugees far from the village, beyond their national borders and often their cultural roots. The world is not composed of sovereign, spatially discontinuous units; and refugees do not simply cross these lines and fall in the cracks. The flow of refugees across the fuzzy spaces gives rise to new questions about personal identity, loss and global culture.

Bonding under threat – refugeehood

One out of every 130 people on earth has been forced into flight. As well as the 23 million who are refugees, 30 million are internally displaced persons (Deng, 1994). Despite these dramatic statistics, there is a relative lack of literature on the feelings of inmates of refugee camps towards their homeland, and about the effects of camp life on cultural survival. The organization of refugee camps takes away the right to choose. This threat to the inmates' cultural traditions may be intensified if elders, bearers of the culture, such as traditional healers, are not permitted to go on with their work in the camp or to pass on their knowledge to the younger generations.

Pressures on camp inmates operate, for the most part, within a context of continuing threats to security, and with memories of death still very strong. Mozambicans in a camp in Malawi were worried that family members they left behind had become victims of ritual murder and that their dead relations' spirits remained 'in trouble' and would attack and possess them. Confined in the camps, the survivors were unable to complete rituals to protect themselves from the spirits. Ugandans faced similar problems during their flight to Sudan and needed to deal with these losses according to their cultural codes. The traditional beliefs were modified with the move to the camps; ancestral lion spirits, for example, previously tied to the land, seem to have 'moved' with Mozambicans into Malawi and they have become severed from the home and the land.[1] In the wake of the war in former Yugoslavia, too, the loss of 'homeland' and the impact on cultural identity was evident (Zivcic, 1993). Children and mothers, particularly the Bosnians, felt pessimistic about whether they would have a homeland to go back to, and this contributed to their sense of loss (Polic *et al.*, 1993).

The trauma of camp life, along with those experienced before and during the flight, can endure long after resettlement. Among Southeast-Asian refugees in the U.S.A., regardless of the number of years spent there, more than five years after resettlement the traumas predicted distress (Chung & Kagawa Singer, 1993). Refugees, wherever they are, may experience homesickness and cultural bereavement. Marjorie Muecke, in her review of refugee health problems, has identified the key health issues of each of three phases — from internal displacement to asylum in a second country to resettlement in a third — and emphasizes the dangers of reducing their health to pathology (Muecke & Sassi, 1992). The conventional way of looking at refugees — as moving from flight to resettlement — is a useful way to track individual biographies, but this view of them is embedded in an ideology that sanctions the ineluctable move from horror to hope offered by absorption into a new country. In the case of Cambodia, this ideology obscures from view the violent stem of cultural bereavement that started during Pol Pot's cultural reconstruction and sensitized Cambodians to a continuing series of violations through famine, flight, internment and resettlement. Cultural fracturing was reinforced by the tendency of Westerners to work with resettled refugees, camp inmates, and people in Cambodia as three separate groups rather than as a dispersed whole.

I suggest that the Cambodians should be regarded as a single cultural group that has been dispersed across three circles, in Cambodia, in the camps, and in Western countries. The cultural identity of the Cambodians occupying each space cannot be considered separately from that of their compatriots who inhabit the other spaces (Eisenbruch, 1994b). Resettled Cambodians with ever-diminishing access to their cultural traditions, including traditional healing, continue to accumulate cultural losses as they move across each circle. Now, there is an emergence once more, of the middle circle — this time inside Cambodia — as returnees have become internally displaced by the continuing war.

---

1   Usually, however, the refugees only maintain the cults of ancestral lineage spirits, adopting or partially accepting the land spirit cults of host populations, and linked to burial sites of the hosts' ancestors (Colson, 1982).

The inner circle: those who stayed at home

Few countries were subjected to such an intense process of cultural realignment as occurred during the fundamentalism of the Pol Pot years. The forced evacuations and marches across the country in April 1975 served to sever people completely from their attachments of birth. Most children over the age of six were taken into Khmer Rouge mobile teams, an artifice that transferred the traditional culture's code of respect for parents and ancestors to the faceless 'high organization' of the Khmer Rouge. Recent history and culture, as embodied by Buddhism, was obliterated; it was replaced by the introduction of a fictive link with the grandeur of ancient Angkor (Chandler, 1992).

The words chosen by a regime shape thought and cultural identity. The Khmer Rouge sought to 'reconstruct' the mentality of the people – by addressing an individual or a commune meeting: "To reconstruct [brainwash] you, to be out of words to reconstruct you, to knock you off with the back of the axe head." If the words failed to do the job, the Khmer Rouge had another way of reconstructing the person, to kill him – in the last line, a macabre play on words, the syllables were rearrangements of 'the back of the axe' (ខ្នង ពូថៅ).

To this day, Cambodian refugees and returnees loathe the use of the term កសាង when it is used of a person. Even the sliding in of the term ធម្មैर (from the Sanskrit) by the Khmer Rouge demonstrated the re-shaping of culture, for this term was substituted for the សាលា which some cadres wrongly told the people was derived from the decadent French language – it was derived from the Pali and used in Buddhism, which the Khmer Rouge wanted to wipe out of people's hearts even more than the French colonial relics. The Khmer Rouge also replaced the old descriptive place names of the districts (ស្រុក), and even the street names, and replaced them with numbers; in this way, they severed the reminders of the origins of the place (see Vickery, 1983; Chandler, 1991). After the liberation in 1979, the use of language to shape culture continued. The Heng Samrin regime introduced the term ធម្មैर អប់រ for re-education or perhaps jailing of political dissidents (the term was associated previously with the training of schoolchildren or people of lower status). Now, some Cambodians revert to a pre-revolutionary term កែប្រ which means to correct or switch something.

The Khmer Rouge's cultural panel-beating and, perhaps, the period after liberation, compelled many to alter their thinking about Cambodian culture and in some cases their memories of its past – and theirs. The central question is how a people such as the Cambodians reconcile the continuing changes in their identity and culture with their collective memory of their history. In this chapter, I make a working assumption that the traditional healers can help to define the Cambodian meaning of home and of homesickness; what aspects of the culture were lost and yet what remains of the traditional beliefs and rituals, which can help people to overcome their losses and cultural bereavement.

The middle circle: refugee and border camps
Until 1993, the second biggest population of Cambodians in the world was concentrated in the Thai-Cambodian border camps. Many inmates, fleeing the aftermath of the Pol Pot period, had been incarcerated for more than a decade, cut off from normal social relations and cultural life, and enduring terror and continuing war. It has been suggested that, officially, 'training in Cambodian culture' was given a low priority (Gyallay-Pap, 1989). The camp culture in Northern Thailand was found seriously to undermine traditional norms and values among the Hmong, with children flouting the authority of clan elders (Boyden, 1994). The Hmong developed a new religious movement, Koom Haum, against the strong pressure in the camps from fundamentalist missionaries to convert (Tapp, 1988). Some, with shaky cultural allegiances, were vulnerable to promises from fundamentalist missionaries in the camps and Western ideologies after resettlement.

Fieldwork in refugee camps
In 1987 I visited the UNHCR refugee camps (Phanat Nikhom and Khao I Dang) in Thailand and the UNBRO displaced persons camps (Site 2 and Site 8) on the Thai-Cambodian border to examine how the Cambodians maintained cultural traditions including traditional healing. A follow-up visit was carried out in 1990. The traditional healers in the UNHCR camps and, after 1989 in Site 2, helped to provide some relief from the pressures of guilt and betrayal, and where possible palliated homesickness, given the limits imposed by camp life (Eisenbruch, 1988). Yet the process of being divested of their culture continued as Cambodians, before leaving the transit camps, underwent medical screening and felt obliged, for example, to remove their magical amulet waist cord. To traditional Cambodians, this cord, made for them by the traditional healer and consisting of rolled squares of lead or tin inscribed with magical Pali letters, protected against illness and danger likely to be encountered on the next journey to 'freedom', but which took them one step further from the land of birth and the placental anchor. But for the apprehensive Cambodian about to be put in front of an X-ray machine the cord, which has radio-opaque metal, suddenly became dangerous – they dreaded the 'shadow' cast by the magical cord would mark them as having tuberculosis and therefore condemn them to the dangers of limbo in 'medical hold'. Many regarded the aim of the medical screening as to protect the host society from contamination by what they had brought with them, and the traditional practice, far from being valued, became something to hide or discard.[2] In the UNBRO border camps, traditional family values embedded in Buddhism and overturned during the Pol Pot times were deformed once more. Many had lost traditional cultural supports. Elderly Cambodians, without their revered status, were unable to pass on their

2 This divesting of culture continued when the refugees arrived in Australia and were ridiculed by health workers for their quaint ritual objects and were told to take them off. Some, complying with the instructions, violated the cultural prescription of their traditional healer, and were possessed at once by ancestral spirits, an experience that tipped some into psychosis. Modern medicine, in this case, re-educated the refugees to believe that, to be healthy in the eyes of the powerful foreigner, you had to abandon your traditional health practices, if not your beliefs.

knowledge; nor were the traditional healers, who had lost their manuals of healing. The women, often widowed, or with husbands in the military, were burdened with the care of children, many of whom were malnourished or neglected. Young people were often encouraged to steal. Few children entered the pagoda to become novice monks and transfer merit to their parents. Adolescent boys were conscripted into a guerrilla army where they would be trained to kill their fellow Cambodians press-ganged into government militia units in Cambodia.

The outer circle: life as refugees after resettlement

Resettlement, even from the awful conditions of the camps, does not necessarily bring relief. In a study of two groups of Cambodian refugee youth, one in Thai camps awaiting resettlement and the other already in the United States, it was found that the level of anxiety symptoms was higher among those in the United States (Muecke & Sassi, 1992). Then there is the complex issue of whether speeding up acculturation helps to reduce stress and morbidity – it should, if one takes a unidimensional view that "the quicker you get used to life in the new country and forget past trauma, the better." Many studies on acculturation show that it is not unidimensional, and that refugees probably do best if they can acculturate and at the same time keep a strong grip on the bedrock of their cultural identity (Cheung, 1995). There is evidence that, when forced to choose between the two cultures, refugees become more alienated at the same time as they 'successfully' adjust to their new lives (Birman & Tyler, 1994). On the other hand, alienation seems lessened when immigrants or refugees can live in their own communities (Eisenbruch, 1986; Moon & Pearl, 1991). The cultural identity of the refugee, as Kondic (1992) has shown among Croatians, has a bearing on symptoms such as anxiety and depression.

Alienation is constructed by the culture, but there are few anthropological studies on the *meaning* of alienation among refugees or how the society's traditions might help to overcome it. Even if alienation diminishes for an individual, new problems can arise for the group: exiled mothers and their children, for example, have different ways of coping with their loss and separation from families and from their cultural roles. If young refugees acculturate more quickly than their elders and, in doing so, the cultural skew within the community may increase.

Homesickness and reactions to loss of culture

There is a vast literature on homesickness and culture shock as it affects all classes of displaced people, such as sojourners, as well as refugees and immigrants, health professionals and missionaries. On the basis of these studies, it would seem that manifestations of homesickness display cultural differences. Culture shock (dealt with in detail by Adrian Furnham in this volume) leads us to consider how refugees after resettlement show *cultural* as well as personal losses. The losses can be made worse by climate and geography confounding the cultural code of conduct. Muslims under the midnight sun of the Arctic Circle, for example, didn't know when to hold the first prayer of the day, which has to be offered before sunrise, or when to break their fast during Ramadan month (Sande, 1991). Reactions to loss of culture, as well as to the trauma itself, may be reactivated later in life, as shown by the example of Vietnamese and Hmong cancer patients (Schriever, 1990). Some refugees react with psychosomatic blindness to the horrors they witnessed (Wilkinson, 1994); this condition can be treated by working through the past losses and traumas (Van Boemel & Rozee, 1992). Another even more dramatic manifestation of the loss of home is found among the Hmong refugees, some of whom, apparently healthy young men, die in the middle of the night (Lemoine, 1983). In this condition, entitled Sudden Unexpected Nocturnal Death Syndrome (SUNDS), it is suggested that nightmare attacks are linked to the inability to practice traditional rituals (Adler, 1994).

It is generally argued that the reactions to the separation from the old culture depend in large part on the person's ability to engage in healthy mourning (Levy Warren, 1987). While mourning the loss of the old culture might be a step in adapting to the new environment, maintenance of links with the old world may help. George Pollock (1989) terms this ambiguity the mourning-liberation process. We know that loss of homeland may cause the refugee to grieve but we do not know how, because bereavement is shaped by culture (Rosenblatt, 1993). The Western assumption is that therapy should encourage grief work by the working through of losses, but 'grief work' might not be universal. And refugees may react to cumulative losses according to their cultural notions of death (Silverman et al., 1995).

Adaptation to life in Western countries
Like flotsam, refugees are washed onto many shores. Around the world there are several hundred thousand Cambodians, most of whom moved to the Thai-Cambodia border and into the camps after 1979 before resettlement in the West. In some centers, such as Long Beach or Paris, there are large communities, but in most settings there were no established Cambodian structures, few Buddhist monks and even fewer traditional healers. In 1983 I worked with an Indo-Chinese children's mental health service in Boston. The Cambodians proved to be appropriate for study because they had suffered a traumatic loss of society and culture and were obliged to adapt rapidly to a new country. Their symptoms were often attributed to post-traumatic stress disorder by Western psychiatrists, and the cultural meanings were missed. I investigated the experiences of 79 Cambodian unaccompanied refugee adolescents, in the United States (1983-84) and Australia (1985-87), looked at the relationship between losses of culture and traditional beliefs and practices, and measured their cultural bereavement (Eisenbruch, 1990a). They seemed to feel that participating in traditional Buddhist and other rituals could combat their painful feelings of loss (89%) and they drew comfort from their beliefs in Buddhism (76%). Sometimes the importance of these feelings is ignored by policy-makers and care-givers, who feel that rapid integration into Western thought, behavior, and religion is better for the young refugees. The promotion of access to Buddhist monks and traditional healers seemed to ameliorate homesickness (Eisenbruch, 1990b).

Cultural bereavement

Cultural bereavement is the total experience of the uprooted person – or group – resulting from loss of old social structures, cultural values and meanings, and self (Eisenbruch, 1984a; Eisenbruch, 1984b). It means that the person – or group – continues to live in the past, is visited by supernatural forces from the past while asleep or awake, suffers feelings of guilt about abandoning culture and homeland, feels pain if memories of the past begin to fade, but also finds constant images of the past (including traumatic images) intruding into daily life, yearns to complete obligations to the dead, and feels stricken by anxieties, morbid thoughts and anger which interfere with the ability to get on with daily life including acculturation to the new society.

Central is the issue of refugee identity during the life cycle. Robertson (1992) cites the example of a Palestinian woman who transformed her identity – as a stigmatized refugee, as accepting her refugee identity, as developing refugee pride, and the death of that identity as it was replaced by a growth of identity as a Palestinian woman with a right to statehood. Political activism may help refugees to overcome their cultural clash with the new country, but it raises new complications, as shown by the example of Afghan refugees whose men suffered from wounded pride (Parvanta, 1992). The socio-political context will also color the bereavement of peoples affected by displacement, as shown by the Yolmo 'song of sadness' which expresses the grief of Sherpa who left Tibet for Nepal (Desjarlais, 1991). And, as George (1995) has shown in Sulawesi, Indonesia, individuals became violent not only because they were angry but also as expression of the attempt by the whole community to deal with its own mourning.

Whatever aspirations immigrant and refugee parents may hold for their children, there is evidence that often (not always) they want to keep their past alive in their children (Dhruvarajan, 1993). Successful Southeast-Asian refugee youths tend to have parents proud of their ethnic identity and belong to a strong ethnic community (Edwards et al., 1994). Even if the parents jettison the past culture, the children may seek to rediscover it (Hadjadj, 1989). Hmong children born in the United States and well adapted to Western life were torn by the expectations away from the Hmong roots (McInnis, 1991).

The traditional culture, transplanted into a suitable refugee setting, can work quite well, as shown by the example of Tibetan refugees in India who, according to Mahmoudi (1992) are uniquely well-adjusted. Traditional medicine remains important for Southeast-Asian refugees after resettlement (Chung & Lin, 1994). Cambodian refugee women, for example, explained illness largely in terms of humoral imbalances and violations of codes of conduct especially about food, and they included traditional medicine as part of the treatment of their children's illnesses (Frye, 1990). People continue to observe sometimes onerous traditions, such as care-giving to the elderly, because of filial obligation or piety, and these customs appear to help the elderly Indochinese refugees to feel less homesick (Tran, 1991). But it is not all one way, for the elderly, in turn, help to transmit the 'lost' culture to the grandchildren. David Suzuki (1995) commented that the evolutionary position of homo sapiens gives the grandparents a role in preparing the young for life. They are best equipped to transmit accumulated cultural data outside the DNA itself. The elderly refugee not only may gain support from the young, but also has the opportunity to pass on first-hand knowledge of the family past, to make it alive for the young.

When war subsides: how traditional healers help survivors cope with homesickness and grief
When war subsides, the survivors are faced with the question of how to heal, and how to deal with their homesickness and grief. In Mozambique, the children said they needed to heal their 'hearts', and they 'reconstructed' them by ritual ceremonies carried out by Synanga or traditional healers in communal ceremonies (Gibbs, 1994). The re-establishment of a local infrastructure helped the reconstruction in the long run. In Kenya, two culturally disrupted tribes lost the ability to grieve effectively, and those who had developed psychosomatic illnesses improved once they were helped to rediscover traditional ways grieving (Banta, 1991).

What happened to Cambodian culture after the Vietnamese liberation in 1979 from the Khmer Rouge? Cambodian self-definitions notions of ethnicity or, at any rate, nationality changed during the Sihanouk, communist, and contemporary political regimes to reflect differing ideas about Khmer-ness (Edwards, 1996). They redefined and re-identified themselves, utilizing traditional forms in new ways and new forms within a traditional framework (Ebihara *et al.*, 1994). There was an impression, on the one hand, that there was suppression of normal Khmer life or even that 'Vietnamisation' or 'ethnocide' continued apace (Martin, 1986). On the other, this view was questioned by some who believed that the regime was doing its best to restore cultural traditions, and there was even a tendency by some to romanticize the 'good old days' before the UNTAC arrived and corrupted everything (Boua, 1994). It would appear that the Cham minorities have rebuilt their culture whereas the Vietnamese float up and down the Mekong, homeless and, as ever, the scapegoats reviled for everyone else's losses.

Reactions to cultural loss can be protected against. It is not surprising that uprooted people sometimes long to participate in traditional ceremonies. In Australia in 1985 I began to work with three Cambodian traditional healers, taking patients who sought traditional healing from them. By making a diagnosis and performing ritual ceremonies such as encircling the house to protect it from entry of evil spirits, and pouring lustral water on the patient to cleanse him of evil spirits, the healers were able to help the refugees, often giving them their first respite since arriving in Australia. Using a semi-structured interview of Cambodian explanatory models for illness (Eisenbruch & Handelman, 1989), I found that the symptoms of anxiety or depression among Cambodian patients attending a community practice were associated with animistic and magical explanations to do with leaving their homeland (Eisenbruch, 1990c). Once again, access to traditional rituals was the antidote to their cultural bereavement and sometimes alleviated their symptoms. And the healers, despite their low numbers and loss of status, mitigated against emotional distress, supported people facing crises such as marital breakdown, sexual abuse, or child abuse, and contributed to understanding the indigenous Cambodian point of view in medico-legal and forensic cases.

Ritual has been shown to have a place in overcoming maladaptive grieving among non-refugees. There is growing recognition of the need to open up, rather than close down, the links with the positive aspects of their homeland and culture (Miller & Billings, 1994). Culturally inappropriate clinical management of the refugee who is suffering cultural bereavement can further undermine the patient's cultural identity and exacerbate his homesickness. Schreiber (1995) reports the mismanagement of an Ethiopian refugee wrongly thought to be psychotic but who responded to traditional healing and rituals to purify the pollution after death associated with the flight from the homeland. Schreiber presents the case as an example of cultural bereavement. One sees a role for traditional healers as 'cultural bereavement therapists', not only with uprooted refugees, but also with communities, which have lost their heritage as a result of modernization; in Tahiti, the *tahua* healer affirms the patient's value of Tahitian culture and identity in the face of the ongoing French presence (Clark, 1993).

Cultural survival in Cambodia today
This chapter opened with the theme of the placenta as emblem of the strength of the rootedness of Cambodian people to home. This anchor is shown in other traditional beliefs and treatments for indigenous illnesses, and reinforces the dangers of forced migration far from the home. Between 1990 and 1996, my Cambodian assistants and I carried out participant observation in every province of Cambodia. I wanted to see how the Cambodians in their own country felt about their identity and culture, and in what ways they felt troubled by feelings such as 'homesickness' or, perhaps, a nostalgia for the pre-1975 world they had lost. And I wanted to know in what ways the traditional healers might be able to help the people redefine themselves as Cambodians with a traditional culture of value in their country. In the course of these six years, my focus necessarily changed: when I started, Cambodia was at war and in need of emergency relief, and people were frightened of the resurgence of the Khmer Rouge; after two years, it was in transition, and the people had to accommodate to the influx of UNTAC and many foreigners; and after two more years, it became a country undergoing development, with further changes to the ecology of village life. Each phase raised new questions about homesickness and cultural survival.

The value of traditional healers
There is a growing literature attesting the value of traditional healers as 'trauma therapists' in countries recovering from war. Bracken *et al.* (1995), writing on the Luwera triangle, noted that, "not only were they providing therapies for sick individuals, but they functioned as a link with the past and thus contributed a sense of continuity to the family."

It seems to me that the traditional healers provide a means for the people to resolve their personal sadness and their problems in the community that sometimes is more acceptable than the methods brought by the West; more than that, the traditional methods are themselves a way of combating feelings of cultural loss caused by ongoing modernization and development projects. As new psychiatric and mental health services take off in Cambodia, the healers could work alongside them, with no detriment to either.

We observed in detail the healing rituals: how the healers embarked on procedures, made objects such as amulets and applied them to the patient, and helped the patient's integration back into their village. After the treatment, we clarified their rationale and choice in examining, diagnosing and treating the person; their nosology of the serious psychiatric illness; and how the psychosocial 'illness' mirrors problems in social and economic development. We noted the position of the healers in their communities, and their accounts of their apprenticeship and healing powers. Some were afraid to use magic openly and claimed to know only traditional herbal medicine because it was similar to Western medicine and did not challenge the health politics (Eisenbruch, 1994a).

The case of 'vanquished by the water-earth'
In the case of 'vanquished by the water-earth', the term for one sort of malaria, unfamiliar elements in the food or in the water of the new environment of the displaced person are believed to conquer the person's body elements. In 'vanquished by guardian spirits', the person out of his familiar village inadvertently upset the local guardian spirits in the new location and they attacked him to cause malaria. The first of these categories showed the danger in journeying far from home. The traditional healers prevented the voyager from getting sick by keeping the old environment alive inside the person, and treated him by putting it back.

These remarks on 'vanquished by the water-earth' are pertinent to many of the inmates from the Thai border camps, who were repatriated to malaria-infected areas in the north-west of the country. At moments like these, one must consider the feelings of guilt and grief of those who migrate and, at the same time, the feelings of those who remained towards their compatriots who left (Grinberg *et al.*, 1989). Sometimes, the people who had never left Cambodia tended to blame the returnees, accusing them of carrying the malarial germ with them and, in this way, as being able to contaminate the homeland. To some extent, this attitude towards the returnees was medically justified, since some had been exposed to virulent falciparum when they were guerrilla soldiers. But it also expressed an ambivalence about their compatriots who had betrayed them by escape and who were 'different from them' after many years of life exposed to Western NGOs in the camps; those who stayed at home, on the other hand, with no thought of escape, had endured more than a decade of privation since 1979 under the Vietnamese-dominated Communist regime.

'Thinking too much' and loss
Like a malfunctioning Tardis, extreme homesickness can trap the uprooted person in a time-warp for the lost past. For Cambodians, this trap shows up as a classical problem people call 'thinking too much', perhaps the most significant marker of grief and an emblem of mental troubles in Cambodia which can lead to 'madness of the feeling' known nowadays as ឆ្កួត សតិ អារម្មណ៍.[3] This term is linked in people's memories with the

---

3 The Khmer Rouge cadres were masters at taking archaic and arcane Pali and Sanskrit terms and using them as part of their speech with the people. In another example, an old Buddhist term was used when a high cadres official wanted to convey to the ordinary people that the Angkar had its

Pol Pot years. Before 1975, people used the term 'madness of thinking' (ឆ្កួត គិត្ត) and it was the Khmer Rouge who popularized a rarefied Sanskrit term to label those thought to be slacking at their toil, an indication of nostalgia.[4] Many healers believed that the central trigger for this disorder was 'thinking too much' because of a web of irreversible losses – of life and family, possessions, status.[5] Thinking too much was found commonly among Cambodian refugees for years after their resettlement, and was linked not only to the traumatic Khmer Rouge regime (Frye & D'Avanzo, 1994) but also to their recollection (perhaps an example of so-called false memory) of the pre-Revolutionary golden years. In a study of 301 unaccompanied Cambodian adolescents, thinking about the homeland contributed to depression (Bemak & Greenberg, 1994). A similar condition to thinking too much, called 'brain fag' syndrome or 'overworking the head', was described among Ethiopian refugees in Israel (Durst *et al.*, 1993).

The role of outside influences in cultural erosion

Some Cambodians, whether in camps or resettled in the West, become victims of a cargo cult and emulate anything Western, and in the process jettison their own ways, and lose touch with their systems of meaning, including their cosmological framework that explains sickness, death, loss and suffering and offers a way to overcome the pain. Eventually they or their children might not want access to their traditional healers and, instead of being spiritual healers, the traditional healers may become relics of something that means nothing to the people.

During the Heng Samrin regime, World Vision International, with the co-operation of the Cambodian Ministry of Health, produced a series of health education pamphlets in easy-to-read Khmer. One was entitled *'Some Traditional Beliefs to be Discarded'* (Thach, 1988). The pamphlet was organized according to common beliefs about child-rearing and the prevention of illness. Each section began with a boxed summary of the beliefs of the 'old folks', and was followed by a rhetorical question, and the reply explained the 'scientific' point of view and concluded that the traditional

---

'high' reasons for doing what it did, but explaining nothing. The term is related to the chain of causation, a well-known Buddhist formula which sums up the principal causes of existence, including, ironically, the causes of suffering and homesickness!

4 Or the term was applied to someone who really was ill with, for example, malaria, and the cadre didn't want to give credibility to the illness. The cadre said the person had 'illness of សតិ អារម្មណ៍'. Either way, it was the first step towards execution.

5 One might add here a comment about 'thinking too much', a concept that westerners sometimes find difficult in their dealings with Cambodians. The wrong interpretation is that Cambodians don't like to think much and they are intellectually lazy. But we can see in the context of Buddhist metaphysics that there is a well-founded fear of using one's mind beyond its boundaries of competence and that this can throw the person into mental disorder.

ways should be discarded. If one is to believe the press, the traditional healers are responsible for killing defenseless endangered species of animals and trees. They are wiping out the gecko population, for example, for medicine, which makes soldiers take their minds off their families at home. They are illiterate liars who use subterfuge to get into hospitals and wreck proper treatments.

Many Cambodians who reached safety were overwhelmed with guilt for wronging their ancestors, and developed psychotic reactions (Hiegel, 1989). Hiegel set up a Khmer traditional medicine centre (TMC) in Khao I Dang (Hiegel & Landrac, 1990). The TMC provided a moratorium for the traditional healer to treat patients outside the domination of Western health systems. For those in the UNHCR camps who had been awarded refugee status and were awaiting resettlement, the moratorium provided, among others, by the traditional healers in the camps could not last. Once they moved to the Phanat Nikhom transit camp, groups had to attend cultural orientation programs. Survival skill training reflected the ideologies of the countries of resettlement.

Displaced and resettled Cambodians were usually assessed in terms of how well they adjusted to their new setting and those who stay in continuing civil war in Cambodia in terms of their ability to accept new influences such as Western methods of hygiene and sanitation. Some refugees in the West, some displaced persons on the border camps, and others in Phnom Pehn actively absorbed aspects of their new surroundings. Of these, some simultaneously preserved or augmented their cultural identity (Cambodians who get enough Western education to understand modern medicine but who still consult traditional healers); and some ditched their affiliation with their culture, becoming alienated from it (Cambodians who shy away from familiar beliefs about health and social conduct and who have blind faith in modern medicine). Some keep a sense of cultural identity, even though they may fail to do well materially, by actively preserving and rediscovering the beliefs and rituals of their culture; and some lose their reference both to their new surroundings and to their own culture, because they do not have enough cultural institutions such as the Buddhist pagoda in their new community. Despite these cultural erosions, the traditional healer in Cambodia, at any rate, still bears the cultural interpretations of illness for his people, understands the ways they signal their distress, and has the power and cultural recipes to treat them. Rather than being a reactionary force against change, he may help the people feel less homesick.

In another example of cultural erosion by foreigners, there was proselytising by certain voluntary agencies in the camps and on the border, which the Cambodian administrators could not curb despite pleas to the missionaries. A series of twenty-five pamphlets was printed in easy-to-read Khmer by Voice of Prophecy Bible Correspondence School in Bangkok, and grafted onto the refugees' plight the promise of Christian Salvation as a better solution than their Buddhism. Today, missionary groups, many of whom worked formerly in the border camps, have moved into Cambodia where they carry out active conversion programs (McNally, 1995; Horner, 1994). Despite the alleged cash incentives to authorities to turn a blind eye, some quarters of government apparently resist the incursion of missionary groups. The Ministry of Cult and Religion State Secretary noted that some of these churches were giving money to people if they joined, and they said that King Sihanouk was evil because he worshipped an idol (Channo, 1995).

Returning home

The case of the Cambodians reveals how homesickness affects a people as a whole and not just as trenches of refugees dispersed around the globe. When I formulated the notion of cultural bereavement in the early 1980s, no-one saw any immediate prospects for a resolution of the political problems in the People's Republic of Kampuchea; and the suggestion that young refugees might yearn to go home was sometimes dismissed not only as out of step with resettlement policy but also as a flight of fancy that had nothing to do with the real world. The refugees could not go back, and that was that. After more than a decade, politics has turned, and people are going back. So the 'theory' of cultural bereavement, originally focusing on how to help refugees adjust to the new place, suddenly takes on a new angle, as some bereft of their homeland now avail themselves of the most potent possible antidote – going home.

UNHCR advocates voluntary repatriation as the ideal durable solution for refugees. Millions have gone back, but did they find themselves at home? There are no data on how they fit into the 'disarticulation of production', which can take many years to repair (Allen, 1994). Warner (1994) points out that the repatriation is not simply to the territorial place, but to 'a concept of home and community'. There will be a historic fit between the group and the land but, in practice, there are rifts. In Cambodia, they may 'go home' to their land because authorities coerce them on pain of withholding food, but the Khmer Rouge burn their houses over and over (Ogden, 1994). And the refugees cannot recreate what was there before, especially if they held unrealistic expectations (Mkhize, 1994). According to some, the nostalgia and homesickness is, if anything, an expression of the denial of these rifts (Warner, 1994). It is apparent that going 'home' is by no means a solution to the mental health problems of many refugees who may feel that they are internal exiles in their own land (Zarzosa, 1996). Harrell-Bond cites examples from Rwanda and warns that repatriation is not the best solution for everyone (Harrell-Bond, 1995).

The repatriation from the camps

In 1992-93, more than 300,000 Cambodians were repatriated across the Thai-Cambodian frontier – many were in a fragile state of mental health for coping with this upheaval (Arnvig, 1994). Many were resettled in areas severely affected by war. One might assume that, ideally, the returnees would resume their life as farmers close to the earth they left behind. Many moved through secondary migration, often to areas where there are high risks such as land mines and no community structure. A year later, 40 per cent of the families could not get enough food to meet basic daily needs, and a huge number was landless. A proportion was placed in Settlement Sites – after more than a decade on the border, more camps. Some refugees, along with their compatriots who never left, become internally displaced persons (IDPs), pried every year out of their homes by Khmer Rouge attacks, and they become forced migrants once more, to seek refuge under conditions said to be little better than in the border camps from which they were repatriated (Dulphy, 1994). They cannot easily feel at home, especially when their homes are re-mined.

Prolonged guerrilla war and displacement force newcomers into flight once more (Sokhet & Whiteside, 1995), with consequences for people's health and behavior (Anyinam, 1995). The returnees and the local population, in north-western Cambodia, are further dislocated by internal displacement and the constant threat of land mines, serious illness, landlessness and poverty. In addressing the UNTAC period, Heder and Ledgerwood (1996) echo my earlier remarks that, given the radical shifts in Cambodian social life since the 1970s, there has been a significant change in what is meant to be Khmer. We revisit the question whether the repatriation, and the spurt of development and Western exposure, helped people to feel in touch with their past and their land again or, on the contrary, more alienated than ever.

An 'emergent' middle circle since repatriation – in north-western Cambodia
Voluntary repatriation seems the ideal durable solution for refugees. Millions have gone back, but do they find themselves at home? Repatriation may signify resettlement in the old country, but not necessarily to a familiar home and community; Instead of dousing feelings of uprooted ness, 'going home' can rekindle them. One stereotype held by expatriate workers is that the villagers want to become modern, but the truth of this assertion has not been systematically tested. The villagers' health appears to be embedded in their beliefs about natural and supernatural forces in the environment of the village and the surrounding fields and forests. Development teams seldom consider how these beliefs may stop the villagers from accepting introduced programs, or how the program could take advantage of the indigenous beliefs. Assuming that the traditional healer is a good source of data about indigenous beliefs concerning village life, the observation of the healers' work with returnees (squandering assets on gambling or being duped into unproductive expenditure) could help tune development to cause the least amount of alienation to the person returning home and to his compatriot who never left.

It is probable that many of the most vulnerable people, such as those in newly created settlements of returnees or of displaced people, are also those who are the most isolated from a community structure. Sometimes in these 'unnatural' villages, there is no pagoda, no market, no traditional healer. The health status of these people is worse than those in natural villages. Further, it is possible that these settlers' needs can be met if they are helped to find traditional healers in neighboring communes.

Choosing to return from resettlement in Western countries
It may seem puzzling why any migrant, long settled into stable lives in Western countries, should uproot to return to economic and social uncertainty in the homeland. It may have to do with living with kinsfolk in their own cultural groups. The decision to return may be triggered by just one event. Even if they do not go back, alienated children of immigrants may, in turn, over-identify with the parental culture, and feel nostalgia and a wish to return to a country they never knew. It is not easy to go back to one's country, and harder for the children who may never have set

foot in that place and who face identity diffusion (Kromayer, 1989). A person with insufficient competence in the parent's culture may become unable to return to his homeland successfully, should he one day be in a position to do so. Instead of dousing the uprootedness, 'going home' can rekindle it. Espin (1992) described her experiences of loss and uprootedness from fleeing her native Cuba and her reactions to a visit. For years she had felt as if her memories had no geography and that Cuba did not have a real existence beyond her memory. Going back, she saw that the place where she feels at home is not fully home any more. Or the returnee may be made to feel guilty for having abandoned the homeland, as if he had committed a crime (Kovalskys, 1988).

Cultural loss and the effects of development projects
People can lose their culture not only when they flee their homeland, but also when massive development projects threaten the old community and ecosystem and isolate them from their land on which they depend to maintain their traditional rituals (Prince, 1993). 'Development refugees' also suffer grief and cultural dislocation, no matter which country or ethnic group, and despite the new economic opportunities (Weist, 1995). Now, in Cambodia, people who are veterans of war and dislocation face imminent damming of the Mekong by UNDP-approved projects, despite the opposition of groups concerned about the impact on local culture (Grainger, 1996). The introduction of Western values into traditional societies, by giving them the tools to rebuild their communities, can open the door for people to overcome their losses. The downside is that development may also disrupt people's self-definitions and social relationships (Fitzgerald, 1990). Sometimes, development, along with the associated cultural losses, drives the people back to traditional healers (Mookherjee & Manna, 1995). In Cambodia, the healers seem best able to respond to their compatriots' feelings of nostalgia and grief for the past, but the quickened pace of culture change associated with development threatens in some ways to increase the distance of the people from their past.

Conclusion

In this chapter it will have become clear to the reader that all classes of displaced persons world-wide are affected by homesickness and culture shock. Manifestations of homesickness are intimately tied to notions of home and community, and to traditional constructs. Traditional beliefs and practices sustain the cultural bonding and hence well-being of displaced persons. In the absence of acknowledgement and expression of such customs, cultural bereavement may worsen, and be exacerbated under the impact of Western cultural paradigms. Indigenous traditions can palliate intrusion and aid displaced persons to cope with the cultural, as well as psychic, losses experienced during exile and on return to their homeland.

Author note

I would like to thank Lam Bun Thar, Cheth Naren, and Chou Sam Ath for their help with the fieldwork in Cambodia, and Thong Thel and Kong Hol for their assistance in Australia and Keo Veth for his help in France. This work was funded in part by a grant from the Australian Research Council.

References

Adler, S. R. (1994). Ethnomedical pathogenesis and Hmong immigrants' sudden nocturnal deaths. *Culture, Medicine and Psychiatry, 18,* 23-59.

Allen, T. (1994). The United Nations and the homecoming of displaced persons. *International Review of the Red Cross, 301,* 340-353.

Anyinam, C. (1995). Ecology and ethnomedicine: Exploring links between current environmental crises and indigenous medical practices. *Social Science and Medicine, 40,* 321-329.

Arnvig, E. (1994). Women, children and returnees. In: P. Utting (Ed.), *Between hope and insecurity: The social consequences of the Cambodian peace process* (pp. 143-182). Geneva, Switzerland: UNRISD.

Banta, L. E. (1991). Major mental illness in two Kenyan outposts. In: Samuel O. Okpaku (Ed.), *Mental health in Africa and the Americas today: A book of conference proceedings* (pp. 187-193). Nashville, TN: Chrisolith Books.

Bemak, F., & Greenberg, B. (1994). Southeast Asian refugee adolescents: Implications for counseling. *Journal of Multicultural Counseling and Development, 22,* 115-124.

Birman, D., & Tyler, F. B. (1994). Acculturation and alienation of Soviet Jewish refugees in the United States. *Genetic, Social, and General Psychology Monographs, 120,* 101-115.

Boua, C. (1994). Reflections on a battle for survival. *Phnom Penh Post,* 3. 25.19.

Boyden, J. (1994). Children's experience of conflict related emergencies: Some implications for relief policy and practice. *Disasters, 18,* 254-267.

Bracken, P. J., Giller, J. E., & Summerfield, D. (1995). Psychological responses to war and atrocity: The limitations of current concepts. *Social Science and Medicine, 40,* 1073-1082.

Chandler, D. P. (1991). *The tragedy of Cambodian history: Politics, war, and revolution.* New Haven, CT: Yale University Press.

Chandler, D. P. (1992). *Brother number one: A political biography of Pol Pot.* Boulder, CO: Westview Press.

Channo, M. (1995). The stones being thrown at Christians. *Phnom Penh Post,* 4. 5.17

Cheung, P. (1995). Acculturation and psychiatric morbidity among Cambodian refugees in New Zealand. *International Journal of Social Psychiatry, 41,* 108-119.

Chung, R. C., & Kagawa Singer, M. (1993). Predictors of psychological distress among Southeast Asian refugees. *Social Science and Medicine, 36,* 631-639.

Chung, R. C., & Lin, K. M. (1994). Help-seeking behavior among Southeast Asian refugees. Special Issue: Asian-American mental health. *Journal of Community Psychology, 22,* 109-120.

Clark, S. S. (1993). Anxiety, cultural identity, and solidarity: A Tahitian ethnomedical encounter. *Ethos, 21,* 180-204.

122

Colson, E. (1982). *The social consequences of resettlement: The impact of the Kariba resettlement upon the Gwembe Tonga.* Manchester, UK: Manchester University Press for the Institute of African Studies, University of Zambia.

Deng, F. (1994). Protecting the dispossessed: Interim report to the United Nations Secretary-General on activities to promote protection and assistance for internally displaced persons. New York: United Nations.

Desjarlais, R. R. (1991). Poetic transformations of Yolmo 'sadness'. *Culture, Medicine and Psychiatry, 15,* 387-420.

Dhruvarajan, V. (1993). Ethnic cultural retention and transmission among first generation Hindu Asian Indians in a Canadian Prairie city. *Journal of Comparative Family Studies, 24,* 63-79.

Dobbs, L. (1994). Old and happy in the far northeast. *Phnom Penh Post,* 3. 24.7

Dulphy, F. (1994). Northwest faces new refugee crisis. *Phnom Penh Post,* 3. 21.1-6.

Durst, R., Minuchin Itzigsohn, S., & Jabotinsky Rubin, K. (1993). 'Brain-fag' syndrome: Manifestation of transculturation in an Ethiopan Jewish immigrant. *Israel Journal of Psychiatry and Related Sciences, 30,* 223-232.

Ebihara, M. M., Mortland, C. A., & Ledgerwood, J. (1994). *Cambodian culture since 1975: Homeland and exile.* Ithaca: Cornell University Press.

Edwards, J. N., Fuller, T. D., Sermsri, S., & Vorakitphokatorn, S. (1994). Why people feel crowded: An examination of objective and subjective crowding. *Population and Environment A Journal of Interdisciplinary Studies, 16,* 149-173.

Edwards, P. (1996). Imaging the other in Cambodian nationalist discourse before and during the UNTAC period. In: S. Heder & J. Ledgerwood (Eds.), *Propaganda, politics, and violence in Cambodia: Democratic transition under United Nations peace-keeping.* (pp. 50-72). Armonk, NY: M. E. Sharpe.

Eisenbruch, M. (1984a). Cross-cultural aspects of bereavement: I. A conceptual framework for comparative analysis. *Culture, Medicine and Psychiatry, 8,* 283-309.

Eisenbruch, M. (1984b). Cross-cultural aspects of bereavement: II. Ethnic and cultural variations in the development of bereavement practices. *Culture, Medicine and Psychiatry, 8,* 315-347.

Eisenbruch, M. (1986). Action research with Vietnamese refugees: Refugee, befriender and researcher relationships. *Journal of Refugee Studies, 7,* 30-51.

Eisenbruch, M. (1988). Report on Cambodian mental health in Site 2, Site 8, Khao I Dang, and Phanat Nikhom camps in Thailand. Submitted to UNHCR Geneva.

Eisenbruch, M. (1990a). Classification of natural and supernatural causes of mental distress: Development of a Mental Distress Explanatory Model Questionnaire. *Journal of Nervous and Mental Disease, 178,* 712-719.

Eisenbruch, M. (1990b). Cultural bereavement and homesickness. In: S. Fisher & C. L. Cooper (Eds.), *On the move: The psychology of change and transition* (pp. 191-205). New York: John Wiley & Sons Ltd.

Eisenbruch, M. (1990c). The physical and mental well-being of the Indo-Chinese communities in Australia. *Journal of Vietnamese Studies, 3,* 78-90.

Eisenbruch, M. (1992). The use of traditional healing for treating children of war: The case of *skan* in Cambodia. *Refugee Studies Programme (Oxford),* 3(abstract)

Eisenbruch M., & Hauff, E. (1994a). Resources and limitations in meeting the mental health needs of the Cambodian population. 19-21 April; Phnom Penh: University of Oslo/IOM.

Eisenbruch, M. (1994b). Mental health and the Cambodian traditional healer for refugees who resettled, were repatriated or internally displaced, and for those who stayed at home. *Collegium Antropologicum, 18,* 219-230.

Eisenbruch, M., & Handelman, L. (1989). Development of an Explanatory Model of Illness Schedule for Cambodian refugee patients. *Journal of Refugee Studies, 2,* 243-256.

Espin, O. M. (1992). Roots uprooted: The psychological impact of historical/political dislocation. Special Issue: Refugee women and their mental health: Shattered societies, shattered lives: I. *Women and Therapy, 13,* 9-20.

Ewing, F. S. J. (1960). Birth customs of the Tawsug, compared with those of other Philippine groups. *Anthropology Quarterly, 33,* 129-133.

Fitzgerald, M. H. (1990). The interplay of culture and symptoms: Menstrual symptoms among Samoans. *Medical Anthropology, 12,* 145-167.

Frye, B. (1990). The process of health care decision making among Cambodian immigrant women. *International Quarterly of Community Health Education, 10,* 113-124.

Frye, B. A., & D'Avanzo, C. D. (1994). Cultural themes in family stress and violence among Cambodian refugee women in the inner city. *Advances in Nursing Science, 16,* 64-77.

Geertz, C. (1960). *The religion of Java.* New York: Free Press.

George, K. M. (1995). Violence, solace, and ritual: A case study from island southeast Asia. *Culture, Medicine and Psychiatry, 19,* 225-260.

Gibbs, S. (1994). Post-war social reconstruction in Mozambique: Re-framing children's experience of trauma and healing. *Disasters, 18,* 268-276.

Grainger, M. (1996). MRC slams 'radical' NGOs, as donors urged to halt funding. *Phnom Penh Post,* 5. 11.9

Grinberg, L., Grinberg, R., & Festinger, N. T. (1989). *Psychoanalytic perspectives on migration and exile.* New Haven, CT: Yale University Press.

Gyallay-Pap, P. (1989). Reclaiming a shattered past: Education for the displaced Khmer in Thailand. *Journal of Refugee Studies, 2,* 257-275.

Hadjadj, S. (1989). Les enfants et les adolescents du palimpseste (Children and adolescents as palimpsests). *Psychanalystes, 31,* 53-66.

Harrell-Bond, B. (1995). Comments on 'New directions to avoid hard problems'. *Journal of Refugee Studies, 8,* 299-300.

Heder, S., & Ledgerwood, J. (1996). Parties of violence: An introduction. In: S. Heder & J. Ledgerwood (Eds.), *Propaganda, politics, and violence in Cambodia: Democratic transition under United Nations peace-keeping* (pp. 3-49). Armonk, NY: M. E. Sharpe.

Hiegel, J., & Landrac, C. (1990). Suicide dans un camp réfugiés Khmers en Thailande: Meurtre du moi et meurtre de soi. *Nouvelle Revue d'Ethnopsychiatrie, 15,* 107-138.

Horner, S. (1994). Biblical recipes for healing pain. *Phnom Penh Post,* 3. 4.13

Kondic, L., & Mavar, M. (1992). Anxiety and depressive reactions in refugees. *Psychologische Beitrage, 34,* 179-183.

Kovalskys, J. (1988). Exilio y desexili (Exile and repatriation). XXI InterAmerican Congress of Psychology (1987, Havanna, Cuba). *Revista Chilena de Psicologia, 9,* (1 (sic))) 51-54.

Kromayer, H. (1989). Reintegrering af tyrkiske unge, der er vokset op i Tyskland: II. Identitetskonflikt og selvopfattelse ved tilbagevenden til Tyrkiet (Reintegration of Turkish youth who grew up in Germany: II. Identity conflict and self-image after return to Turkey). *Skolepsykologi, 26,* 251-265.

Laderman, C. (1983). Wives and midwives: Childbirth and nutrition in rural Malaysia. Berkeley: University of California Press. 1 p. Comparative studies of health systems and medical care, vol. 7. 0-520-06036-9.

Lemoine, J. (1983). La malediction des hmong en exil: Les rêves qui tuent. *Actuel,* 106-191.

Levy Warren, M. H. (1987). Moving to a new culture: Cultural identity, loss, and mourning. In: Jonathan Bloom-Feshbach & Sally Bloom-Feshbach (Eds.), *The psychology of separation and loss: Perspectives on development, life transitions, and clinical practice.* (pp. 300-315). San Francisco, CA: Jossey-Bass Inc.

Mahmoudi, K. M. (1992). Refugee cross-cultural adjustment: Tibetans in India. *International Journal of Intercultural Relations, 16,* 17-32.

Martin, M. A. (1986). Vietnamised Cambodia: A silent ethnocide. *Indochina Report, 7,* 1-31.

McInnis, K. (1991). Ethnic-sensitive work with Hmong refugee children. *Child Welfare, 70,* 571-580.

McNally, D. (1995). Mormons pedal the Word to Khmers. *Phnom Penh Post,* 4. 16.14

Miller, K. E., & Billings, D. L. (1994). Playing to grow: A primary mental health intervention with Guatemalan refugee children. *American Journal of Orthopsychiatry, 64,* 346-356.

Mkhize, H. (1994). Mental health of women political repatriates. *Women and Therapy, 15,* 101-116.

Mookherjee, H. N., & Manna, S. (1995). Psychoemotional responses to the existing social systems in tribal populations in India. In: Rumi Kato Price, Brent Mack Shea, & Harsha N. Mookherjee (Eds.), *Social psychiatry across cultures: Studies from North America, Asia, Europe, and Africa.* (pp. 51-59). New York: Plenum Press.

Moon, J. H., & Pearl, J. H. (1991). Alienation of elderly Korean American immigrants as related to place of residence, gender, age, years of education, time in the U.S., living with or without children, and living with or without a spouse. *International Journal of Aging and Human Development, 32,* 115-124.

Muecke, M. A., & Sassi, L. (1992). Anxiety among Cambodian refugee adolescents in transit and in resettlement. *Western Journal of Nursing Research, 14,* 267-291.

Ogden, J. (1994). Refugees return to mines, destruction. *Phnom Penh Post,* 3. 13.17

Parvanta, S. (1992). The balancing act: Plight of Afghan women refugees. Special Issue: Refugee women and their mental health: Shattered societies, shattered lives: I. *Women and Therapy, 13,* 113-128.

Polic, M., Zabukovec, V., Strnisa, Z., & Majcen, V. (1993). Perception of war and its consequences. *Studia Psychologica, 35,* 276-283.

Pollock, G. H. (1989). On migration - voluntary and coerced. *Annual of Psychoanalysis, 17,* 145-158.

Prince, R. H. (1993). Psychiatry among the James Bay Cree: A focus on pathological grief reactions. *Transcultural Psychiatric Research Review, 30,* 3-50.

Rice, P. L. (1994). When I had my baby here! In: P.L. Rice (Ed.), *Asian mothers, Australian birth - Pregnancy, childbirth and childrearing: The Asian experience in an English-speaking country.* Melbourne, Australia: Ausmed Publications.

Robertson, E. B., Skinner, M. L., Love, M. M., & Elder, G. H. (1992). The Pubertal Development Scale: A rural and suburban comparison. *Journal of Early Adolescence, 12,* 174-186.

Rosenblatt, P. C. (1993). Cross-cultural variation in the experience, expression, and understanding of grief. In: D. P. Irish, K. F. Lundquist, & V. Jenkins Nelsen (Eds.), *Ethnic variations in dying, death, and grief: Diversity in universality.* (pp. 13-19). Washington, DC: Taylor & Francis.

Sande, H. (1991). Muslims under the midnight sun. *Nordisk Psykiatrisk Tidsskrift, 45,* 243-245.

Schreiber, S. (1995). Migration, traumatic bereavement and transcultural aspects of psychological healing: Loss and grief of a refugee woman from Begameder County in Ethiopia. *British Journal of Medical Psychology, 68,* 135-142.

Schriever, S. H. (1990). Comparison of beliefs and practices of ethnic Viet and Lao Hmong concerning illness, healing, death and mourning: Implications for hospice care with refugees in Canada. *Journal of Palliative Care, 6,* 42-49.

Silverman, P. R., Nickman, S., & Worden, J. W. (1995). Detachment revisited: The child's reconstruction of a dead parent. In: K. J. Doka (Ed), *Children mourning, mourning children* (pp. 131-148). Washington, DC: Hospice Foundation of America.

Sokhet, R. (1994). Hostages alive but losing weight. *Phnom Penh Post*, 3. 20.20

Sokhet, R., & Whiteside, D. (1995). Vengeance on a scale not seen in a long time. *Phnom Penh Post*, 4.20

Suzuki, D. (1995). (BBC series on DNA and genetics).

Tapp, N. (1988). The reformation of culture: Hmong refugees from Laos. *Journal of Refugee Studies, 1,* 20-37.

Thach, S. (1988). Customs which should be discarded. Phnom Penh. World Vision International.

Tran, T. V. (1991). Family living arrangement and social adjustment among three ethnic groups of elderly Indochinese refugees. *International Journal of Aging and Human Development, 32,* 91-102.

Van Boemel, G. B., & Rozee, P. D. (1992). Treatment for psychosomatic blindness among Cambodian refugee women. Special Issue: Refugee women and their mental health: Shattered societies, shattered lives: II. *Women and Therapy, 13,* 239-266.

Vickery, M., Chandler, D. P., & Kiernan, B. (1983). *Democratic Kampuchea - Themes and variations (First ed.).* New Haven, CT: Yale University Southeast Asia Studies. 99 p. Revolution and its aftermath in Kampuchea: Eight essays.

Warner, D. (1994). Voluntary repatriation and the meaning of the return to home: A critique of liberal mathematics. *Journal of Refugee Studies, 7,* 160-174.

Weist, K. M. (1995). Development refugees: Americans, Indians and the big dams. *Journal of Refugee Studies, 8,* 163-184.

Wilkinson, A. (1994). A changed vision of God. *New Yorker,* 52-68.

Zarzosa, H. L. (1996). The impact of return migration: The case of Chile. *Refugee Participation Network,* 34-35.

Zivcic, I. (1993). Emotional reactions of children to war stress in Croatia. *Journal of the American Academy of Child and Adolescent Psychiatry, 32,* 709-713.

9 Children's Coping with Homesickness: Phenomenology and Intervention

CHRISTOPHER A. THURBER

Children's coping with homesickness: Phenomenology and intervention

How children and adolescents[1] cope with homesickness deserves careful study for several reasons. First, homesickness is experienced by millions of children who spend time away from home and family. In children separated from home, self-reported prevalence rates of homesickness hover around 75%, depending on sample and environment characteristics (e.g., Fisher, 1989; Thurber, 1995a). The emotional distress, behavior problems, and deleterious physical, cognitive, and social consequences of homesickness have been well documented in young people (Burt, 1993; Fisher et al., 1990; Fisher & Hood, 1987; Fisher et al., 1986; Fisher et al., 1985; Thurber, 1995a).

Second, an understanding of how children cope with homesickness will guide interventions. Certainly, established treatments for the related constructs of depression and anxiety will influence interventions for homesickness. However, homesickness is a uniquely complex construct, in part because the stress of transition involves separation from familiar entities home; attachment figures; native culture) and integration into a novel environment. This complexity warrants a thorough understanding of what children themselves are doing to cope with homesickness, and specifically, which of their ways of coping are effective.

Third, coping with homesickness involves, by definition, the uniquely stressful circumstance of separation from primary caregivers. This circumstance is steeped in research from the related domains of attachment (e.g., Ainsworth et al., 1978; Bowlby, 1969), temperament (e.g., Kagan, 1994), psychobiology (e.g., Hofer, 1994), and affect regulation (e.g., Calkins, 1994). From these literatures, we may hypothesize that insecure, inhibited, autonomically labile children who rely heavily on their parents for regulation of emotion will be more likely to experience distress upon separation, or become homesick, than their secure, outgoing, autonomically steady, self-reliant peers. Clearly, these affiliated literatures lend predictive power to an investigation of coping by identifying characteristics that may place children at risk for maladjustment to separation. Perhaps children's coping instinctively compensates for some of these risk factors. For example, some children may be able to form new attachments in novel environments. However, there may be some risk factors, such as autonomic reactivity, that transcend children's coping skills. The empirical study of children's

---

1 Henceforth referred to collectively as 'children.'

128

coping with homesickness complements the literatures cited above by describing the processes children can and do use in the circumstance of separation to adjust themselves and return to a state of psychological and physiological equilibrium.

After reviewing research on the phenomenology of homesickness in children, I will outline theories of stress and coping relevant to separation and homesickness. Next, I will summarize several descriptive studies of children's coping with homesickness. Finally, I will discuss the implication of these studies on interventions for homesickness.

The experience and expression of homesickness in children

Although homesickness surely has existed ever since people were separated from some place they called home, Hippocrates (*ca* 460 – *ca* 377 B.C.) may have been the first Western author to write about the condition. This Greek physician believed that homesickness was due to an imbalance in the black bile humor. Some 2200 years after Hippocrates's death, British, American, and French physicians, writing during the American War for Independence and the French Revolutionary War, repeatedly documented homesickness in soldiers (see Bachet, 1950; Rather, 1965; and Zwingmann, 1959 for reviews). During the American Civil War, in the 1860's, residential summer camping[2] for children began to blossom in the United States. Today, more than 5 million American children leave home to attend summer camps each year. Not surprisingly, documentation of the phenomenology of homesickness in children has grown.

In his 1923 book, *Camp Management*, H. W. Gibson's total coverage of homesickness was: "Early in the season look out for homesick boys. Keep them busy" (p. 10). Subsequent publications in the nursing and camping literatures have given homesickness more careful consideration (Baier & Welch, 1992; Pravda, 1995; Winland-Brown & Maheady, 1990). Yet it was not until the 1980's that Fisher and her colleagues conducted the first systematic, empirical research on homesickness in children attending boarding schools (Fisher *et al.*, 1984, 1986, 1990). Replicating many findings in previous studies of homesickness in adult university students, Fisher's group found: (1) about three-quarters of boys and girls spending time away from home experienced homesickness (Fisher *et al.*, 1986, 1990); (2) both boys and girls defined homesickness as a state of negative affect combined with a cognitive

---

2 According to Macleod (1983), organized residential (i.e., overnight) summer camping began in 1861 when William Frederick Gunn marched a group of boys from Connecticut to Long Island (New York) to participate in a military-style bivouac camp. During the industrial revolution that followed the American Civil War, the popularity of residential camping grew dramatically. Today, there are over 1,500 residential summer camps accredited by the American Camping Association. Children typically spend 2-8 weeks living in tents or cabins in rural areas with university students who act as counselors, supervising games, crafts, sports, field trips, and intercamp athletic competitions.

preoccupation with returning home and being reunited with primary caregivers (Fisher *et al.*, 1986, 1990); (3) homesick children reported more non-traumatic physical ailments than their non-homesick peers (Fisher *et al.*, 1986); (4) homesickness may be exacerbated by perceptions of high environmental demand and low perceived control (Fisher *et al.*, 1990); and (5) maturing age and previous experience away from home dramatically reduced the likelihood of homesickness. No strong or reliable gender differences emerged in the self-reported definition or experience of homesickness.

My own research has continued to explore both the phenomenology (Thurber, 1995a) and etiology (Thurber, 1995b) of homesickness. I have chosen to study childhood homesickness at residential summer camps because the separation is discrete yet substantial in time, and objectively uncontrollable in many respects, yet ethical in nature. A recent study (Thurber, 1995a) with 329 boys ages 8-16 who were spending two weeks away at camp found that: (1) homesickness was prevalent and varied in intensity. Eighty-three percent of the boys reported some homesickness on at least one day during their stay, and 5.8% experienced severe depression and anxiety, as measured by standardized clinical research questionnaires; (2) homesickness was experienced as a combination of depression and anxiety, particularly the former; (3) younger boys and boys with less experience at summer camp were at greater risk for homesickness than older, more experienced boys; and (4) homesickness presented most often as internalizing behavior and was sometimes detectable to observers who knew the boys. Sixty-three percent of the boys with moderate or high self-reported levels of homesickness were judged by observers to be homesick. A recently completed study at a summer camp for girls has replicated these findings (Thurber & Weisz, 1997). As in Fisher *et al.* (1990), I found that girls reported experiencing a slightly higher intensity of homesickness compared to boys, averaged over the course of two weeks.

Inconsistent with popular notions, the most homesick boys and girls in three separate samples of mine have become progressively more homesick over the course of their separation, experiencing a significant drop in homesickness two days before reuniting with parents. Speculation in the residential camping literature on the course of homesickness had previously been based on notions of how long it typically took children at camp to make friends and get maximally involved in activities. Various authors had cited findings that, for children who experienced it, homesickness was most severe on the first day (Cohen, 1990); the first two days (Ditter, 1990); the first three days (Hamessley, 1977; Winters, 1989); or the first four days (Mitchell *et al.*, 1977). These time windows for peak homesickness were markedly narrower than those suggested in studies of boarding school students (e.g., Fisher *et al.*, 1984), although authors in the camping literature offered no data to support their speculations. Of note is the overall shape of the homesickness course curve, which authors in the residential camping literature had described as showing an immediate onset and increase after separation, followed by remission in three to four days. The fact that the most homesick children in my samples began their stays away from home more homesick than their peers and then became progressively more homesick prompted numerous questions about how children cope (or fail to cope) with the stressor of separation from home.

Theories of stress and coping

Considering the quantity and magnitude of different circumstances that can and do stress children, it is not surprising that research efforts have long focused on describing the impact of stress. Only in the past two decades have researchers begun to concentrate on how children cope with this impact. These efforts have supplied provocative data on how children cope with a variety of stressors, including everyday hassles (e.g., Band & Weisz, 1988; Seiffge-Krenke, 1993), chronic illness (e.g., Band & Weisz, 1990; Hauser et al., 1993), painful medical procedures (e.g., Curry & Russ, 1985; Weisz et al., 1994), hospitalization (reviewed by Rutter, 1981) and separated families (e.g., Radovanovic, 1993; Wallerstein, 1983). Surprisingly, considering its frequency and impact, research on how children cope with homesickness was limited to one anecdotal description of boys' use of distraction to cope with homesickness at boarding school (Harris & Guz, 1986).

As I noted, children's coping with homesickness is complex because the stress of transition involves, by definition, separation from the familiar (home; attachment figures; native culture) as well as integration into a novel environment. The discomfort of separation and the demands of a novel environment can understandably leave some children perceiving a reduced sense of control (Cooper, 1990). In turn, children's low perceived control may result in negative affect (Weisz et al., 1987; Weisz et al., 1989) and vice versa (Skinner, 1995). Not surprisingly, low perceived control has been associated with maladjustment to transitions (Fisher & Cooper, 1990), and specifically to childhood homesickness (Fisher et al., 1985; Fisher et al., 1990; Thurber & Weisz, 1997; but cf. Fisher et al., 1986). Low perceived control is also associated with homesickness in adults (Burt, 1993). Specifically, perceived control over the decision to leave home ('decision control') has been shown to predict adjustment in adults (Davidson & O'Connor, 1990; Fisher et al., 1985; Reinardy, 1992). Although the association between decision control and homesickness in children is uncertain (Fisher et al., 1984, 1986; Fisher et al., 1990), perceived control in this and other domains seemed worthy of investigation. For these reasons, control beliefs theory (Weisz, 1990), and in particular the two-process model of control (Rothbaum et al., 1982), offers a useful framework for studying the complexities of children's coping with homesickness[3].

The two-process model of control distinguishes between *primary control* -modifying objective conditions to fit oneself- and *secondary control* -adjusting oneself to fit

---

3   The control theory of coping has its roots in Piaget's (1929) constructs of assimilation and accommodation, as well as in motivational theory (White, 1959).

131

objective conditions. *Relinquished control* coping -giving up or simply emoting- is not a process of exerting control, but is a third way to categorize coping. In operationalizing these concepts, it is helpful to distinguish between coping *methods* and coping *goals* (Weisz *et al.*, 1994). Simply stated, methods are ways of acting or thinking; goals are the ends toward which coping methods are directed. On a macroscopic level, methods are codable either observable or unobservable behavior (cf. Compas, 1987). On a microscopic level, methods can be extremely diverse, even in children (Band & Weisz, 1988). However, the concepts of primary and secondary control apply *only* to coping goals because only goals have an object of control: either one's self (secondary control) or the objective conditions (primary control).

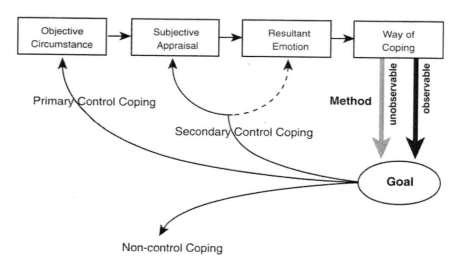

Figure 9.1.   The merging of lazarus' theory of stress and coping with Rothbaum *et al.'s* two process model of control

Figure 9.1 illustrates how Weisz's model of control coping merges with a widely used model of stress developed by Lazarus and his colleagues (e.g., Lazarus & Folkman, 1984a, 1984b). Lazarus's theory (in boxes) states that an emotion results from the subjective appraisal of an objective circumstance (also called the 'person-environment relationship' (1993, p. 35)). Coping, then, is an effortful response to the (negative) emotion in question. According to Lazarus, "coping is best defined as efforts to manage demands that tax or exceed our resources" (1993, p. 34). As *Figure 9.1* illustrates, each way of coping is composed of a method which may be either observable (e.g., playing a game; running away; crying) or unobservable (e.g., thinking about ice cream; wondering about what causes homesickness) and a goal which may be either primary control (e.g., returning home; winning a game), secondary control (e.g., forgetting about homesickness; reconsidering the importance of losing a game), or relinquished control (e.g., simple emoting; ruminating) (see Heckhausen & Schulz, 1995 for a review). Note that coping methods and goals can be mutually determined, i.e., method choice can depend on goal choice and goal choice can depend on method choice. Note, too, that some children explain their secondary control goals as unelaborated attempts to 'feel better' or 'not feel so bad.' In this case, secondary control may be aimed directly at influencing emotions, bypassing subjective appraisal altogether. This route is indicated by a dotted line in *Figure 9.1*.

The coping methods and goals that children use are determined in part by their perception of control, their motivations and intentions, and the specific emotion generated (Lazarus, 1993). Coping methods and goals are also determined by a person's response repertoire, the range of possible outcomes, and the controllability of the circumstance and resultant emotions. Some researchers have suggested that perceived control prompts primary control coping, whereas intensity of emotion prompts secondary control coping (Compas *et al.*, 1991). This is an intriguing notion. However, most children and adults simultaneously apply a combination of primary and secondary control strategies to most stressors (Folkman *et al.*, 1986; Weisz *et al.*, 1994), so this is a challenging notion to test. Other factors that certainly influence both the methods and the goals of coping include socialization, cultural context, temperament, and previous experience with the stressor in question. To complicate matters further, the influence of these factors on the nature of coping varies developmentally. As children grow older, ethnic identity is enhanced and challenged, peer group identity fluctuates, independence is fostered, and metacognitions about emotions develop and mature (Harris, 1989). Also, children's beliefs about the contingency of events become more realistic with age, their competence increases in a variety of domains, and, as a result, their perceptions of control shift (Weisz, 1983; Rothbaum & Weisz, 1989).

A few studies of children's coping have suggested that using secondary control or emotion-focused coping is the most adaptive choice when stressors are largely uncontrollable (Compas *et al.*, 1988; Radovanovic, 1993; Weisz *et al.*, 1994). Indeed, it is tempting to conclude that optimal outcome is always achieved by employing primary control coping for controllable stressors and secondary control coping for uncontrollable stressors. Learned helplessness theory (Abramson *et al.*, 1978) and common sense suggest that attempts to change an unchangeable circumstance are the definition of futility and often lead to feelings of helplessness and depression.

In reality, however, this neat correspondence between coping control and stressor control is complicated by several factors. First, even circumscribed stressors have controllable *and* uncontrollable elements; thus 'mixed' primary-secondary coping, applied simultaneously, and customized to fit the variegated elements of a single stressor, may be most adaptive (Weisz *et al.*, 1994). A related form of adaptive customization may be sequentially 'layered' coping, where one sort of coping is replaced by another sort if the first proves ineffective. A second complicating factor is the context in which the stressor occurs. For example, there may be cultural preferences for primary and secondary control, which, if violated, can themselves become stressors (Azuma, 1984; Kojima, 1984; Seginer *et al.*, 1993; Weisz *et al.*, 1984). Third, age and cognitive sophistication may play key roles in explaining children's inclination to use primary vs. secondary coping. A review by Compas *et al.* (1991) summarizes evidence that primary control coping, which requires basic causal understanding, emerges around ages 4-5 and increases until children are about 8 to 10 years old. By contrast, secondary control coping, which requires metacognitive sophistication, may emerge between ages 6-8 and increase through adolescence. Together, these findings suggest that efficacious coping should be mixed, layered, culturally acceptable, and cognitively appropriate. In sum, there are robust developmental trends in the ways children cope, but there may not be a simple relationship between the perceived controllability of a given stressor and type of control coping used.

Children's coping with separation and homesickness

Two interview studies and one questionnaire study on children's coping with homesickness may be all that comprise the extant descriptive literature on the topic. Harris (1989) described an unpublished interview study involving two groups of 8- and 13-year-old boys at an English boarding school (Harris & Guz, 1986). Some of the questions boys were asked focused on what they did to change feelings of homesickness. Although exact percentages were not noted, two frequently reported ways of coping were: (1) letter-writing and telephoning (both observable methods) in order to re-establish contact with home (a primary control goal); and (2) engaging in distracting activities (either observable or unobservable methods) in order to forget about separation and homesickness (a secondary control goal). The notion that the positive emotions associated with distracting activities could replace the negative emotions associated with homesickness prompted Harris (1989) to consider whether boys believed consciousness had a limited capacity. One 8-year-old boy remarked, that "thinking about other things than home helps ... cos it takes your mind off feeling sad. It occupies your mind. I don't think you can think two things at once" (p. 163). Some 13-year-olds expressed a similar sentiment. Boys of both ages "warned of the danger or futility of thinking about home or making contact with home" (p. 164; cf. Rubin, 1949; Mitchell *et al.*, 1977). Both the potency of distraction and the futility of rumination echo Gibson's early warning about homesick boys: "Keep them busy."

One intriguing question that Harris (1989) raised was how boys learn these and other ways of coping with homesickness. He concluded that "use of the cognitive suppression [coping strategy] depends on a contribution both from the boys and from the institution" (p. 166). The boys have "some insight into the limited capacity of consciousness [and] might infer that a distraction or blocking strategy would be effective, try it out, and become convinced of its utility" (p. 166). Moreover, "the institution provides an organized schedule that governs most waking hours" (p. 166). There are many similarities between the coping skills of these boys at a boarding school and the coping skills of 56 boys I interviewed at a residential summer camp (Thurber, 1997).

Because little had been reported formally about how children cope with homesickness, the primary goals of the study were: (1) to use a split method-goal coding scheme based on the two-process model of control to describe how boys cope with homesickness and competitive loss. Secondarily, this study sought: (2) to explore possible relationships among coping goals and subsequent adjustment; and (3) to discover whether boys' coping practices were congruent with their advice to other boys faced with the same stressors. The 56 boys, ages 8- to 16-years-old, were interviewed about their coping methods and goals for homesickness and the comparison stressor of competitive loss (i.e., losing a game or a match).

Results indicated that very few boys (4 out of 56) coped with homesickness by relinquishing control. Only 2 of 56 relinquished control for competitive loss. Many boys reported *mixed* coping, comprised of both primary *and* secondary control goals. For the stressor of homesickness, 16% of the boys had exclusively primary control goals; 34% had mixed primary/secondary goals; 43% had exclusively secondary control goals; and 7% relinquished control or responded only with displays of emotion. Boys' coping was also *layered*. The modal boy reported two different ways of coping ways for both stressors.

Consistent with the 57 boys in Compas *et al.* (1988), there was a developmental trend in the generative aspect of boys' layered coping. Age correlated moderately with the total number of secondary control coping goals that boys of different ages reported using for homesickness ($r = .36$; $p < .01$). Paralleling this generative developmental trend, there was a developmental trend in the percent of secondary control coping goals that boys of different ages reported using. Consistent with Band and Weisz (1988), this increase in secondary coping appeared to happen at about age 10. Overall, the correlation between age and the percent of boys' method repertoires that had secondary control goals was .33 ($p < .05$). *Table 9.1* lists the five most frequently reported method-goal combinations for homesickness. All the boys in the study reported having experienced homesickness, yet overall levels of distress were low and varied little, precluding meaningful analysis of whether certain coping goals were associated with better adjustment than others.

The distribution of advice given for both homesickness and competitive loss closely resembled the distributions of actual methods that boys used to cope with these two stressors. Only four boys (7%) advised others to do something they themselves were not doing either for homesickness or for competitive loss.

Based on the results of this interview study, a survey questionnaire was designed using a popular pediatric stress and coping questionnaire (KIDCOPE; Spirito *et al.*, 1988) as a model. Employing this questionnaire, called Ways of Coping with Homesickness (WOCH; Thurber & Weisz, 1997), and various measures of perceived control and homesickness, a second study was conducted with 315 boys and 717

Table 9.1. Five most frequent method-Goal coping combinations for homesickness

Method	Goal	Example
1. Physical activity	*Cognitive avoidance*	Play baseball in order to forget about homesickness
2. Direct problem solving	*Direct problem solving*	Write a letter home in order to renew contact with home and receive a letter back
3. Cognitive adjustment	*Cognitive adjustment*	Thinking that two weeks is not a very long time in order to make the end of a camp closer
4. Cognitive adjustment	*Cognitive avoidance*	Thinking how beautiful the lake is in order to forget about homesickness
5. Direct problem solving	*Cognitive adjustment*	Look at the family picture in order to focus on positive thoughts of family

a *Note.* Goals appear in italics. The sample comprised 56 boys participating in semi-structured coping interviews (Thurber, 1997). A coding manual for coping interviews is available from Thurber and Weisz (1993).

girls who were spending two or four weeks away from home at single-gender residential summer camps in the northeast United States. The WOCH included 14 descriptions of ways to cope with homesickness. Near the end of their first two weeks at camp, children were asked to rate, on a three-point scale of frequency ('not at all,' 'some,' or 'a lot'), how much they employed each item. Then, on an identically constructed three-point scale, children were asked to rate the effectiveness of each way of coping they employed. The 14 WOCH items are summarized below in the key to *Figure 9.2*.

Like its precursor, this study sought to describe children's coping with homesickness. With a larger sample size, wider variability in levels of distress was ensured, permitting comparisons of various coping profiles on key outcome measures, such as intensity of homesickness. The summer camp setting also provided a uniquely uncontrollable circumstance of separation for these children. As is often the case with American residential summer camps, contact with home was limited to letter writing, and children were not allowed to return home except for severe medical, conduct, or emotional problems, all of which were rare.

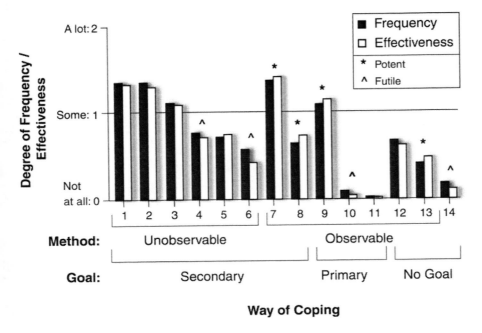

Figure 9.2.   Mean Frequency and Effectiveness Ratings for the 14 Closed-Ended Items on the Ways of Coping with Homesickness Questionnaire. See text and Table *9.2* for explanation.

Children's coping was found again to be mixed (involving both primary and secondary goals) and layered (involving more than one method). The modal child gave a 'some' or 'a lot' rating to 7 of the 14 closed-ended WOCH items. A mere 5 out of the 1032 children sampled (0.5%) did *not* report using a combination of primary control and secondary control coping. The mean frequency and effectiveness of the various ways that the entire sample (N=1032) reported coping with homesickness are depicted in *Figure 9.2*. This figure illustrates that five of the 14 items had mean frequency and mean effectiveness ratings greater than the midpoint ('some') on the three-point scales. These items closely resembled the most frequent and effective method-goal combinations uncovered in the interview study (see *Table 9.1*).

The five WOCH items with the highest frequency endorsements by the entire sample were, in descending order: (1) doing something fun in order to forget about being homesick; (2) thinking positively in order to feel better; (3) simply changing feelings in order to be happy; (4) reframing time; and (5) renewing a connection with home (e.g., writing to parents) in order to feel closer to home.

Not surprisingly, the 254 children with high levels of homesickness (averaging more than 5 on a scale from 0 to 10) reported coping more frequently than the 778 children with low levels of homesickness or no homesickness at all. On average, the girls reported coping more frequently than the boys.

Table 9.2.   Key to items on the way of coping with homesickness questionnaire

1	I tried to feel better by thinking about the good side of things, like about all the fun to do at camp	- -	Unobservable method Secondary goal
2	I just changed how I felt, and tried to be happy and have fun	- -	Unobservable method Secondary goal
3	I reminded myself that my stay at camp was not that long after call and I would be home pretty soon	- -	Unobservable method Secondary goal
4	I tried to forget about being homesick by just not thinking about my home, my parents, and other things I missed	- -	Unobservable method Secondary goal
5	I thought about the people who care about me, and what they might say to make me feel less homesick	- -	Unobservable method Secondary goal
6	I wished that things were different, like that I had never felt homesick at all, or that things here were more like at home	- -	Unobservable method Secondary goal
7	I did something fun to forget about being homesick, like to go an activity, play a game, or read a book - not just sit around	- -	Observable method Secondary goal
8	I did something to feel closer to home, like hang out with kids from home, write a letter to my parents, or look at a picture of my family or my pets	- -	Observable method Secondary goal
9	I went to see someone who could talk with me and help me feel better, like a leader or one of my friends	- -	Observable method Primary goal
10	I did something to try to go back home, like run away, or write to my parents and tell them to come get me	- -	Observable method Primary goal
11	I did something angry or mean to try to get sent home, like get in a fight, or destroy some camp property on purpose	- -	Observable method Primary goal
12	I spent time by myself	- -	Observable method No explicit goal
13	I just let my feelings out, maybe by crying or yelling	- -	Observable method No explicit goal
14	I did not do anything. Nothing would have helped	- -	No explicit method No explicit goal

Specifically, the largest gender effects indicated that girls relied on social support more than boys and that boys coped in aggressive ways more often than girls. The former is a common finding in the coping literature (e.g., Frydenberg & Lewis, 1991, 1993). The latter was rare for both genders. The two most frequent ways of coping by the most homesick children were: letting feelings out (item 13) and wishful thinking (item 6).

As expected, indices of perceived control (over homesickness, over separation from home, and in general) were positively correlated with overall quality ratings of boys' and girls' stays at camp and negatively correlated with self-reported homesickness. To test the relationship between ways of coping on ratings of both quality of stay and homesickness, children were first categorized into one of four coping profiles. Categorization into profiles called 'primary dominant,' 'secondary dominant,' and 'relinquished dominant' were based on each child's most frequently reported coping goal. The 'non-dominant' profile was a category for children who did not have a penchant for one of the three coping goals.

Results are summarized in *Figure 9.3*. The vast majority (83%) of children adaptively chose to cope with their objectively uncontrollable separation from home and resultant homesickness by setting mostly secondary control goals. Homesickness was highest for the 8% of the sample in the relinquished dominant category. Children in the secondary dominant category rated their camp stays the highest among the four groups. There was also a main effect of perceived control. Those children who perceived low control over homesickness were significantly more homesick than those who perceived high control, regardless of the dominant coping profile. Perhaps most fascinating was the significant interaction between coping profile and perceived control on level of homesickness. As *Figure 9.3* illustrates, the most homesick children in the low perceived control group were those with primary dominant profiles those who tried to influence this rather uncontrollable separation. By contrast, the most homesick children in the high perceived control group were those with relinquished dominant profiles those who just let their feelings out, gave up, or ruminated about their homesickness.

Summary and treatment implications

We may draw a few tentative conclusions from the available studies on children's coping with homesickness.

1. Like most stressors, homesickness is multifaceted, with controllable and uncontrollable aspects. Separation from home and family, exposure to novel people and novel environments, and the associated negative affect can all tax or exceed the resources of children. Not surprisingly, children report coping with homesickness in a wide variety of ways.

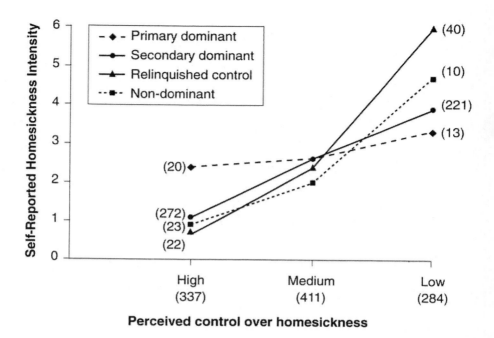

Figure 9.3. The interaction between perceived control over homesickness and dominant goal of self-reported homesickness intensity (Boys and girls, N=1032). *Note*: Numbers in parentheses are group sizes.

2. The goals of children's methods for coping with homesickness appear to be determined, in part, by the controllability (perceived and objective) of the stressful circumstance. Most children have a mixed and layered coping approach that appears to entail repeatedly responding to the controllable and uncontrollable aspects of the stressful circumstance and the resultant emotions.

3. Children's coping with homesickness also varies by age and gender. Older children are less homesick in general than younger children, and so it is not surprising to find that older children report less frequent, more effective coping. Girls report more social support coping than boys; boys report more aggressive coping than girls.

4. Some ways of coping are more effective than others. Relinquishing control by simply emoting or anxiously ruminating is often futile. By contrast, potent coping can have either primary or secondary goals. Secondary control coping for homesickness is largely favored over primary control coping.

5 Finally, some children appear more skilled at coping than others, but the transactional relationships among coping goals, perceived control, and adjustment are particularly complex. These and other complexities, such as the chronological development of stressful circumstances, resultant emotions, and perceived control remain for future research to unravel.

Should future research also be aimed at developing interventions for homesickness? In answering this question, we must differentiate the symptoms of homesickness from the phenomenon itself. Treatments for anxiety (e.g., deep relaxation) and depression (e.g., cognitive-behavioral therapy) may provide effective relief from the *symptoms* of homesickness (Cooper, 1990). However, before we attempt to eliminate the *phenomenon* of homesickness, we must consider its possible functions. First, displays of distress associated with homesickness may adaptively elicit the very care giving whose paucity or absence invoked homesickness in the first place (Thurber, 1995a). Second, successful coping may satisfy a fundamental need for competence (White, 1959; Skinner, 1995), as well as bring relief from symptoms. When coping is cast in such a functional light, intervention beyond sensitive, ethical treatment of symptoms seems contraindicated. Perhaps allowing children to return home early from a camp stay undermines their confidence, competence, and perceived control. Skinner argued that " 'coping' is one label for how people re-establish control that has been challenged or lost, and in so doing discover and create a more competent self" (1995, p. 122). And Parmelee reasoned that minor illnesses and 'other life perturbations' (such as homesickness) "can expand children's personal and social experiences in ways beneficial to their behavioral development" (1986, p. 1). In sum, homesickness naturally promotes growth. Yet, caregivers usually are inclined to help children overcome homesickness. Moreover, some cases of homesickness can be so severe that symptoms of distress overwhelm a child's ability to reestablish control and enhance competence. What, then, is the developmentally appropriate response to homesickness?

Returning home eliminates homesickness[4]. Ethics demand that caregivers consider this option when children are severely distressed and returning home is possible. Ethics also demand that caregivers help children find relief from the symptoms of homesickness. Descriptive research such as that summarized above is a first step in the search for effective relief. We now know what some children have found to be the most effective ways of coping with homesickness at boarding schools and summer camps. These and future findings surely can guide caregivers in assisting children who persevere with futile ways of coping. The dilemma comes in weighing the potential risks of forcing continued separation (e.g., aversion to future separations, attachment problems with caregivers) and the potential risks of returning home earlier than planned (e.g., overdependence, reduced sense of competence and control) against the obvious benefits of separation (e.g., independence, enhanced sense of competence and control, reduced risk for future homesickness) and the obvious benefit of returning home: symptom relief. Parents, teachers, camp staff, and other caregivers would be wise to consider this dilemma carefully when evaluating the decision to return a child home.

---

4   Even the *anticipation* of returning home can reduce homesickness (Thurber, 1995; Corp, 1791, cited in Rather, 1965).

Returning home is sometimes not an option, as with immigrant and refugee children, foster children, and homeless children. Of course, a wide variety of additional stressors in these cases (e.g., foreign languages, poverty, hunger, maltreatment, substance abuse) can compound the stress of homesickness and must be coped with in their own right. Nevertheless, homesickness itself can be influenced by a variety of preventive and palliative strategies when returning home is decided against or is simply not an option.

Authors in the camping literature (e.g., Pravda, 1995; Winters, 1989) have suggested numerous preventive strategies, including: (1) educating children about the normality and etiology of homesickness; (2) educating children about effective coping; (3) allowing children to participate in the decision to leave home initially; (4) educating children about the novel environment where they will be; (5) encouraging children to practice separations by spending several days at friends' or relative's homes; (6) establishing realistic methods of maintaining contact with home, such as letter writing; (7) pairing inexperienced children with more experienced children; and (8) involving children in the novel environment once separation has occurred (Burrow, 1992; Gibson, 1923; Mitchell et al., 1977).

Involvement in the novel environment may take several forms. Fisher's 'competing resource' model emphasizes the importance of encouraging children's *commitment to* and *distraction by* elements of the novel environment. According to the model, commitment and distraction work synchronously to "attenuate homesickness because the information generated by the new environment competes effectively for a limited capacity [attentional] resource" in children (Fisher, 1990, p. 309). Boys' comments in Harris and Guz's (1986) study support this notion, as do boys' and girls' effectiveness ratings for physical distraction (Thurber, 1997; Thurber & Weisz, 1997).

Motivating children to distract themselves from homesickness through commitment to a novel environment must go beyond explanation. Some of the most homesick children whom I have interviewed at summer camps have given me detailed explanations of why they are homesick and what they should think and do to assuage the condition. Yet somehow they seemed paralyzed to act. Instead of repeatedly engaging in various primary and secondary control coping, they withdrew, ruminated, and emoted. Others were so surprised and upset by the intensity of their homesickness that their initial distress was compounded, making it even more difficult for them to mobilize their coping resources or invest themselves in the novel environment.

If perceived control motivates action, then one possible way to minimize homesickness without diluting its value as a growth experience might be to enhance the novel environment in ways that make it easy for children to experience control. This technique moves beyond prevention and symptom relief, addressing the phenomenon of homesickness from an environmental perspective, *in situ*. Surrogate caregivers may be able to structure environments in ways that significantly reduce the distress associated with homesickness, yet still provide children with meaningful separation experiences. Skinner (1995) suggested that providing contingent, consistent structure, attentive caregiver involvement, and support of autonomy can promote successful coping in novel environments by increasing control experiences. By contrast, chaos, caregiver neglect, and coercion all reduce control and therefore undermine coping. Naturally, the exact shape of Skinner's suggested environmental enhancements will vary by institution.

Of course, in the environments and cultures in which they have been studied, many children *are* motivated and *do* cope effectively without changes to the environment. Understanding what distinguishes these children from their maladjusted peers will provide additional insight into ways of minimizing the pain and maximizing the gain from separation and homesickness.

Author Notes

This research was supported in part by grants from Sigma Xi, the Scientific Research Society, the Colin Brown Fund, and National Research Service Award MH10920-01 from the National Institutes of Health. Foremost, I wish to thank Marian D. Sigman and John R. Weisz for their enthusiasm and insightful comments about the design and documentation of this research. Warmest thanks also to Allison Wohlfiel for her assistance in coding interviews and questionnaires; Caryn and Gene Clark, Tom Giggi, Judy Snell, Audrey Vorperian, and the parents of all the campers, for their enormous support of this research; the cabin leaders and camp staffs, for their affable diligence; and the campers themselves, for their inspiration, time, and honesty.

References

Abramson, L. Y., Seligman, M. E. P., & Teasdale, J. D. (1978). Learned helplessness in humans: Critique and reformation. *Journal of Abnormal Psychology, 87,* 49-74.

Ainsworth, M. D., Blehar, M., Waters, E., & Wall, S. (1978). *Patterns of attachment: A psychological study of the Strange Situation.* Hillsdale, NJ: Erlbaum.

Azuma, H. (1984). Secondary control as a heterogeneous category. *American Psychologist, 39,* 970-971.

Bachet, M. (1950). Etude sur les états de nostalgie. *Année Medicale et Psychologique, 108,* 11-34; 559-587.

Baier, M., & Welch, M. (1992). An analysis of the concept of homesickness. *Archives of Pediatric Nursing, 6,* 54-60.

Band, E. B., & Weisz, J. R. (1988). How to feel better when it feels bad: Children's perspectives on coping with everyday stress. *Developmental Psychology, 24,* 247-253.

Band, E. B., & Weisz, J. R. (1990). Developmental differences in primary and secondary control coping and adjustment to juvenile diabetes. *Journal of Clinical Child Psychology, 19,* 150-158.

Bowlby, J. (1969). *Attachment and Loss, Volume I: Attachment.* New York: Basic Books.

Burrow, D. (1992). *How to be a great camp counselor.* Shirley, MA: McElroy.

Burt, C. D. B. (1993). Concentration and academic ability following transition to university: An investigation of the effects of homesickness. *Journal of Environmental Psychology, 13,* 333-342.

Calkins, S. D. (1994). Origins and outcomes of individual differences in emotion regulation. In: N. A. Fox (Ed.), *The development of emotion regulation* (pp. 53-72). Chicago, Ill: University of Chicago.

143

Compas, B. E. (1987). Coping with stress during childhood and adolescence. *Psychological Bulletin, 101,* 393-403.

Compas, B. E., Banez, G. A., Malcarne, V., & Worsham, N. (1991). Perceived control and coping with stress: A developmental perspective. *Journal of Social Issues, 47,* 23-34.

Compas, B. E., Malcarne, V. L., & Fondacaro, K. M. (1988). Coping with stressful events in older children and young adolescents. *Journal of Consulting and Clinical Psychology, 56,* 405-411.

Cooper, C. L. (1990). Coping strategies to minimize the stress of transitions. In: S. Fisher & C. L. Cooper (Eds.), *On the move: The psychology of change and transition* (pp. 315-327). New York: John Wiley and Sons.

Curry, S. L., & Russ, S. W. (1985). Identifying coping strategies in children. *Journal of Clinical Child Psychology, 14,* 61-69.

Ditter, B. (1990, April). In the trenches. *Camping Magazine, 9.*

Fisher, S. (1989). *Homesickness, cognition, and health.* Brighton: Lawrence Erlbaum.

Fisher, S., & Cooper, C. L. (1990). *On the move: The psychology of change and transition.* New York: John Wiley and Sons.

Fisher, S., & Hood, B. (1987). The stress of the transition to university: A longitudinal study of psychological disturbance, absent-mindedness and vulnerability to homesickness. *British Journal of Psychology, 78,* 425-441.

Fisher, S., Elder, L, & Peacock, G. (1990). Homesickness in a school in the Australian Bush. *Children's Environments Quarterly, 7,* 15-22.

Fisher, S., Frazer, N., & Murray, K. (1984). The transition from home to boarding school: A diary-style analysis of the problems and worries of boarding school pupils. *Journal of Environmental Psychology, 4,* 211-221.

Fisher, S., Frazer, N., & Murray, K. (1986). Homesickness and health in boarding school children. *Journal of Environmental Psychology, 6,* 35-47.

Fisher, S., Murray, K, & Frazer, N. A. (1985). Homesickness, health, and efficiency in first year students. *Journal of Environmental Psychology, 5,* 181-195.

Folkman, S., Lazarus, R. S., Dunkel-Schetter, C., DeLongis, A., & Gruen, R. J. (1986). Dynamics of a stressful encounter: Cognitive appraisal, coping, and encounter outcomes. *Journal of Personality and Social Psychology, 50,* 992-1003.

Frydenberg, E., & Lewis, R. (1991). Adolescent coping: The different ways in which boys and girls cope. *Journal of Adolescence, 14,* 199-133.

Frydenberg, E., & Lewis, R. (1993). Boys play sports and girls turn to others: Age, gender and ethnicity as determinants of coping. *Journal of Adolescence, 16,* 253-266.

Gibson, H. W. (1923). *Camp management: A manual for camp directors.* Cambridge, MA: Murray Printing.

Hamessley, M. L. (1977). *Handbook for camp nurses and other camp health workers.* New York: The Tiresias Press.

Harris, P. L. (1989). *Children and Emotion.* Oxford, UK: Basil Blackwell.

Harris, P. L., & Guz, G. R. (1986). *Models of emotion: How boys report their emotional reactions upon entering an English boarding school.* Unpublished paper, Department of Experimental Psychology, University of Oxford, UK.

Hauser, S. T., DiPlacido, J., Jacobson, A. M., Willett, J, & Cole, C. (1993). Family coping with an adolescent's chronic illness: An approach and three studies. *Journal of Adolescence, 16,* 305-329.

Heckhausen, J. & Schulz, R. (1995). A life-span theory of control. *Psychological Review, 102,* 284-304.

Hofer, M. A. (1994). Hidden regulators in attachment, separation, and loss. In: N. A. Fox (Ed.), *The development of emotion regulation* (pp. 192-207). Chicago, Ill: University of Chicago.

Kagan, J. (1994). On the nature of emotion. In: N. A. Fox (Ed.), *The development of emotion regulation* (pp. 7-24). Chicago, Ill: University of Chicago.

Kojima, H. (1984). A significant stride toward the comparative study of control. *American Psychologist, 39*, 972-973.

Lazarus, R. S. (1993). Why we should think of stress as a subset of emotion. In: L. Goldberger & S. Breznitz (Eds.), *Handbook of stress* (pp. 21-39). New York: The Free Press.

Lazarus, R. S., & Folkman, S. (1984a). Coping and adaptation. In: W. D. Gentry (Ed.), *The handbook of behavioral medicine* (pp. 282-325). New York: Guilford.

Lazarus, R. A., & Folkman, S. (1984b). *Stress, appraisal, and coping.* New York: Springer.

Macleod, D. I. (1983). *Building character in the American boy: The Boy Scouts, YMCA, and their forerunners, 1870-1920.* Madison, WI: University of Wisconsin Press.

Mitchell, A. V., Robberson, J. D., & Obley, J. W. (1977). *Camp counseling.* Philadelphia, PA: W. B. Saunders.

Pravda, M. (1995). Homesickness: Dispelling the myths. *Camping Magazine, 67*, 18-20.

Radovanovic, H. (1993). Parental conflict and children's coping styles in litigating separated families: Relationships with children's adjustment. *Journal of Abnormal Child Psychology, 21*, 697-713.

Rather, L. J. (1965). *Mind and body in 18th century medicine: A study based on Jerome Gaub's De regimine mentis.* Los Angeles, CA: University of California Press.

Rothbaum, F., Weisz, J. R., & Snyder, S. (1982). Changing the world and changing the self: A two-process model of perceived control. *Journal of Personality and Social Psychology, 42*, 5-37.

Rothbaum, F., & Weisz, J. R. (1989). *Child psychopathology and the quest for control.* London: Sage.

Rubin, R. (1949). *The book of camping.* New York: Association Press.

Rutter, M. (1981). Stress, coping, and development: Some issues and some questions. *Journal of Child Psychology and Psychiatry, 22*, 323-356.

Seginer, R., Trommsdorff, G., & Essau, C. (1993). Adolescent control beliefs: Cross-cultural variations of primary and secondary orientations. *International Journal of Behavioral Development, 16*, 243-260.

Seiffge-Krenke, I. (1993). Coping behavior in normal and clinical samples: More similarities than differences? *Journal of Adolescence, 16*, 285-303.

Skinner, E. A. (1995). *Perceived Control, Motivation, and Coping.* Thousand Oaks, CA: Sage.

Spirito, A., Stark, L. J., & Williams, C. (1988). Development of a brief checklist to assess coping in pediatric patients. *Journal of Pediatric Psychology, 13*, 555-574.

Thurber, C. A. (1995a). The experience and expression of homesickness in preadolescent and adolescent boys. *Child Development, 66*, 1162-1178.

Thurber, C. A. (1995b). Managing homesickness at residential summer camps. *CompassPoint, 5*, 8-11.

Thurber, C. A. (1997). Describing boys' coping with homesickness using a two-process model of control. *Anxiety, Stress, and Coping, 10*, 181-202.

Thurber, C. A., & Weisz, J. R. (1993). *Coding manual for coping with competitive loss and separation from home.* Unpublished manuscript, University of California at Los Angeles, Department of Psychology.

Thurber, C. A.., & Weisz, J. R. (1997). "You can try or you can just give up": The impact of perceived control and coping style on childhood homesickness. *Developmental Psychology, 33*, 508-517.

Weisz, J. R. (1990). Development of control-related beliefs, goals, and styles in childhood and adolescence: A clinical perspective. In: K. W. Schaie, J. Rodin, & C. Scholler (Eds.), *Self-directedness and efficacy: Causes and effects throughout the life course* (pp. 103-145). New York: Erlbaum.

Weisz, J. R., McCabe, M. A., & Dennig, M. D. (1994). Primary and secondary control among children undergoing medical procedures: Adjustment as a function of coping style. *Journal of Consulting and Clinical Psychology, 62*, 324-332.

Weisz, J. R., Rothbaum, F., & Blackburn, T. (1984). Standing out and standing in: The psychology of control in America and Japan. *American Psychologist, 39*, 955-969.

Weisz, J. R., Stevens, J. S., Curry, J. F., Cohen, R., Craighead, W. E., Burlingame, W. V., Smith, A., Weiss, B., & Parmelee, D. X. (1989). Control-related cognitions and depression among inpatient children and adolescents. *Journal of the American Academy of Child and Adolescent Psychiatry, 28,* 358-363.

Weisz, J. R., Weiss, B., Wasserman, A. A., & Rintoul, B. (1987). Control-related beliefs and depression among clinic-referred children and adolescents. *Journal of Abnormal Psychology, 96,* 58-63.

White, R. W. (1959). Motivation reconsidered: The concept of competence. *Psychological Review, 66,* 297-333.

Winland-Brown, J. E., & Maheady, D. C. (1990). Using intuition to define homesickness at a summer camp. *Journal of Pediatric Health Care, 4,* 117-121.

Winters, C. (1989, May). Summer camp: Off to a great start. *Parents,* 82-88.

Zwingmann, C. A. (1959). 'Heimweh' or 'nostalgic reaction': A conceptual analysis and interpretation of a medico-psychological phenomenon. Unpublished doctoral dissertation, Stanford University, Palo Alto, CA.

10 Homesickness after Relocation during Early Adolescence

ERIC M. VERNBERG AND CAMILLE J. RANDALL

Homesickness after relocation during early adolescence

The early adolescent years (11-14 years of age) are notable for major biological, cognitive, and social transitions. Relocation to a new community during this period creates an additional set of demands for the adolescent and his or her family, yet research on the ways relocation may influence adolescent development remains sparse. Conceptual models of homesickness potentially contribute to a clearer understanding of possible effects of relocation during early adolescence. This chapter applies these conceptual models within the context of major developmental features of early adolescence.

Three propositions organize this effort. First, homesickness models may provide needed guidance for future research on relocation. Second, currently available research on relocation in early adolescence may be profitably reformulated in terms of homesickness models. Third, developmental features of early adolescence must be considered in research on homesickness after relocation during this age.

Defining homesickness in early adolescence

Adopting the general definition of homesickness as a complex cognitive-motivational state primarily centered on missing family, friends, and physical aspects of the home environment (Fisher & Hood, 1988), it becomes necessary to specify how this state is likely to be expressed in early adolescence after relocation to a new community. In describing this complex state, it seems useful to consider expressions of homesickness in multiple domains, including behavioral, somatic, cognitive, and affective (Van Tilburg et al., 1996). Before considering domain-specific expressions, however, it is necessary to address the issue of whether, how often, and for how long issues related to missing people or other aspects of the previous environment are significant concerns among teenagers who have relocated.

Research on this issue is very sparse. The limited evidence available suggests that some, but not all, adolescents note missing friends or other people from the previous community as a worry or concern after relocation. Our research with a sample of 71 recently relocated 12- to 14-year-old adolescents found that 25% noted concerns or difficulties related to leaving friends or relatives about three months after relocating, but only 2% reported missing familiar settings (Abwender et al., 1991). Making new friends was a concern for 55% of the adolescents, suggesting some dissatisfaction with their friendship networks in the first few months after relocating. This study utilized responses to an open-ended question about the respondents' 'biggest struggles having to do with settling in after the move,' and thus may underestimate reports of missing people or places that might be obtained with more structured questions probing for these types of concerns. Since reporting these preliminary findings, we have gathered additional information on an additional 125 recently relocated adolescents. Analyses are currently in progress regarding the worries and concerns relating to relocation over the course of the year after relocating. One initial finding from these analyses is that, when asked 11 months after relocating, 43% of the 196 adolescents indicated that, if given the choice, they would rather be living in their previous communities. This suggests that longing for the previous community persists for at least a year for a substantial percentage of relocated adolescents.

Among the many factors that may shape whether or not longing for the previous community occurs after relocation, several seem particularly germane. One is whether adolescents who relocate to a new community anticipate living again in their previous communities. Do adolescents who do not anticipate living again in their previous community experience periods in which a sense of missing the previous community produces homesickness? Is longing for a previous community more likely to occur, or persist, when the possibility of return exists? A related factor is whether relocation co-occurs with a loss of contact with a parent or parent-surrogate because of divorce, bereavement, or occupational demands. Relocation is a relatively common occurrence after divorce, and separation from a parent as well as friends seems likely to be particularly difficult. In addition to the strain of separation from a parent, the possibility of return may be higher when one parent remains in the previous community, thus complicating issues of commitment to relationships in the new community. Finally, success in establishing close relationships in the new community may be very important in determining whether significant longing for the previous community occurs.

As with evidence about missing people or other aspects of the previous community, research on the symptomatology that may be attributed to homesickness is sparse. Behavioral expressions of homesickness have generally been proposed to center around withdrawal or lack of engagement in the new environment (Van Tilburg et al., 1996). One developmental consideration here is that recent evidence suggests that symptoms of withdrawal and lack of engagement (including timid, fearful behavior) in general are significantly more frequent among 12- to 14-year-olds than 9- to 11-year-olds (McDermott, 1996). Two possible implications of this developmental trend seem salient. First, following relocation during the early adolescent period, parents may attribute an increase in withdrawal or lack of engagement as a result of relocation, when these symptoms may instead be the result of normative developmental changes. Second, if children entering early adolescence are prone to develop these types of symptoms, the stresses of relocation may intensify their expression. Evidence already exists that active rejection by peers and lower levels of intimacy in friendships after relocation contributes to increased social avoidance and distress (Vernberg *et al.*, 1992). It remains to be demonstrated that these symptoms are more common in relocated adolescents compared to residentially stable adolescents.

Somatic complaints associated with homesickness, such as stomachaches, fatigue, and sleep disturbances, have been reported as responses to stressful events and 'daily hassles' in numerous studies with early adolescents. Complicating the issue of identifying somatic complaints that may be due to homesickness is the fact that early adolescence is typically a period of rapid physical growth and puberty-related hormonal change (Malina, 1990). These physical changes by themselves contribute to increased moodiness, physical discomfort, and fatigue (Nottleman *et al.*, 1990), causing potential misattribution of increased somatic complaints during this age to stressful events such as relocation. Nonetheless, conceptual models for psychosomatic symptoms during early adolescence emphasize the complex interplay of physical changes with the concomitant social and cognitive changes that mark this period of life (Kager *et al.*, 1992). It is entirely possible that homesickness in early adolescence may result in somatic complaints, yet research on somatic symptoms after relocation must take into account the unique features of early adolescence in sorting out normative increases in somatic symptoms from those related specifically to the stresses surrounding relocation.

Cognitive aspects of homesickness after relocation are believed to include negative thoughts about the new community, obsessional, idealized thoughts about the previous environment, and absent-mindedness or other signs of cognitive disengagement (Van Tilburg *et al.*, 1996). The cognitive advances of early adolescence make this element of homesickness especially interesting. For many youngsters, recently improved capacities for social comparison and social perspective-taking may make unpleasant changes in their social experiences seem particularly salient (Lapsley *et al.*, 1986). Close friendships typically increase markedly in intimacy during the transition from childhood to adolescence (Buhrmester & Furman, 1987), and the sense of loss (and longing) for missing friends may be exceptionally acute because cognitive advances may allow the adolescent to think and reason about these experiences in ways that would have been impossible just a few years earlier. These thoughts, because they may be new in the adolescent's mental life, may be experienced as exceptional and unique, and hence more intense or troubling than might be the case for an older adolescent. In addition, early adolescents may lack some of the cognitive capacities that enable older individuals to cope with adversity, such as a stronger sense of identity and a more objective third party approach to evaluating social behavior (Lapsley, 1990).

Do the cognitive elements of homesickness occur after relocation during early adolescence, and are there age-specific qualities? The evidence available thus far is sketchy. There seems to be little doubt that friendship relationships require several months after relocation to approximate the quality and quantity of relationships in the previous community, and that active rejection by peers is more frequent for boys after relocation (Vernberg, 1990a; Vernberg *et al.*, 1994). Thus, there frequently does seem to be a decline, perhaps just temporarily, in the quality of relationships with peers after relocation during this age range. It remains to be established whether these changes in social experiences lead to negative thoughts about the new community and longing for the previous one. The finding reported earlier in this paper that 43% of the early adolescents in our sample expressed a preference for the previous rather than current community 11 months after relocating suggests that these cognitive elements may occur frequently. However, it is not clear whether these cognitions occur more frequently or intensely for early adolescents in comparison to younger or older ages, nor whether a stated preference for living in the previous community necessarily indicates negative thoughts about the new community and idealized thoughts about the old.

Affective components of homesickness typically are postulated to include internalizing (as opposed to externalizing) symptoms, most of which fall within the broad realm of mood disturbances and anxiety (Van Tilburg et al., 1996). It is becoming increasingly clear that most, if not all, symptoms of mood disturbance and anxiety found in adults can also be exhibited by early adolescents, including negative cognitions such as those that characterize homesickness in adults (Cantwell & Baker, 1991; Compas et al., 1993; Garber et al., 1993). From this, it is plausible to expect that the affective symptoms associated with homesickness in adults and older adolescents could also be shown by early adolescents. At the same time, symptoms of depression become more common as youngsters move from middle childhood to early adolescence (Compas et al., 1993; Rutter, 1991). This provides ample opportunity for misattribution for the onset of affective symptomatology to a disruption such as relocation, when these symptoms instead may be driven by maturation-related biological, cognitive, and social forces. As with other domains of homesickness symptoms, caution is needed to avoid mistaking developmental changes with changes in life circumstances.

Despite this caveat, there is also ample reason to expect increases in internalizing symptomatology when peer or parental relationships become unsatisfactory during the early adolescent years. To the extent that relocation may contribute to difficulties in interpersonal relationships, relocation may contribute to increases in the types of internalizing symptoms characteristic of homesickness. In a mixed sample of residentially stable and recently relocated adolescents (total N=76), for example, causal analyses indicated that depressive symptoms, as measured by the Child Depression Inventory, rose over a six-month period as rejection by peers increased and intimacy and companionship with a best friend decreased (Vernberg, 1990b). A later study done exclusively with relocated adolescents (N=68) over an eight-month period found similar results for social anxiety (Vernberg et al., 1992). Finally, a recent cross-sectional study with 130 relocated early adolescents indicated that self-reported loneliness was higher for those who were more frequent targets of taunts, physical aggression, and ostracism by peers (Vernberg et al., 1995).

Thus far, there is no convincing evidence to indicate that the relationship between peer experiences and internalizing symptoms is stronger for relocated adolescents than for residentially stable adolescents, nor that internalizing symptoms characteristic of homesickness are more common among relocated adolescents as a group is than among residentially stable peers. However, there is some evidence that the simultaneous occurrence of school changes (i.e., the normative transition from elementary school to junior high or high school), family changes (e.g., divorce, serious illness), and the onset of puberty predicts relatively enduring increases depressive symptomatology during adolescence (Petersen *et al.*, 1991). Relocation during early adolescence that is perceived as a negative, stressful experience and co-occurs with the onset of puberty and with undesirable changes in family structure or processes seems particularly likely to contribute to the emergence of the affective symptoms characteristic of homesickness.

Explaining homesickness in early adolescence

Current formulations of homesickness propose several possible explanations for the phenomenon, including disruptions of attachment relationships, interruption of life style, reduced control, role change, and approach/avoidance conflicts (Fisher, 1989, 1990; Van Tilburg *et al.*, 1996). Each of these has possible application to the early adolescent years, with special consideration for developmental issues characteristic of this period.

Disruptions of Attachment Relationships. Just as the infant's attachment relationships promote autonomy, the early adolescent's attachment relationships can be said to promote a stable identity, a key developmental expectation of adolescence (Erikson, 1968). Early adolescent friendships emulate the early parent-child attachment bond in that they regulate proximity to preferred others (Buhrmester & Furman, 1987), as well as foster a sense of security which enables identity development (Brown, 1989; Youniss, 1980). When adolescents must move away from established friendships, as in the case of residential relocation, a portion of their protective base for identity exploration, in a sense, is lost. Homesickness after a residential move may manifest itself as a longing for this base, or as feelings of anxiety (separation distress) in absence of this base.

Indeed, parents and siblings also provide early adolescents with a sense of security, yet the reciprocal nature of adolescent friendships may serve a unique function in identity development (Youniss, 1980). Reciprocity refers to the characteristic equality of adolescent relationships, which is believed to promote development via cooperation and reflection. In contrast, familial relationships are more hierarchical. Perhaps indicative of parents' understanding of the unique role of friendship attachments in early adolescence, some evidence suggests that parents, following a residential move, actively help their adolescent children reestablish friendship networks in the new community (Vernberg *et al.*, 1993). Such efforts seek to alleviate the 'attachment homesickness' that may be characteristic of early adolescents who move to new communities just as their intimate friendships begin to burgeon.

Finally, it is important to consider the potential impact of the disruption of a parent-child attachment relationship in early adolescence, as may occur when the child of divorced parents moves between parents' residences. Although intimacy ratings of friendships increase from childhood into adolescence, intimacy ratings of mothers and fathers are stable across time, indicating that parental relationships remain important and influential to the early adolescent (Hunter & Youniss, 1982). The reduced proximity to the noncustodial parent, which may result from, an intercommunity move may be perceived as a loss to the early adolescent and may contribute to the adolescent's feelings of homesickness. This sense of loss may be compounded by the loss of the adolescent's existing friendship network.

Interruption of life style. By early adolescence, a sizable proportion of an individual's time is spent with peers and in peer activities (Berndt, 1982). The early adolescent, then, may become accustomed to engaging in mutually satisfying activities with a particular group of friends and to the provision of certain 'hangouts' or certain types of activities. After an intercommunity move, the adolescent may find himself or herself in terra incognita. For example, a move from a suburban to a rural community may find the adolescent without a favorite store or restaurant chain, or without shopping malls, altogether. A move from a rural to an urban community, similarly, may find the adolescent without access to an agriculture-oriented club or to the type of part-time job for which he or she is qualified (e.g., farm or ranch work). If the two communities are similar, however, lifestyle disruption may be limited to not being able to engage in favored activities with particular friends and not being able to enjoy particular friends' perspectives on favored activities.

Further, the adolescent's existing schemata for cliques and surroundings may be challenged. An individual raised in a relatively homogenous small town may find fitting into a peer group difficult, in the midst of the 'freaks,' 'jocks,' 'druggies,' 'brains,' and 'elites' characteristic of larger, more urban communities. Early adolescent friendships are formed largely on the basis of similarity (Epstein, 1989; Kandel, 1978), and an adolescent's perceived loss of 'similar' peers or cliques in a new surrounding may hinder the formation of new peer networks which, then, may contribute to the adolescent's perceived loss of and longing for continuity. The adolescent may also desire the continuity of place. For instance, the recent urban inductee may miss ostensible horizon lines. Or the newly suburbanized adolescent may miss the hustle and bustle and visual noise of the large city to which he or she was accustomed. In comparison, the new community may seem monotonous and limiting.

Finally, international moves may place adolescents in (literally) foreign environments in which the language and customs deviate markedly from the prior locale. Language and social barriers may make transitions especially difficult for these youngsters. Homesickness, then, may occur when the adolescent longs for the lifestyle and culture in which he or she was acclimated.

Reduced control. The interruption of life style, which may accompany residential relocation, relates to the (sense of) reduced control, which an early adolescent may experience in his or her new surroundings. An adolescent may have enjoyed proficiency in navigating the social idiosyncrasies of the previous location. However, the new community is likely to have a new set of rules and most certainly will have a new set of peers for which established patterns of interpersonal relations may be insufficient. For instance, diminished control, or sense of efficacy, is likely following an adolescent's unsuccessful attempts to break into a 'closed' circle of friends. Such exposure to peer rejection may be a real threat, post move (Vernberg, 1990a; Vernberg *et al.*, 1994). Too, an otherwise socially-gifted adolescent who has moved between countries may lack a common language, which would enable entry into a new peer group, and may thus diminish this adolescent's sense of social efficacy. Homesickness, in this case, may equate to the early adolescent's desire to return to a predictable and self-mastered social milieu.

As early adolescents progress into reciprocal, egalitarian relationships with peers, they become accustomed to contributing to interpersonal decision-making in a real way. The structure of junior high and high schools also enables early adolescents' decisions regarding course electives and extracurricular activities (Epstein, 1989). Early adolescents may enjoy increased decision-making opportunities within their family environments, as well, although a decision to make an intercommunity move may be beyond their control. Our data on adolescent mobility reveal a constituency of adolescents who disagreed with their parents about the acceptability of relocation. In our previously-mentioned sample of 196 relocated adolescents, 37% reported that they did not want to move. In the families of adolescents opposed to relocation, 75% included at least one parent who favored the move. Parental job transfers or wishes to move to more a diverse setting or closer to relatives, in most cases, override the adolescent's wishes to remain in an established friendship network in a familiar social environment. Circumstances such as an intercommunity move, which adolescents may perceive to limit their decision-making opportunities in the home, may subsequently decrease early adolescents' self-esteem and motivation at a time when, developmentally, they expect to have more decision-making control (Eccles *et al.*, 1993).

The adolescent's perceived loss of control over interpersonal and intrafamilial circumstances, which may accompany a residential move, may be characterized as a poor stage-environment fit (Eccles *et al.*, 1993). That is, during a time when autonomy and perceived control should be increasing, especially within friendships (Furman & Buhrmester, 1985), the changes afforded by a move may significantly decrease autonomy and control by limiting opportunities to master the social environment and to participate in decision-making in the home. Post move, an adolescent may miss the emergent independence fostered by his or her previous surroundings and may experience this discrepancy as homesickness. Empirical efforts, to this date, have not addressed whether, or how often, relocation leads to decreases in adolescents' perceived autonomy and control.

Role change. In addition to possibly acquiring a more subordinate position in the familial decision-making hierarchy, as discussed previously, the residentially-mobile early adolescent may experience other types of role change, or role loss. For instance, the lofty role provided by popularity among peers may be partially or entirely lost after a move. Established peer hierarchies in the new setting may be difficult for an adolescent to change. Some evidence suggests that, by about 11 months post move, a portion of early adolescents have not established levels of intimacy (e.g., trust, support, loyalty, openness) and companionship (e.g., frequency and types of contact, shared activities) in their friendships comparable that found for residentially-stable adolescents (Vernberg, 1990a). The adolescent once known to peers as the interpersonal arbiter, eternal friend, and ever ready companion may not be able to acquire sufficient levels of intimacy and companionship in his or her friendships immediately post move to be able to offer much support to new friends. Too, the general role of 'friend' may be difficult to retrieve due to the increased likelihood of rejection, post move (Vernberg, 1990a). It is not known how long it takes for mobile adolescents to return to comfortable levels of intimacy and companionship in their friendships. It is likely, however, that some early adolescents will experience significant changes in their friendship experiences after relocating. The role confusion resulting from this marked discrepancy may be expressed as homesickness for a known and relatively static niche within a peer network.

Additionally, the meaning of 'adolescent' may vary from community to community. For instance, the transition into junior high signifies, to many, the transition into early adolescence itself. Several attributes of junior high schools promote autonomy and individuation (e.g., choice of classes, choice of peer group, self-management; Eccles *et al.*, 1993). However, a seventh-grade student in junior high may move to a new community in which seventh-grade is part of elementary school, and thus may suffer a loss of the spoils which accompany junior high status. Conversely, a seventh-grade student in elementary school who is accustomed to being looked up to by younger students and to feeling comparatively mature may feel displaced after a move to a community in which seventh-grade occupies the lowest position in junior high. Role loss may be especially extreme if the grades within the new school are competitive and older students expose the adolescent to age-insulting taunts. Finally, a community's general conception of adolescence may figure into an adolescent's perception of role loss following a move. An adolescent who moves from a rural community which values young teenagers as responsible farm help or as caretakers for younger siblings to a community which perceives adolescents to be irresponsible and apathetic may feel displaced and wrongly disrespected.

Intercommunity moves, because they disrupt adolescent friendships, may also increase an adolescent's dependence on parental support. While parents are still important intimacy sources and instrumental aid providers for adolescents (Furman & Buhrmester, 1985), the increased dependency on parents, which may accompany a move, is counter to what is expected at this time and may engender feelings of role loss as adolescents return to (perceived) preadolescent levels of dependence. Homesickness in early adolescence, then, may be akin to desiring a previously established status within the peer group, community, and/or family.

Approach-Avoidance conflicts. As discussed previously, friendships are important harbingers of the developmental needs and skills of early adolescents. The natural propensity in adolescence is toward intimate and companionate experiences with peers (Berndt, 1982; Youniss, 1980). Adolescents who experience an intercommunity move are expected to pursue new friendships due to friendship's developmental salience, although they may be incapacitated to do so because of real and perceived social obstacles. Such an approach/avoidance conflict may precipitate homesickness in early adolescence.

Real obstacles to friendship development following a move may include peer rejection experiences, especially for males (e.g., physical or verbal aggression; Vernberg, 1990a). Rejection possibilities for residentially-mobile adolescents may be caused by developmental trends in peer group formation, rather than by the adolescents' inability to successfully master new social situations. For instance, a study on friendship stability indicates that early adolescents lose more friends than they gain across an academic year (Berndt & Hoyle, 1985). This finding supports a developmental trend to limit the size of friendship networks in early adolescence, possibly in order to facilitate intimacy (smaller groups of friends may be more conducive to disclosing personal thoughts and feelings). The newly relocated adolescent, however, may be at a special disadvantage due to this emergent trend; younger children may be better able to fit into an existing friendship network and, thus, may not experience the characteristic approach/avoidance conflict of early adolescent relocates.

Social anxiety may also present an approach-avoidance conflict in relation to friendship development following a move. The limited data available suggest that social anxiety and withdrawal may serve a protective function for the relocated early adolescent by limiting exposure to peer rejection, which is somewhat more likely following a move (Vernberg et al., 1992). However, social anxiety and withdrawal also decrease the likelihood of establishing intimate friendships, which may be emotionally and maturationally beneficial to the adolescent (Vernberg et al., 1992). Real and perceived threats to establishing friendships in a new community place the residentially-mobile adolescent in a dilemma: is it better to approach a new group of peers, or is it better to shrink from social contacts to avoid rejection and its negative psychological sequelae? (see East et al., 1987; Vernberg, 1990b). The mobile adolescent may be homesick for a time, place, and status ('residentially-stable'), which did not require such difficult decisions.

Directions for research on homesickness in early adolescence

Although early adolescents appear capable of experiencing homesickness similar to that shown by older adolescents and adults, it is important to note that an intercommunity move at this age does not automatically confer symptoms of homesickness. Despite the fact that relocation in early adolescence is a major life transition during a sensitive developmental period, there is little documentation of the proportion of early adolescents who experience homesickness after relocation or the conditions giving rise to this complex cognitive-motivational state. Developmental theory and research provides strong justification for intensive investigation of these issues.

A conceptual model for investigating homesickness after relocation in this stage of life must incorporate factors at the level of the individual, the family, and the circumstances surrounding the move (cf. Vernberg & Field, 1990). The theoretical perspectives that have informed research on homesickness with older adolescents and adults offer suggestions for identifying potentially important variables within each of these broad factors. Incorporating a developmental perspective adds additional specificity in identifying variables that seem most important to consider.

It may also prove useful to distinguish between variables that enable early adolescents to negotiate key tasks after relocation (e.g., friendship formation) and those that influence the relationship between experiences and adaptation (e.g., coping style or resources). For example, some evidence suggests that sophistication in interpersonal negotiation strategies influences how quickly relocated adolescents are able to establish new friendships that are similar to pre-move friendships in terms of intimacy and companionship (Vernberg et al., 1994). It remains unclear, however, whether the formation of new friendships altogether precludes feelings of homesickness following an intercommunity move or attenuates homesickness by providing a sense of continuity and reducing the number of post-move stressors. More highly developed perspective-taking skills, while possibly helpful in the task of forming friendships, have also been implicated in the normative rise of negative thoughts and troubling feelings during adolescence (Lapsley, 1990).

Several individual characteristics seem important to consider in research on homesickness in early adolescence. The occurrence of rapid biological changes related to puberty just prior to or after relocation seems particularly important to consider (Petersen et al., 1991). It is not clear whether rapid pubertal development influences an adolescent's experiences with peers after moving, or instead places additional demands on adolescent's coping resources (or both). Gender also may play a role. Girls typically begin puberty earlier than boys, and also begin to show more internalizing symptoms than boys during adolescence (Compas et al., 1993; Petersen et al., 1991). However, girls also may experience fewer difficulties in forming new friendships after a move and do not appear to run the risk that boys do of becoming more frequent targets for aggression from peers (Vernberg, 1990a; Vernberg et al., 1995).

At the cognitive level, skills in social reasoning and problem-solving, as noted above, seem important to consider. Finally, affective and behavioral features of the adolescent (e.g., depression, social avoidance) are implicated in influencing how quickly friendships are formed (Vernberg, 1990b; Vernberg et al., 1992). Moreover, adolescents with depressogenic explanatory styles may be particularly susceptible to developing internalizing symptoms, including homesickness, when unpleasant events occur (Garber et al., 1993).

Among family characteristics, the quality of parent-adolescent relationships seems likely to play a role in how an adolescent responds to the challenges of relocation. An adolescent who is emotionally close to friends but psychologically distant from his or her parents may perceive the loss of contact with friends after relocation as especially traumatic and disruptive, whereas an adolescent with close ties to his or her parents may fare better emotionally and socially. In addition to overall quality of parent-adolescent bonds, specific family behaviors may also be important in affecting the nature of post-move peer experiences. Family attempts to facilitate friendship formation for their adolescent after relocation appear to influence the quality of adolescents' relationships 11 months after moving, even after controlling for the quality of premove friendships (Vernberg et al., 1993). Other potentially important family features may include the adolescent's involving in decision-making about the move, family responses to pubertal changes, and socioeconomic resources.

Potentially important circumstances surrounding the move include concurrent life events, daily hassles, cultural or ethnic differences between the new and old communities, and expectations regarding the permanence of relocation. As noted earlier, the simultaneous occurrence of rapid pubertal change, normative school transition, and major family changes appears to set the stage for increased levels of depression through middle adolescence (Petersen et al., 1991). The transition to a new community along with peak pubertal change and major family changes (e.g., divorce, bereavement) seems even more challenging. Further, research on the relationship between life events and adolescent adjustment suggests that the daily hassles that accompany major events contribute to changes in adjustment during adolescence (Compas et al, 1989).

Marked change in culture or ethnicity may also complicate the process of establishing friendships, in part because discrepancies in social schemes that occur from these changes (Mandler, 1990). Our research team has conducted one study to test this assumption, and found that the degree of change in the ethnic composition between the new and old communities predicted success in establishing friendships after relocating, even after controlling for premove friendships (Maqueda, 1996). In this study, moving into a community where a significantly smaller proportion of the population, compared to the previous community, were of the same ethnicity as the adolescent predicted difficulties in friendship formation. An earlier study, using distance moved as a proxy for cultural change, found that adolescents who moved greater distances had poorer post move friendships than those who moved locally or within state (Vernberg & Daugherty, 1988). To our knowledge, no specific connections have been documented between cultural and ethnic changes and the emergence of homesickness in relocated early adolescents. Such connections, however, seem likely.

Issues related to commitment to the new versus prior community also are important to consider. Adolescents who have moved to new communities several times before, such as children of military personnel, may lack the extensive schema of home which adolescents who have resided in the same community for most of their lives may possess. An extensively mobile adolescent may have experienced several different types of communities in several regions of the country and consequently may have a more diverse notion of place, or of home. Without such an idealized and static concept of home, the early adolescent who has moved several times may not expect continuity and may not experience much dissonance in a new community. However, it may be rare that an individual has moved several times while in early adolescence. Given the unique characteristics and functions of friendships in this developmental stage, perhaps no amount of moving experience would prepare the adolescent for parting with close friends at this time, and thus would not prevent feelings of homesickness. Experience with moves, then, may only be a buffer to the extent that it allows adolescents to be more flexible in their expectations of place. Adolescents' expectations of home may inevitably include remembrances of the close friends that peopled the previous location.

Finally, it is important to note that homesickness following an intercommunity move may be a transitional state that may lead to positive outcomes for the early adolescent. Homesickness is orienting and motivating, in that it creates a negative emotional state that the early adolescent may seek to eliminate by increasing efforts to establish friendships and to learn more about the new community. If the adolescent successfully alleviates his or her homesickness by actively meeting peers or becoming familiar with the new environment, then the adolescent's sense of self-efficacy may be enhanced. Residential stability, in contrast, is less likely to offer such mastery exercises to the early adolescent. Positive emotional experiences are posited to accompany successful schema accommodation, such as that which may be uniquely afforded by an intercommunity move (Mandler, 1990). Too, manifestation of homesickness following a move may prompt an adolescent's parents to facilitate his or her transition into the new community. While such active measures by parents seem to increase dependence, they may foster independence in the long run by enhancing or expediting the adolescent's formation of egalitarian relationships and friendships with peers (see Berndt, 1982; Vernberg *et al.*, 1993).

References

Abwender, D. A., Vernberg, E. M., Beery, S. H., & Ewell, K. K. (March, 1991). *Adolescents' concerns following relocation: Comparison with parents' perceptions.* Paper presented at the Annual Convention of the Southeastern Psychological Association, New Orleans, LA.

Berndt, T. J. (1982). The features and effects of friendship in early adolescence. *Child Development, 53,* 1447-1460.

Berndt, T. J., & Hoyle, S. G. (1985). Stability and change in childhood and adolescent friendships. *Developmental Psychology, 21,* 1007-1015.

Brown, B. B. (1989). The role of peer groups in adolescents' adjustment to secondary school. In: T. J. Berndt & G. W. Ladd (Eds.), *Peer relationships in child development* (pp. 188-215). New York: John Wiley & Sons.

Buhrmester, D., & Furman, W. (1987). The development of companion-ship and intimacy. *Child Development, 58,* 1101-1113.

Cantwell, D. P., & Baker, L. (1991). Manifestations of depressive affect in adolescence. *Journal of Youth and Adolescence, 20,* 121-133.

Compas, B. E., Ey, S., & Grant, K. E. (1993). Taxonomy, assessment, and diagnosis of depression during early adolescence. *Psychological Bulletin, 114,* 323-344.

Compas, B. E., Howell, D. C., Phares, V., Williams, R. A., & Ledoux, N. (1989). Parent and child stress: An integrative analysis. *Developmental Psychology, 25,* 550-559.

East, P. L., Hess, L. E., & Lerner, R. M. (1987). Peer support and adjustment of early adolescent peer groups. *Journal of Early Adolescence 7,* 153-163.

Eccles, J. S., Midgley, C., Wigfield, A., Buchanan, C. M., Reuman, D., Flanagan, C., & Mac Iver, D. (1993). Development during adolescence: The impact of stage-environment fit on young adolescents' experiences in schools and in families. *American Psychologist, 48,* 90-101.

Epstein, J. L. (1989). The selection of friends. In: T. J. Berndt & G. W. Ladd (Eds.), *Peer relationships in child development* (pp. 158-187). New York: John Wiley & Sons.

Erikson, E. H. (1968). *Identity: Youth and crisis.* New York: W. W. Norton.

Fisher, S. (1989). *Homesickness, cognition, and health.* London: Erlbaum.

Fisher, S. (1990). The psychological effects of leaving home: Homesickness, health, and obsessional thoughts. In: S. Fisher & C. L. Cooper (Eds.), *On the move: The psychology of change and transition* (pp. 153-170). Chichester, UK: Wiley.

Fisher, S., & Hood, B. (1988). Vulnerability factors in the transition to a university: Self-reported mobility history and sex differences as factors in psychological disturbance. *British Journal of Psychology, 79,* 309-320.

Furman, W., & Buhrmester, D. (1985). Children's perceptions of the personal relationships in their social networks. *Developmental Psychology, 21,* 1016-1024.

Garber, J., Weiss, B., & Shanley, N. (1993). Cognitons, depressive symptoms, and development in adolescents. *Journal of Abnormal Psychology, 102,* 47-57.

Hunter, F. T., & Youniss, J. (1982). Changes in functions of three relations during early adolescence. *Developmental Psychology, 18,* 806-811.

Kager, V. A., Arndt, E. K., & Kenny, T. J. (1992). Psychosomatic problems of children. In: C. E. Walker & M. C. Roberts (Eds.), *Handbook of Clinical Child Psychology* (2nd ed.) (pp. 303-317). New York: John Wiley & Sons.

Kandel, D. B. (1978). Similarity in real-life adolescent friendship pairs. *Journal of Personality and Social Psychology, 36,* 306-312.

Lapsley, D. K. (1990). Egocentrism theory and the 'new look' at the imaginary audience and personal fable in adolescence. In: R. M. Lerner, A. C. Petersen, & J. Brooks-Gunn (Eds.), *The encyclopedia of adolescence* (pp. 281-286). New York: Garland.

Lapsley, D. K., Milstead, M., Quintana, S., Flannery, D., & Buss, R. (1986). Adolescent egocentrism and formal operations: Tests of a theoretical assumption. *Developmental Psychology, 22,* 800-807.

160

Malina, R. M. (1990). Physical growth and performance during the transitional years (9-16). In: R. Montemayor, G. R. Adams, & T. P. Gullotta (Eds.), *From childhood to adolescence: A transitional period?* (pp. 41-62). Newbury Park, CA: Sage.

Mandler, G. (1990). Interruption (discrepancy) theory: Review and extensions. In: S. Fisher & C. L. Cooper (Eds.), *On the move: The psychology of change and transition* (pp. 13-32). New York: John Wiley & Sons.

Maqueda, M. (1996). *Influence of ethnic, educational, and economic features of a new community on adolescents' adjustment following relocation.* Unpublished master's thesis, University of Miami, Coral Gables, FL.

McDermott, P. A. (1996). A nationwide study of developmental and gender prevalence for psychopathology in childhood and adolescence. *Journal of Abnormal Child Psychology, 24,* 53-66.

Nottlemann, E. D., Inoff-Germain, C., Susman, E. J., & Chrousos, G. P. (1990). Hormones and behavior at puberty. In: J. Bancroft & J. M. Reinisch (Eds.), *Adolescence and puberty* (pp. 88-123). New York: Oxford University Press.

Petersen, A. C., Sarigiani, P. A., & Kennedy, R. E. (1991). Adolescent depression: Why more girls? *Journal of Youth and Adolescence, 20,* 247-271.

Rutter, M. (1991). Age changes in depressive disorders: Some developmental considerations. In: J. Garber & K. A. Dodge (Eds.), *The development of emotional regulation and dysregulation* (pp. 273-300). Cambridge, UK: Cambridge University Press.

Van Tilburg, M. A. L., Vingerhoets, A. J. J. M., & Van Heck, G. L. (1996). Homesickness: A review of the literature. *Psychological Medicine, 26,* 899-912.

Vernberg, E. M. (1990a). Experiences with peers following relocation during early adolescence. *American Journal of Orthopsychiatry, 60,* 466-472.

Vernberg, E. M. (1990b). Psychological adjustment and experiences with peers during early adolescence: Reciprocal, incidental, or unidirectional relationships? *Journal of Abnormal Child Psychology, 18,* 187-198.

Vernberg, E. M., Abwender, D. A., Ewell, K. K., & Beery, S. H. (1992). Social anxiety and peer relationships in early adolescence: A prospective analysis. *Journal of Clinical Child Psychology, 21,* 189-196.

Vernberg, E. M., Beery, S. H., Ewell, K. K., & Abwender, D. A. (1993). Parents' use of friendship facilitation strategies and the formation of friendships in early adolescence: A prospective study. *Journal of Family Psychology, 7,* 356-369.

Vernberg, E. M., & Daugherty, T. K. (August, 1988). *Predictors of social experiences and adjustment following relocation during early adolescence.* Paper presented at the Annual Convention of the American Psychological Association, Atlanta, GA.

Vernberg, E. M., Ewell, K. K., Beery, S. H., & Abwender, D. A. (1994). Sophistication of adolescents' interpersonal negotiation strategies and friendship formation after relocation: A naturally occurring experiment. *Journal of Research on Adolescence, 4,* 5-19.

Vernberg, E. M., Ewell, K. K., Beery, S. H., Freeman, C. F., & Abwender, D. A. (1995). Aversive exchanges with peers and adjustment during early adolescence: Is disclosure helpful? *Child Psychiatry and Human Development, 26,* 43-59.

Vernberg, E. M., & Field, T. (1990). Transitional stress in children and young adolescents moving to new environments. In: S. Fisher & C. L. Cooper (Eds.), *On the move: The psychology of change and transition* (pp. 127-151). New York: John Wiley & Sons.

Youniss, J. (1980). *Parents and peers in social development.* Chicago, Ill: University of Chicago Press.

11 Personality, Temperament, and Homesickness

GUUS L. VAN HECK, AD J.J.M. VINGERHOETS, AAFKE VOOLSTRA,
IRMA GRUIJTERS, HANNIE THIJS, AND MIRANDA A.L. VAN TILBURG

Introduction

Homesickness is a condition familiar to most people. The main characteristic is the pervasive feeling of sadness that happens universally to all age groups, under conditions of being away from home. Despite the universality of homesickness, little research has been done on this specific condition or its outcomes (Baier & Welch, 1992). Arising from the currently available literature reviews, conceptual analyses and empirical studies are many research questions focusing at antecedents and consequences of homesickness. A major question that should be asked concerns personality factors as preceding factors of homesickness.

It certainly is not a voluminous literature that examines the links between homesickness, on the one hand, and temperament and personality traits, on the other hand. As a matter of fact, only a few studies focus directly on these particular relationships. For instance, dependency, predominantly on family and parents, was found to be a characteristic feature of homesick students (Carden & Feicht, 1991). Also, in a longitudinal study, it has been shown that individual differences in dependency were systematically related to homesickness (Brewin et al., 1989). In a way, these findings suggest a possible linkage of homesickness to separation anxiety.

Of course, dependency is not the only personality characteristic that has received attention of researchers in the field of homesickness. In a group of first-year university students, Fisher (1989) found substantial links between introversion, depression, and obsession, on the one hand, and homesickness, on the other hand. She showed that introverts reported slightly more homesickness experiences than extraverts. She also demonstrated convincingly that levels of depression and obsession were already heightened in homesick persons *prior to leaving home*, indicating the existence of a vulnerability factor.

Eurelings-Bontekoe et al. (1994) compared homesick military conscripts with groups of normal controls and conscripts with different psychiatric symptoms. They reported the following characteristics of homesick military conscripts: (i) high levels of rigidity, somatization, and introversion, (ii) low levels of dominance and self-esteem, (iii) a high need for social support together with a lack of adequate social skills, and (iv) from an early age onwards, homesick experiences, serious problems with separation from parents, a strong emotional bond with parents, fewer of shorter holidays and stays without parents or alone, and avoidance of dating and going out. Rigidity proved to be the best predictor of homesickness. Moreover, it was shown that homesick conscripts prefer to maintain their old habits. They were strongly attached to a very regular life, tending to avoid, as much as possible, new situations that require psychological adaptation.

In a study with male soldiers, homesick subjects appeared to be less extraverted, less dominant and less assertive, but more rigid (Eurelings-Bontekoe et al., 1995). Compared with controls, women with either chronic feelings of homesickness or episodic attacks of homesickness were less assertive, less extraverted and more rigid, but did not differ in terms of dominance scores (Eurelings-Bontekoe et al., 1996).

In line with the Dutch psychiatrist Rümke's (1940) view that neurotic individuals are more vulnerable with respect to homesickness, Bergsma (1963) found relatively more neurotic characteristics in Dutch homesick military conscripts compared with non-homesick soldiers. In another Dutch Army investigation, Fontijn (1990) also reported a positive relationship between neuroticism and homesickness. Gasselsberger (1982), in a study on boarding school children, has provided additional empirical support for such a link between neuroticism and homesickness. Finally, Stroebe et al. (2002) conducted two studies on antecedents and consequences of homesickness, one in the Netherlands, and one in the UK. In both studies, emotional instability (neuroticism) was linked to higher levels of self-reported homesickness.

With regard to self-esteem, somewhat contradictory results have been reported. Hojat and Herman (1985), Eurelings-Bontekoe et al. (1994), as well as Stroebe et al. (2002) found lower self-esteem among homesick adults. Furthermore, Benn et al. (2005) found that recalling one's parents as rejecting was directly associated with increased homesickness. They suggest that recall of parental rejection may also generate feelings of inferiority that may lead to distress when moving into new environments. Fisher (1989), however, obtained no differences in self-esteem between homesick and non-homesick students. The latter finding possibly reflects cultural differences or differences in the assessment of homesickness and self-esteem. Overall, research provides substantial support for significant links between homesickness and low scores on self-esteem measures.

Verschuur et al. (2003) investigated the relationships between homesickness and the temperament and character dimensions of Cloninger's psychobiological model of personality (Cloninger, 1986; Cloninger et al., 1993). Homesickness was in general characterized by higher scores on Harm Avoidance, reflecting a link between severity of homesickness and a tendency to respond intensely to signals of aversive stimuli that leads to avoidance of punishment and non-reward. Severity of homesickness was also positively associated with Reward Dependence. People high on the latter trait are persistent: they continue to act in ways that produce reward. In addition, severe homesickness was characterized by lower Self-Directedness and, to a lesser extent, higher Self-Transcendence. Thus, homesickness is related to a poor ability to control, regulate and adapt behavior to fit the situation in accord with individually chosen goals and values. Furthermore, homesickness seems to be related to a relatively strong ability to experience spiritual ideas. Verschuur et al. (2003) have also reported that high scores on Rigidity, one of the subscales of their Homesickness Vulnerability Questionnaire (HVQ; Verschuur *et al.*, 2001), predicted severity of homesickness.

Related to the personality theory of Cloninger (e.g., Cloninger *et al.*, 1993) are the personality systems of Eysenck (1967) and Zuckerman (1991). Schmitz (1997; see also this volume) studied homesickness as an indicator of reactions to acculturative stress among immigrants. Using questionnaires based on the models of Eysenck and Zuckerman, he could demonstrate that homesickness was positively related to neuroticism, extraversion, sociability, anxiety and hostility, and negatively to impulsivity and sensation seeking.

Mohamed (1996), examining homesickness in postgraduate students, assessed appraisal and coping styles, together with personality scores. Subjects high in neuroticism and introversion tended to be more homesick. A pessimistic life orientation and adoption of confrontive coping and self-blame were also associated with homesickness. Students who were high on neuroticism and low on extraversion appeared to be susceptible to homesickness, largely because of their somewhat dysfunctional cognitive stress processes. So, coping appeared to be more important than personality.

Van Tilburg *et al.* (1999) conducted a study that examined the impact of coping strategies and basic personality styles, and timely recovery of homesickness. It was found that a particular coping style, i.e., mental escape, and neuroticism predicted homesickness chronicity. Also daydreaming and fantasies about home and wishful thinking were significantly associated with homesickness chronicity. In contrast to the findings of Mohamed (1996), the interference of neuroticism on timely recovery of homesickness was greater than the effect of any coping style. Consequently, it can be concluded that in this case personality is a more important antecedent of homesickness than personal preferences to deal with stressful events. In this study, Van Tilburg *et al.* (1999) used the Five-Factor Personality Inventory (FFPI; Hendriks, 1997). The FFPI is a questionnaire that covers the five-dimensional trait space of the Five-Factor Model of personality (FFM; e.g., see McCrae & John, 1992; Wiggins, 1996). The FFM proposes the domain of Extraversion, Agreeableness, Conscientiousness, Neuroticism and Openness as the basic dimensions underlying individual differences, features that relate in a gross way to Power, Love, Work, Affect and Intellect (Goldberg, 1990). It is this model that enjoys an unprecedented level of interest in personality research and practice (Paunonen & Ashton, 2001). Therefore, in the following part of this chapter, we will focus on this unified framework for trait research by further exploring individual differences in homesickness.

Homesickness and the five-factor model of personality

Recently, taxonomic research in personality psychology has focused on the development of a parsimonious way of describing the full range of personality traits, attempting to establish an integration of the diversity of existing individual difference measures. In this context, the five-factor approach has achieved appreciable popularity. This five-factor structure of trait descriptors has been reported by various researchers pursuing the so-called lexical strategy (Goldberg, 1982; John *et al.*, 1988; Norman, 1963; Tupes & Christal, 1961). The five global factors incorporate "hundreds, if not thousands of traits" (Goldberg, 1993, p. 27). This trait taxonomy has been traditionally labeled as the *Big Five*.

Extraversion reflects such traits as sociability, assertiveness, and activity level, while introversion reflects silence, passivity and reserve (Goldberg, 1993). Agreeableness reflects a preference for a particular way of dealing with other people. Individuals with high scores on Agreeableness are helpful, friendly, considerate, warm, etc.; low-scorers are quarrelsome, demanding, rude, egocentric, cynical, etc. Conscientiousness contrasts such traits as industry, order, reliability, self-discipline with characteristics like careless, negligent, undependable, disorganized, unreliable. Neuroticism includes such traits as nervousness, anxiety, hostility, depression, vulnerability. The fifth factor, in the early days of the Big Five interpreted as Intellect, has been labeled more recently as Openness to Experience, a broad construct that implies, amongst others, receptivity to many varieties of experience (McCrae, 1994). According to their advocates, this structure of five dimensions of interpersonal and intrapersonal conduct "... captures, at a broad level of abstraction, the commonalities among most of the existing systems of personality description, and provides an integrative descriptive model for personality research" (John, 1990, p. 96). The adoption of the FFM as the universal framework for personality description has been propagated by many personality psychologists who are convinced that these five factors "are both necessary and reasonably sufficient for describing at a global level the major features of personality" (McCrae & Costa, 1986, p. 1001).

High-scorers on Neuroticism have a low self-esteem. They tend towards anxiety and depression, worry, and are preoccupied with things that might go wrong. Distinguishing aspects of homesickness are ruminative activity and feelings of insecurity (Bell & Bromnick, 1998). Therefore, it is reasonable to expect that Neuroticism is associated with homesickness. Furthermore, it seems reasonable to expect that Openness to Experience, the fifth of the Big Five, should be related to measures of homesickness as well. Open individuals are not only characterized by a broader and deeper scope of awareness, but also by a need to enlarge and examine experiences. They are, amongst others, exploring, curious, and unconventional (McCrae & Costa, 1991). Because of these characteristics, it is plausible to assume that high-scorers on Openness to Experience will have fewer difficulties in adapting to new environments, taking into account that "failure to cognitively assimilate new experiences" is a characteristic of homesickness (Bell & Bromnick, 1998, pp. 745-746), and also taking into account the fact that Schmitz (1997; this volume) found a sizeable positive correlation between homesickness and a measure of Rokeach's (1960) concept 'closed-mindedness', a general personality trait which is related to the ability to form new cognitive systems of various kinds: perceptual, conceptual and aesthetic. However, one should not expect very high correlations between openness and homesickness, because open people experience both the good and the bad more intensely (Costa & McCrae, 1984).

It is much more difficult to conceive of possible associations between Extraversion, Agreeableness and Conscientiousness and homesickness. There are insufficient theoretical reasons to suspect that there may be structural associations between these basic personality variables and homesickness.

Homesickness and temperament

There are good reasons to expect that there are also systematic links between temperament and homesickness. Temperaments, forming a special class of personality traits, are the constitutional origins of personality and can be conceived of as the most fundamental aspects in which individuals differ from each other (Buss & Plomin, 1984). They are largely hereditary in origin. Pointing at person-environment interactions, Buss and Plomin (1984, p. 155) have suggested that temperaments "might influence the environment by choice of environments, contributing to social contexts, and modifying the impact of environments." Taking this into account, significant relationships between homesickness and temperaments, in as far as they reflect susceptibility to environmental stimulation and preferences for particular social episodes and behavioral contexts, can be expected.

Finding evidence for a substantial role for temperaments would reveal *built-in* tendencies towards homesickness. An implication of this would be a certain degree of 'resistance' to modifications via therapy, training, etc. Especially those temperamental variables that reflect adaptability, that is, the ways people react to new or altered situations, seem to be relevant in this context. In the pediatric approach to temperament, which has been dominated by Thomas and colleagues, *adaptability* is one of the major dimensions of temperament (Thomas *et al.*, 1963). This dimension also plays a crucial role in the Pavlovian perspective on temperament (see, e.g., Strelau, 1983), which focuses on strength of excitation, strength of inhibition, and mobility. Strength of excitation reflects the strength of the nervous system expressed mainly by its working capacity, namely endurance of intense and/or prolonged excitation without passing into defensive inhibition. Individuals high on strength of excitation are not held back by threatening situations; under intense circumstances, they are not inclined to stand by with folded arms. They love to undertake risky activities. Furthermore, they lack emotional disturbances in stressful situations. When they have to perform under severe social or physical pressure, then, they are still able to behave in highly efficient ways. Moreover, they are better able to withstand fatigue during conditions of intense or long-lasting stimulation. Finally, they can operate in an adequate way, even when they are under severe emotional strain. Strength of inhibition refers to the capacity of the nervous system for conditioned inhibition. Strength of inhibition concerns the ability of restraining from emotional, verbal, or motor reactions. People high on scales for strength of inhibition, compared with low-scorers, can easily delay their actions and are less disturbed when interrupted. Mobility reflects the degree of mobility or flexibility in the nervous system, manifested in the individual's capacity for responding quickly and adequately to all sorts of changing environmental conditions.

Summarizing, it can be said that the picture of the role of personality factors in the development of homesickness is far from complete (see also Van Tilburg *et al.*, 1996; Eurelings-Bontekoe, this volume). Until now there still is a limited scientific literature on systematic attempts to relate homesickness to the major individual difference variables of modern temperament and personality psychology. Therefore, the major aim of the research reported in this chapter was to fill this gap. For instance, information on Extraversion and Neuroticism, the 'Big Two' in the current five-factor approach of personality, is still rather limited, and information on the other basic factors in the five-factor model is even scarcer. The use of this FFM in homesickness research deserves more attention, because the personality characteristics in this model represent individual differences in the qualities or resources individuals can draw upon to solve adaptive problems (Buss, 1996).

The present research

For the investigations reported here, participants were recruited via announcements in local newspapers. Three hundred and thirty persons agreed to participate and asked for sending a test-booklet. Two hundred and six persons (62%) returned the mailed set of questionnaires. The age of the subjects ranged from 18 to 73 years. Fifty-five subjects were males. Their average age was 45.3 years ($SD = 14.6$). The group of females consisted of 149 persons with an average age of 40.0 years ($SD = 14.5$). In the case of two subjects no information regarding gender was available.

The following measures were employed. Homesickness was measured using a scale (Gruijters, 1992) constructed according to the Stimulus-Response Questionnaire methodology (cf. Endler *et al.*, 1962; Van Heck, 1981; see for a critical review Furnham & Jaspars, 1983). By means of this type of questionnaire data can be collected on cognitions, feelings and behaviors of individuals, sifted according to different reaction forms, in a series of situations. Each individual reports the intensity of every response variable for every situation.

Gruijters (1992) presented 12 hypothetical situations (see *Table 11.1*) to participants and asked them to imagine being in such a situation and to indicate the intensity of their homesickness symptoms, using seven-point scales ranging from 1 (*Not at all*) to 7 (*Very much*).

Table 11.1.   Situations of the S-R Homesickness Inventory

Item nr.	Duration	Situations		
		Company (with)	Distance
7	A few days	Partner and/or familiar persons	1
3	A few days	Partner and/or familiar persons	2
12	A few days	Familiar persons	1
1	A few days	Familiar persons	2
8	A few days	Alone	1
6	A few days	Alone	2
2	A couple of months	Partner and/or familiar persons	1
11	A couple of months	Partner and/or familiar persons	2
9	A couple of months	Familiar persons	1
5	A couple of months	Familiar persons	2
4	A couple of months	Alone	1
10	A couple of months	Alone	2

Note. Distance 1 = close to home; Distance 2 = far away from home.

The 12 situation descriptions differed systematically in terms of *distance* (nearby versus far away), *length of stay* (short versus long), and *companionship* (alone versus with acquaintances or close persons).

Fourteen response forms were used in the S-R Homesickness Inventory reflecting cognitions, feelings, bodily reactions, and behaviors indicating homesickness (see *Table 11.2*).

Table 11.2.   Response Forms of the S-R Homesickness Inventory

Item nr.	Responses
1	Keeping your mind on your activities
2	Your stomach is giving you troubles
3	Yearning for home
4	Being able to adopt to the new environment
5	Not fancying something
6	Thinking of home
7	Having lack of appetite
8	Trying to get in touch with home
9	Feeling at home in the new environment
10	Being interested in the new things surrounding you
11	Missing home
12	Having sleep problems
13	Withdrawing
14	Feeling homesick

Gruijters (1992) found that the situation Short/Nearby/With Familiar Persons was indicated as arousing the least homesick feelings and Long/Far Away/Alone the most. More interesting, however, was the observation that length of stay and type of companionship were more important than distance, as can be seen from an inspection of the means and standard deviations in *Table 11.3*.

The S-R Homesickness Inventory assesses homesickness in a very reliable way. The internal consistency coefficients for each situation range between a lowest value of 0.86 and a highest coefficient of 0.93.

In the present study, extraversion, agreeableness, conscientiousness, emotional stability, and openness to experience were measured by using a set of 60 bipolar standard markers, 12 for each of the Big-Five factors, as proposed by Goldberg (1989). Items were administered with 9-step rating scales. The bipolar rating scales ranged from (1) *Very* [Trait A], through (5) *Neither* [Trait A] *nor* [Trait B], to (9) *Very* [Trait B]. In the bipolar inventory, the items were ordered such that those expected to be associated with the same factor were separated by items from each of the other four factors (cf. Goldberg, 1989).

Table 11.3. Means and standard deviations of homesickness scores for the 12 situations of the S-R Homesickness Inventory

Item	Mean	SD
Couple of months-alone-far away from home	44.5	16.3
Couple of months-alone-close to home	42.2	16.5
Couple of months-with familiar persons-far away from home	41.3	16.0
Couple of months-with familiar persons-close to home	38.8	15.2
Few days-alone-far away from home	36.8	16.3
Couple of months-partner/familiar persons-far away from home	33.7	14.4
Few days-with familiar persons-far away from home	32.4	13.6
Few days-alone-close to home	32.2	14.3
Few days-with familiar persons-close to home	30.7	13.8
Couple of months-partner/familiar persons-close to home	28.9	12.1
Few days-with partner/familiar persons-far away from home	26.5	12.9
Few days-with partner/familiar persons-close to home	23.8	10.2

The Pavlovian temperament variables were assessed with the Pavlov Temperament Survey (PTS; Strelau et al., 1990; Strelau et al., 1999) with three scales, Strength of Excitation (SE), Strength of Inhibition (SI and Mobility (MO), designed to assess specific properties of the nervous system by means of their behavioral manifestations. It contains 20 items for each subscale, making it a 60-item questionnaire. It is a reliable instrument: Cronbach alpha coefficients are 0.88, 0.78 and 0.91 for SE, SI and MO, respectively. The intercorrelations are $r_{SE\,SI} = 0.35$, $r_{SE\,MO} = 0.64$, and $r_{SI\,MO} = 0.25$ (Van Heck et al., 1993).

Finally, the Dutch Personality Questionnaire (DPQ; Luteijn, 1974; Luteijn *et al.*, 1985) was used in order to test earlier findings regarding neuroticism, rigidity and self-esteem. The DPQ is a questionnaire containing 133 *True - ? - False* items arranged in 7 scales: Neuroticism, Social Inadequacy, Rigidity, Hostility, Self-sufficiency, Dominance, and Self-esteem. The questionnaire is based upon the California Psychological Inventory (CPI; Gough, 1987).

The correlations among the self-descriptions obtained with the list of 60 bipolar trait scales were subjected to exploratory factor analysis. A principal components analysis resulted in a five-factor solution. The number of extracted factors was five, based upon the Scree plot of eigenvalues (Cattell, 1966). The five Varimax factors accounted for 44.7% of the total variance.

Table 11.4. Factor analysis with Varimax rotation; bipolar trait scales
Note Items within a factor are given in order of strength of loading, with the most influential items first. Only secondary loadings exceeding |0.30| are presented. Primary loadings are printed in bold.

Bipolar Trait Scales	I	II	III	IV	V
Introverted – Extraverted	**0.76**				
Reserved – Spontaneous	**0.69**	0.33			
Silent – Talkative	**0.67**				
Timid – Bold	**0.66**		0.31		
Inhibited – Impulsive	**0.64**				
Submissive – Assertive	**0.49**		0.42		
Temperamental – Even tempered	**-0.39**	0.33	0.34		
Unkind – Kind		**0.70**			
Uncooperative – Cooperative		**0.64**			
Inconsiderate – Considerate		**0.61**			
Unfriendly – Friendly		**0.60**			
Cold – Warm		**0.56**			
Unsociable – Sociable		**0.54**	0.32		
Selfish – Unselfish		**0.53**			
Inflexible – Flexible		**0.51**	0.40		
Stingy – Generous	0.30	**0.50**	0.31		
Irresponsible – Responsible		**0.49**		0.44	
Unenthusiastic – Enthusiastic		**0.48**		0.39	
Rude – Polite		**0.46**	0.40		
Distrustful – Trustful		**0.46**			
Imperceptive – Perceptive		**0.33**		0.33	

- *to be continued* -

Table 11.4 continued

Bipolar Trait Scales	I	II	Factor III	IV	V
Rash – Cautious			**0.68**		
Frivolous - Serious			**0.58**		
Unfair – Fair			**0.55**		
Negligent – Conscientious			**0.53**	0.31	
Unrefined – Refined		0.38	**0.53**		
Unpredictable – Predictable			**0.48**		
Careless – Thorough			**0.47**	0.41	
Disorganized – Organized			**0.44**	0.34	
Extravagant – Thrifty			**0.43**		
Boastful – Modest			**0.42**		
Unreflective – Reflective			**0.41**		
Shallow – Deep			**0.33**		
Insecure - Stable	0.39			**0.75**	
Unstable – Stable				**0.74**	
Tensed – Relaxed				**0.72**	
Unassured – Self-confident	0.44			**0.67**	
High-strung – Imperturbable				**0.66**	
Nervous – At ease				**0.65**	
Irritable – Good natured				**0.58**	
Self-pitying – Spartan				**0.58**	
Unenergetic – Energetic		0.37		**0.55**	
Emotional – Unemotional				**0.55**	
Discontented – Contented		0.33		**0.55**	
Inefficient – Efficient			0.35	**0.52**	
Angry – Calm	-0.41			**0.50**	
Passive – Active		0.41		**0.45**	0.34
Envious – Not envious				**0.44**	
Lazy – Hardworking				**0.43**	
Unsophisticated - Sophisticated					**0.81**
Uncreative – Creative					**0.80**
Not artistic – Artistic					**0.72**
Not innovative – Innovative					**0.58**
Unimaginative – Imaginative	0.34				**0.58**
Not analytical – Analytical			0.30		**0.35**
Impractical – Practical					**0.55**
Undependable – Reliable		0.39	0.40		**0.42**
Not adventurous – Adventurous			-0.33		**0.36**

Inspection of the Varimax-rotated factor-solution (see *Table 11.4*) revealed that the five dimensions did not correspond completely with the usual Big Five pattern. Two striking things happened. First, the surgency aspect of extraversion, as measured by markers such as *Unenergetic—Energetic, Passive—Active*, had a primary loading on Emotional Stability. Second, also some Conscientiousness markers, for instance, *Lazy—Hardworking*, moved to Emotional Stability. In spite of these peculiarities, the five factors clearly reflect the Big Five.

Therefore, Factor I is conventionally labeled Extraversion, Factor II Agreeableness, Factor III Conscientiousness, Factor IV Emotional Stability, and Factor V Openness to Experience. Cronbach alpha's were rather satisfactory: 0.71 (Extraversion), 0.85 (Agreeableness), 0.73 (Conscientiousness), 0.89 (Emotional Stability), and 0.78 (Openness to Experience).

Table 11.5 contains the correlations of the Big Five scores with a Total Homesickness score (average score over all situations for 13 response forms, excluding the 'Feeling homesick' item; see *Tables 11.1 and 11.2*). *Table 11.4* reveals that the pattern of relationships is more or less the same for males and females. For the total group significant correlations were found in the case of Extraversion, Emotional Stability, and Openness to Experience. The data reveal that introverted, neurotic persons who are closed to new experiences are especially vulnerable. The correlations between PTS scores and the Total Homesickness score are presented in *Table 11.6*.

Strength of Excitation correlated negatively with homesickness. Looking at different aspects of Strength of Excitation (data not shown in *Table 11.6*), it was found that the highest correlations were obtained for a facet of Strength of Excitation reflecting the fact that having to act under social pressure and/or physical load does not evoke emotional disturbances ($r = -.45, p < .001$, for males as well as females).

With respect to Strength of Inhibition, we see a modest negative correlation with homesickness. But here the gender effect is clear. Only female respondents produced significant correlations. The highest correlations were obtained for females in the case of items that reflect difficulties in waiting with task performance when delay of such performance is expected.

For obvious reasons, in the case of Mobility, the highest correlations were expected. These expectations were confirmed by the results. Substantial negative correlations, for males as well as females, were found between Mobility and homesickness, especially for Mobility-items regarding adaptation to new surroundings.

The correlations between DPQ scores and homesickness are presented in *Table 11.7*. With the exception of self-sufficiency, all variables correlated significantly with homesickness. The analysis of the total data set revealed relatively high positive correlations between neuroticism and social inadequacy and homesickness.

172

Table 11.5. Correlations between Personality and Homesickness: Big Five (FFPI) data

FFPI scales	Total (N=199)	Males (N=55)	Females (N=142)
Extraversion	-0.24***	-0.37***	-0.22**
Agreeableness	-0.09	-0.16	-0.08
Conscientiousness	-0.05	0.09	0.01
Emotional stability	-0.42***	-0.29*	-0.42***
Openness to experience	-0.02***	-0.29*	-0.21***

* p <0.05; ** p <0.01; ***; p <0.001.

Table 11.6. Correlations between Temperament and Homesickness; Pavlov Temperament Survey (PTS) data

PTS scales	Total (N=205)	Males (N=55)	Females (N=148)
Strength and Excitation (SE)	-0.49**	-0.41**	-0.49**
Strength of Inhibition (SI)	-0.22**	-0.08	-0.23*
Mobility (MO)	-0.57**	-0.55**	-0.57**

* p <0.01; ***; p <0.001.

Table 11.7. Correlations between Personality and Homesickness: Dutch Personality Questionnaire (DPQ) data

DPQ scales	Total (N=205)	Males (N=55)	Females (N=148)
Neuroticism	0.49***	0.32**	0.50***
Social Inadequacy	0.45***	0.41***	0.45***
Rigidity	0.21***	0.04	0.29***
Hostility	0.15**	-0.01	0.24**
Self-sufficiency	0.05	-0.10	0.12
Dominance	-0.31***	-0.24*	-0.30**
Self-esteem	-0.47***	-0.45***	-0.46***

* p <0.05; ** p <0.01; ***; p <0.001.

Furthermore, it was found that homesickness was negatively related to dominance and self-esteem. In separate analyses for males and females, the same pattern was obtained for the two groups. However, in the case of females there were also positive links with rigidity and hostility.

Discussion

The results reported here provide positive evidence for links between basic individual difference variables and homesickness. According to the correlations in the *Tables 11.6 and 11.7* homesick individuals, males as well as females, are relatively introverted, emotional unstable, and closed to new experiences. Furthermore, they have less ability to act in adequate ways under emotional strain, they have difficulties with restraining from emotional, verbal or motor reactions. They further lack the capacity to adapt to changing environmental conditions. Finally, they have a negative view of themselves as reflected in low scores on self-esteem. In addition, female homesick persons are also inclined towards rigidity and submissiveness. The picture that emerges from these characterizations represents an extension of our knowledge regarding the role of personality in homesickness. Earlier found associations, especially those regarding extraversion-introversion and emotional stability-neuroticism (e.g., Bergsma, 1963; Eurelings-Bontekoe *et al.*, 1994, 1995, 1996; Fisher, 1989; Fontijn, 1990; Gasselsberger, 1982), could be replicated. In addition to these replications, new information could be obtained with respect to other broad supertraits, such as Openness to Experience, and temperamental factors reflecting important formal characteristics of behavior, such as Mobility in nervous system processes.

Van Tilburg *et al.* (1996) have proposed a distinction between (i) homesickness that is linked to the adversity of the new environment and (ii) homesickness that reflects missing the old environment or significant persons. It is conceivable that both types of homesickness are related to different personality characteristics. For instance, it can be expected that scores on the fifth dimension of the Big Five, Openness to Experience, be more substantially linked to the first type of homesickness than to the second type. Thus an interesting issue for research would be the extent to which personality is related to different types of homesickness.

We would like to conclude by suggesting ways in which research on homesickness phenomena might be improved. We belief that future investigations could benefit by clarifying and defining the concept of homesickness and by developing a comprehensive theoretical framework. Scheier and Bridges (1995) have pointed to this in the broader context of the mediating and moderating roles of personality with respect to stress–illness relationships: "Often variables are included in protocols simply because the relevant measures are readily available. This gives rise to a disjointed literature that is hard to integrate and understand. Future research needs to be more focused and more systematic. To accomplish this task, more comprehensive biobehavioral models are needed that integrate psychological and biological characteristics and mechanisms" (Scheier & Bridges, 1995, p. 266). Taking this statement seriously, we would like to point to two theoretical frameworks that might have a high relevance for further research on the role of personality in homesickness, because both models make it possible to study personality as an organized system or a complex of systems with many different components.

The first model has been suggested by McCrae and Costa (1996) in an attempt to construct a metatheoretical framework for personality theories. This framework contains five categories of personality variables: (i) *basic tendencies* which define the individual's potential and direction and which include the five major personality dimensions but also physical characteristics, cognitive capacities, physiological drives, and focal vulnerabilities; (ii) *characteristic adaptations* such as learned behaviors, interpersonal adaptations, acquired competencies, attitudes, beliefs, and goals; (iii) the *self*-concept; (iv) the *objective biography*, and (v) *external influences* reflecting the impact of developmental factors such as parent-child relations, peer socialization and education, as well as micro-environmental (e.g., situational constraints, motivational pressure) and macro-environmental influences (e.g., culture, subculture, neighborhood).

The second model is the model of ecological congruence, developed by Hobfoll (1988), which states that *resources* (e.g., social support personality resources, coping strategies) will reduce or increase psychological and physical strains or will have no effect on psychological distress and physical symptoms, depending upon the fact whether the resource complex meets, does not meet, or interferes with task demands, emotional demands and biological demands made on the individual. Crucial in this framework is the *fit of resources with demands*, which will depend on several factors, such as environmental constraints, personal and cultural values, perceptions of degree of threat, assessment of need, and perceptions of the availability and suitability of potential support as seen by the individual for a given situation.

Both models pave the way for studying personality-homesickness relationships from an integral ecological perspective. We strongly believe that only by focusing on the person's unique patterns of adjustment to the environment, we will deepen our understanding of the 'forgotten' phenomenon of homesickness.

References

Baier, M., & Welch, M. (1992). An analysis of the concept of homesickness. *Archives of Psychiatric Nursing, 6*, 54-60.

Bell, J., & Bromnick, R. (1998). Young people in transition: The relationship between homesickness and self-disclosure. *Journal of Adolescence, 21*, 745-748.

Benn, L., Harvey, J. E., Gilbert, P., & Irons, C. (2005). Social rank, interpersonal trust and recall of parental rearing in relation to homesickness. *Personality and Individual Differences, 38*, 1813-1822.

Bentley, D. L. (1986, April). *Social support during a transition: Longitudinal analysis of gender differences.* Paper presented at the Annual Convention of the Southwestern Psychological Association, Fort Worth, TX. (ERIC Document Reproduction Service No. ED 276 966).

Bergsma, J. (1963). *Militair heimwee* [Homesickness in the army]. Unpublished Ph.D. thesis. Groningen, The Netherlands: Groningen University.

Brewin, C. R., Furnham, A., & Howes, M. (1989). Demographic and psychological determinants of homesickness and confiding among students. *British Journal of Psychology, 80*, 467-477.

Buss, A. H., & Plomin, R. (1984). *Temperament: Early developing personality traits.* Hillsdale, NJ: Erlbaum.

Buss, D. M. (1996). Social adaptation and five major factors of personality. In: J. S. Wiggins (Ed.), *The five-factor model of personality. Theoretical perspectives* (pp. 180-207). New York: The Guilford Press.

Carden, A. I., & Feicht, R. (1991). Homesickness among American and Turkish college students. *Journal of Cross-Cultural Psychology, 22,* 418-428.

Cattell, R. B. (1966). The scree test for the number of factors. *Multivariate Behavior Research, 1,* 140-161.

Cloninger, C. R. (1986). A unified biosocial theory of personality and its role in the development of anxiety states. *Psychiatric Developments, 3,* 167-226.

Cloninger, C. R., Svrakic, D. M., Przybeck, T. R. (1993). A psychobiological model of temperament and character. *Archives of General Psychiatry, 50,* 975-990.

Costa, P. T., Jr., & McCrae, R. R. (1984). Personality as a lifelong determinant of well-being. In: C. Malatesta & C. Izard (Eds.), *Affective processes in adult development and aging* (pp. 141-157). Beverley Hills, CA: Sage.

Endler, N. S., Hunt, J. McV., & Rosenstein, A. (1962). An S-R Inventory of Anxiousness. *Psychological Monographs, 536,* 1-31.

Eurelings-Bontekoe, E. H. M., Tolsma, A., Verschuur, M. J., & Vingerhoets, A. J. J. M. (1996). Construction of a homesickness questionnaire using a female population with two types of self-reported homesickness: Preliminary results. *Personality and Individual Differences, 20,* 415-421.

Eurelings-Bontekoe, E. H. M., Verschuur, M., Koudstaal, A., Van der Sar, S., & Duijsens, I. J. (1995). Construction of a homesickness questionnaire: Preliminary results. *Personality and Individual Differences, 19,* 319-325.

Eurelings-Bontekoe, E. H. M., Vingerhoets, A. J. J. M., & Fontijn, A. (1994). Personality and behavioral antecedents of homesickness. *Personality and Individual Differences, 16,* 229-235.

Eysenck, H. J. (1967). *The biological basis of personality.* Springfield, Ill: Thomas.

Fisher, S. (1989). *Homesickness, cognition, and health.* London: Erlbaum.

Fontijn, A. J. (1990). *Heimwee als een stress-reactie* [Homesickness as a reaction to stress]. Unpublished M.A. thesis. Leiden, The Netherlands: Leiden University.

Furnham, A., & Jaspars, J. (1983). The evidence for interactionism in psychology. A critical analysis of the situation-response inventories. *Personality and Individual Differences, 4,* 627-644.

Gasselsberger, K. (1982). Depressionsfördernde soziale und territoriale Faktoren von Heimweh-Reaktionen [Depression-related social and territorial factors of homesickness reactions]. *Zeitschrift für Klinische Psychologie, Forschung und Praxis, 11,* 186-200.

Goldberg, L. (1982). From Ace to Zombie: Some explorations in the language of personality. In: C. D. Spielberger & J. N. Butcher (Eds.), *Advances in personality assessment* (Vol. 1, pp. 203-234). Hillsdale, NJ: Erlbaum.

Goldberg, L. R. (1989, June). *Standard markers of the Big-Five factor structure.* Invited Workshop on Personality Language. Groningen, The Netherlands: Groningen University.

Goldberg, L. R. (1990). An alternative 'Description of personality': The Big-Five factor structure. *Journal of Personality and Social Psychology, 59,* 1216-1229.

Goldberg, L. R. (1993). The structure of phenotypic personality traits. *American Psychologist, 48,* 26-34.

Gough, H. G. (1987). *The California Psychological Inventory administrator's guide.* Palo Alto, CA: Consulting Psychologists Press.

Gruijters, I. (1992). *Heimwee en situatiekenmerken* [Homesickness and situation characteristics]. Unpublished M.A. thesis. Tilburg, The Netherlands: Tilburg University.

Hendriks, A. A. J. (1997). *The construction of the Five-Factor Personality Inventory (FFPI).* Unpublished doctoral thesis. Groningen, The Netherlands: Groningen University.

Hobfoll, S. E. (1988). *The ecology of stress.* New York: Hemisphere Publishing Corporation.

176

Hojat, M., & Herman, M. W. (1985). Adjustment and psychosocial problems of Iranian and Filipino physicians in the U.S. *Journal of Clinical Psychology, 41*, 130-136.

John, O. P. (1990). The 'Big Five' factor taxonomy: Dimensions of personality in the natural language and in questionnaires. In: L. A. Pervin (Ed.), *Handbook of personality. Theory and research* (pp. 66-100). New York/London: The Guilford Press.

John, O. P., Angleitner, A., & Ostendorf, F. (1988). The lexical approach to personality: A historical review of trait taxonomic research. *European Journal of Personality, 2*, 171-203.

Luteijn, F. (1974). *De constructie van een persoonlijkheidsvragenlijst* [The construction of a personality questionnaire]. Unpublished doctoral dissertation. Groningen, The Netherlands: Groningen University.

Luteijn, F., Starren, J., & Van Dijk, H. (1985). *Handleiding bij de NPV (Herziene uitgave)* [Manual of the Dutch Personality Questionnaire (rev. ed.). Lisse, The Netherlands: Swets & Zeitlinger.

McCrae, R. R. (1994). Openness to experience: Expanding the boundaries of Factor V. In: B. De Raad & G. L. Van Heck (Eds.), *The fifth of the Big Five*. Special issue of the *European Journal of Personality, 8*, 251-272.

McCrae, R. R., & Costa, P. T., Jr. (1986). Clinical assessment can benefit from recent advances in personality psychology. *American Psychologist, 41*, 1001-1003.

McCrae, R. R., & Costa, P. T., Jr. (1991). Adding Liebe und Arbeit: The full Five-Factor Model and well-being. *Personality and Social Psychology Bulletin, 17*, 227-232.

McCrae, R. R., & Costa, P. T., Jr. (1996). Toward a new generation of personality theories: Theoretical contexts for the five-factor model. In: J. S. Wiggins (Ed.), *The five-factor model of personality. Theoretical perspectives* (pp. 51-87). New York: The Guilford Press.

McCrae, R. R., & John, O. P. (1992). An introduction to the five-factor model and its applications. *Journal of Personality, 60*, 175-215.

Mohamed, A. A. R. (1996). *Stress processes in British and overseas students*. Unpublished doctoral dissertation. Dundee, Scotland: University of Dundee.

Norman, W. T. (1963). Toward an adequate taxonomy of personality attributes: Replicated factor structure in peer nomination personality ratings. *Journal of Abnormal and Social Psychology, 66*, 574-583.

Paunonen, S. V., & Ashton, M. C. (2001). Big Five factors and facets and the prediction of behavior. *Journal of Personality and Social Psychology, 81*, 524-539.

Rokeach, M. (1960). *The open and closed mind*. New York: Basic Books.

Rümke, H. C. (1940). Over heimwee [On homesickness]. *Nederlands Tijdschrift voor Geneeskunde, 84*, 3658-3665.

Scheier, M. F., & Bridges, M. W. (1995). Person variables and health: Personality predispositions and acute psychological states as shared determinants for disease. *Psychosomatic Medicine, 57*, 255-268.

Schmitz, P. G. (1997). Individual differences in acculturative stress reactions: Determinants of homesickness and psychosocial maladjustment. In: M. A. L. Van Tilburg & A. J. J. M. Vingerhoets (Eds.), *Psychological aspects of geographical moves: Homesickness and acculturation stress* (pp. 103-117). Tilburg University Press.

Strelau, J. (1983). *Temperament – personality – activity*. New York: Academic Press.

Strelau, J., Angleitner, A., Bantelmann, J., & Ruch, W. (1990). The Strelau Temperament Inventory Revised (STI-R): Theoretical considerations and scale development. *European Journal of Personality, 4*, 209-235.

Strelau, J., Angleitner, A., & Newberry, B. H. (1999). *Pavlovian Temperament Survey (PTS). An international handbook*. Seattle, WA: Hogrefe & Huber Publishers.

Stroebe, M., Van Vliet, T., Hewstone, M., & Willis, H. (2002). Homesickness among students in two cultures: Antecedents and consequences. *British Journal of Psychology, 93*, 147-168.

Thomas, A., Chess, S., Birch, H., Hertzig, M., & Korn, S. (1963). *Behavioral individuality in early childhood.* New York: New York University Press.

Tupes, E. C., & Christal, R. E. (1961). *Recurrent personality factors based on trait ratings* (USAF ASD Tech. Rep. No. 61-97). Lackland Air Force Base, TX: U.S. Air Force. Reprinted in *Journal of Personality* (1992), 225-251.

Van Heck, G. L. (1981). *Anxiety: The profile of a trait.* Unpublished doctoral dissertation. Tilburg, The Netherlands: Tilburg University.

Van Heck, G. L., De Raad, B., & Vingerhoets, A. J. J. M. (1993). De Pavlov Temperament Schaal (PTS) [The Pavlov Temperament Survey (PTS)]. *Nederlands Tijdschrift voor de Psychologie, 48,* 141-142.

Van Tilburg, M. A. L., Vingerhoets, A. J. J. M., & Van Heck, G. L. (1996). Homesickness: A review of the literature. *Psychological Medicine, 26,* 899-912.

Van Tilburg, M. A. L., Vingerhoets, A. J. J. M., & Van Heck, G. L. (1999). Determinants of homesickness chronicity: Coping and personality. *Personality and Individual Differences, 27,* 531-539.

Verschuur, M. J., Eurelings-Bontekoe, E. H. M., & Spinhoven, Ph. (2001). Construction and validation of the Homesickness Vulnerability Questionnaire. *Personality and Individual Differences, 30,* 11-19.

Verschuur, M. J., Eurelings-Bontekoe, E. H. M., Spinhoven, Ph., & Duijsens, I. J. (2003). Homesickness, temperament and character. *Personality and Individual Differences, 35,* 757-770.

Wiggins, J. S. (Ed.) (1996). *The five-factor model of personality. Theoretical perspectives.* New York: The Guilford Press.

Zuckerman, M. (1991). *Psychobiology of personality.* Cambridge, UK: Cambridge University Press.

12 Homesickness: Personality, Attachment and Emotional Correlates

ELISABETH H.M. EURELINGS-BONTEKOE

Definition

Homesickness can be described as a depression-like reaction to leaving a familiar environment, characterized by ruminative thoughts about home and the desire to go back to the familiar environment. Dijkstra and Hendrix (1983) define homesickness as "a for humans normal state of being, characterized by a depressed mood, physical complaints and a ruminative thinking about the familiar environment and/or familiar people."

It is important to make a distinction between homesickness occurring when being separated form the home situation as a *state* and as an *enduring vulnerability* to react with grief each time when being away from the familiar environment. Verschuur *et al.* (2004) studied the association of both conceptualizations with related concepts, such as anxiety, depression and anger. The latter conceptualization can rather be considered as an enduring trait and does not specifically refer to actual feelings of depression. We compared these two conceptualizations of homesickness in a random sample from the Dutch population (n=485) by assessing their uni- and multivariate associations with anger, anxiety, depression, and anxiety-sensitivity. Both conceptualizations of homesickness were associated with anxiety and depression and with (the externalization of) anger. No association was found between internalization of anger or control over internalized and externalized anger for either conceptualization of homesickness. The pattern of multivariate associations between homesickness and these emotional correlates was similar for both conceptualizations, although homesickness as a state appeared to have a stronger association with depression, whereas the tendency to develop homesickness showed a particularly strong association with anxiety. It is concluded that homesickness can be considered as a mixed emotion of anxiety and depression ("Cothymia") but that depression is more characteristic of homesickness as a state, whereas anxiety is more important if homesickness is conceptualized as an enduring tendency.

In addition, it is important to make a distinction between homesickness as a rather normal and highly prevalent emotional reaction to the stress of adaptation to a new environment and a more pathological form leading to a severe state of depression and dysfunctioning. Such a distinction is similar to the one that can be made between normal and pathological mourning. The intensity of the experience of homesickness may vary widely, as reflected in the number of symptoms and the way it may manifest itself. Fisher (1989) makes a distinction between four different manifestations of homesickness:

1. *Physical complaints*, which most frequently entail stomach and bowel problems, headaches, loss of appetite, sleeplessness and a strange sensation in the legs.
2. *Cognitive manifestations* of homesickness, such as obsessively missing home, an inability to concentrate on daily activities, and a negative evaluation of the present environment.
3. At the *behavioral level*, homesick people are often apathetic, lack interest in their new environment, usually take little initiative and tend to withdraw socially.
4. The *emotional manifestations* of homesickness are often characterized by feelings of depression and fatigue and even suicidal ideation.

In conclusion, homesickness seems to be a complex cognitive-motivational-emotional state, which, in its most severe form, overlaps substantially with major depressive disorder according to criteria of DSM-IV (American Psychiatric Association, 1994).

Prevalence

Because the state of homesickness may vary from a common emotional experience to a severe form of depression and/or separation anxiety, it is difficult to provide exact prevalence figures. The prevalence of homesickness is dependent upon the characteristics of the environment, the way homesickness has been operationalized and assessed and the population under study. Fisher (1988) presents data on boarding school children, indicating that, dependent on the seriousness of the symptoms and whether or not the question is prompted, incidence figures vary from 16 to 91%. Estimates for first-year university students range from 19% (Carden & Feight, 1991) to 95% (Lu, 1990). Serious forms of homesickness are estimated to occur in 10 to 15% of the population. Verschuur *et al.* (2004) found that serious, recurrent homesickness occurred among 13% of a large sample of the Dutch population. Thijs (cited in Vingerhoets *et al.*, 1993) found that in a sample of 206 adults, only 7% indicated that they had never experienced homesickness.

Homesickness appears to be far more prevalent among military conscripts who called for the assistance of the military psychologist than among primary mental health care patients in general. Eurelings-Bontekoe *et al.* (1994) found that 54% of conscripts with psychological problems suffered from homesickness. The prevalence in a second study among military conscripts (Eurelings-Bontekoe *et al.*, 1995) was 53%. Both studies used a 9-item checklist, covering symptoms of depression and a strong desire to a former home situation, to identify the presence of homesickness.

In a study among 171 employees of an international company in the Netherlands (Eurelings-Bontekoe *et al.*, 2000) the prevalence of homesickness, defined on the basis of the 9-item checklist was 10.6%. However, when homesickness was defined on the basis of self-report the prevalence was 29.4%. Taking the self-report measure of homesickness as the 'golden standard,' the specificity of the 9-item checklist appeared to be high (95%) and the sensitivity low (25.5%). That is, of all respondents classified as non-homesick according to the self-report 95% were classified as non-homesick by the 9-item checklist as well. The sensitivity of 25% implies that only 25% of those with self-reported homesickness where as such identified by the 9-item checklist. These figures imply: (1) that prevalence figures indeed depend upon the way homesickness is operationalized and assessed, and (2) that the 9-item checklist taps particularly the more serious cases of homesickness, which may mean that the 9-item checklist is inappropriate for screening purposes. The relatively low prevalence of serious, depression-like homesickness among the employees is probably due to a selection bias: the majority of those who suffer from severe homesickness will probably have returned home.

The role of person variables

Fisher (1989) has emphasized that homesickness is a function of both personality features as well as characteristics of the new environment. One may postulate that neurotic and unstable people are more prone to develop homesickness as a reaction to the stress of having to adapt to new environments. The same holds for people who are rigid and therefore strongly attached to familiar habits and to an environment with a high level of predictability. In addition, it can be hypothesized that avoidant and socially inadequate people experience more difficulties during the process of adaptation to new environments. In contrast, extraverts and people with a high interest in new experiences generally will not suffer from homesickness. Insecure attachment may also play a role: attachment disturbances can be described along a continuum ranging from close, preoccupied patterns of relating, expressed in either compulsive care seeking or compulsive care giving, to distant, detached patterns of relating, expressed in either compulsive self reliance or generalized anger towards attachment figures (West *et al.*, 1994). As Glickauf-Hughes and Wells (1997) describe, an overattached, dependent style is mainly observed among those who as a child were inconsistently treated, dependent upon the parents' moods and needs, i.e., the parents were intermittently rewarding interspersed with punishment or rejection. A detached attachment style is observed among those who as a child were chronically neglected or whose true self has been systematically neglected, by providing love only if the child met the parents' self object needs. A disturbed attachment may give rise to a disturbance in separation and individuation. Moreover, it seems reasonable to assume that personality and attachment style may indirectly influence the vulnerability to develop homesickness and adaptation difficulties by virtue of their influence on the capacity to obtain and profit from social support (Eurelings-Bontekoe, *in press*). This capacity is probably related to stable personality characteristics as attachment style, introversion-extraversion, social competence, mastery and the capacity of intimacy (Cohen & Syme, 1985; Eurelings-Bontekoe, in press; Heller, 1979; Heller & Swindle, 1983; Hobfoll & Stokes, 1988; see also Van Heck, this volume). This chapter will focus on personality, attachment variables and emotional correlates of homesickness. The empirical data will be discussed from a psychodynamic frame of reference, linking homesickness and separation difficulties to separation anxiety and narcissistic vulnerability. Finally, some suggestions will be made concerning the clinical detection and management of homesickness.

Homesickness and personality traits

In literature, the following personality features have been investigated in relation to homesickness.

Dependency: Brewin *et al.* (1989) found in a longitudinal study, that a high level of dependency is a predictor of homesickness. Carden and Feicht (1991) demonstrated that being dependent upon particularly the parents was characteristic of homesick students. Eurelings-Bontekoe *et al.* (1994) found a strong emotional tie to the parents to be characteristic of military conscripts suffering from homesickness. According to Verschuur *et al.* (2003) showed a high level of *Reward Dependence* as measured with the Temperament and Character Inventory developed by Cloninger *et al.* (1994) to be predictive of homesickness severity. A high level of Reward Dependence implies a strong dependence upon the emotional support of others. According to Verschuur *et al.* (2001), a strong tendency to seek social support and to express emotions is characteristic of homesick individuals.

Introversion-extraversion: with respect to the dimension introversion-extraversion results are not clear-cut: Eurelings-Bontekoe found in several studies (Eurelings-Bontekoe *et al.*, 1994; 1995; 1996; Verschuur *et al.*, 2001) that homesick individuals tend to be less extravert than non-homesick persons. Both Fisher (1989) and Voolstra (1992) reported a negative correlation between homesickness and extraversion as well. However, Gasselsberger (1982) failed to find a clear relationship between homesickness and extraversion.

Rigidity: a high level of rigidity appears to be characteristic of people suffering from homesickness as well. Some researchers consider rigidity to be important only among females (Voolstra, 1992; Gruijters, 1992). Eurelings-Bontekoe, however, found a high level of rigidity among homesick males and females (Eurelings-Bontekoe *et al.*, 1994; 1995; 1996; Verschuur *et al.*, 2001; 2003).

Dominance: in contrast to homesick males, who are less dominant than their non-homesick counterparts, dominance does not play a role in homesick females (Eurelings-Bontekoe *et al.*, 1996). This might be due to a kind of 'bottom-effect.' Women in general tend to be less dominant than men, implying that any dominance related effects on homesickness should be stronger among males than among females.

Subassertiveness and social withdrawal: a lack of self-esteem and subassertiveness appears to be characteristic of homesick persons as well (Carden & Feight, 1991; Eurelings-Bontekoe *et al.*, 1994; 1995; 1996; Voolstra, 1992). Verschuur *et al.* (2003) found a low level of *Self-Directedness* as measured with the Temperament and Character Inventory developed by Cloninger *et al.* (1994) to be predictive of homesickness severity. This lack of self-confidence may underlie the strong tendency of homesick subjects to avoid social contacts. Bergsma (cited in Dijkstra and Hendriks, 1983) found that 81% of homesick military conscripts had not made new friends during their stay in the army as compared with 11% of the non-homesick soldiers. In addition, Bergsma reported that 55% of the homesick subjects did not have any friends at home either, as opposed to 20% of the non-homesick subjects. Brewin *et al.* (1989) provided evidence that especially the depressed and anxious homesick students tend to socially withdraw, unless the social interaction was related in some way to feelings of homesickness.

Neuroticism: several investigators have found a positive association between neuroticism and homesickness (Eurelings-Bontekoe *et al.*, 1994; Gasselsberger, 1982; Rümke, cited in Gruijters, 1992). Voolstra (1992) in a study among 206 males and females from the general population even found neuroticism to be the best predictor of homesickness. These results strongly suggest that homesick individuals tend to be unstable, tense, anxious, worrying and irritable.

It is important to note that a low level of extraversion and assertiveness and a high level of rigidity appear to accompany homesickness in men (Eurelings-Bontekoe *et al.*, 1994; 1995) and women (Eurelings-Bontekoe *et al.*, 1996). However, in the studies among males a checklist had been used to identify the presence of homesickness (homesickness as a state), whereas in the study among females the focus was on self-reported homesickness of either a chronic (state) or an episodic nature. Individuals with the latter type of homesickness were not in an actual state of homesickness, but they did nevertheless display corresponding personality characteristics as the females who were chronically homesick. These results thus suggest (1) that the personality factors extraversion, rigidity and assertiveness are important markers of the vulnerability to develop homesickness irrespective of sex and the way homesickness has been operationalized and assessed and (2) that the personality variables found to be associated with homesickness are not the consequences of being in a state of homesickness.

Homesickness and personality disorders

Eurelings-Bontekoe *et al.* (1994) demonstrated that homesick military conscripts were socially withdrawn and tied to their parental home already from an early age on: characteristic for homesick conscripts was that they had spent fewer vacations without parents or alone. Moreover, they disliked school excursions, frequently stayed home and evaluated visiting friends as less pleasant. They suffered from homesickness already from the age of eight on. Homesickness experiences early in life were also found to be characteristic of homesick females (Eurelings-Bontekoe *et al.*, 1996).

This latter finding led us to formulate the hypothesis that the proneness to develop homesickness may be related to a structural vulnerability of personality. If this is indeed the case, there is the possibility that homesickness might also be associated with certain personality disorders. This hypothesis was examined in two studies: the first one compared the prevalence of personality disorders among soldiers suffering from homesickness with the prevalence found among soldiers with psychological problems of a different nature and among a healthy control group (Eurelings-Bontekoe *et al.*, 1996). The second study was carried out among females with two types of self-reported homesickness: a group of females suffering from chronic feelings of homesickness, e.g., due to a residential move, and a group of females suffering from episodic attacks of homesickness, each time they leave their homes for holidays or during stay-overs (Eurelings-Bontekoe *et al.*, 1998). Personality disorders and personality disorder traits were assessed by means of the Questionnaire on Personality Traits (Vragenlijst voor Kenmerken van de Persoonlijkheid (VKP), Duijsens *et al.*, 1993 a, b), a newly developed self-report for the assessment of personality disorders according to DSM-III-R (APA, 1987) and ICD-10 (WHO, 1993). This self-report is based on the International Personality Disorder Examination, a semistructured interview for the assessment of personality disorders according to DSM-III-R and ICD-10 (IPDE; Diekstra *et al.*, 1993; World Health Organization, 1993).

ICD-10 and DSM-III-R are different, but overlapping classification systems (see *Table 12.1* for a comparison of the classification of personality disorders according to the two systems). DSM-III-R groups 11 personality disorders into three clusters: the A ('odd,' severe psychopathology) cluster, including the paranoid, schizoid and schizotypal personality disorders, the B ('impulsive, dramatic') cluster, which includes the histrionic, narcissistic, borderline and antisocial personality disorders and, finally, the C ('anxious') cluster, including the avoidant, dependent, obsessive compulsive and passive aggressive personality disorders. ICD-10 does not explicitly use these three clusters, although a similar grouping can be made. Although the DSM-III-R antisocial personality disorder parallels the ICD-10 dyssocial disorder, there is a substantial conceptual difference between the two disorders: DSM-III-R emphasizes lawbreaking and criminal acts, while ICD-10 includes concepts like lack of empathy, the inability to profit from experiences and the inability to maintain enduring relationships. The questions of the VKP are based on the DSM-III-R and ICD-10 criteria. If a DSM-III-R and a ICD-10 criterion slightly differ from each other, the ICD-10 criterion is used. Most criteria are investigated by one question, 20 criteria are investigated by more than one question. The VKP assesses

Table 12.1. Comparison of classification of personality disorders in DSM-III-R and ICD-10

DSM-III-R	ICD-10
Paranoid	Paranoid
Schizoid	Schizoid
Schizotypical	Absent here, classified with schizophrenia and delusional disorders
Antisocial	Dissocial
Borderline	Emotionally unstable: borderline type
	Emotionally unstable: impulsive type
Histrionic	Histrionic
Narcissistic	Absent in ICD-10
Avoidant	Anxious
Dependent	Dependent
Obsessive-compulsive	Anankastic
Passive aggressive	Absent in ICD-10

all 13 DSM-III-R personality disorders, including the self-defeating and sadistic disorder (American Psychiatric Association, 1987) and nine ICD-10 personality disorders (World Health Organization, 1993). The VKP consists of 174 items, all to be answered with true ((2), ? (1)) or false (0) and in some cases with 'not applicable' (0). All questions are positively formulated. Although this increases the risk of response bias and of artificially high correlations among the personality disorder scales, it has been a deliberate choice to do so in order to maximize the correspondence with the classification systems and the IPDE. Although the reliability of this instrument in terms of internal consistency and temporal stability appears to be relatively modest, reliability figures are comparable to those found with other criterion based instruments (Duijsens *et al.*, 1996). In addition, Duijsens *et al.* (1996) compared the VKP with the IPDE and found the VKP scales to have good convergent and discriminant validity. Although the VKP-subscales were intercorrelated, the highest correlations were found with the corresponding IPDE-scales; correlations between scales measuring different concepts were rather low.

Results of the first study revealed that the prevalence of personality disorders among homesick conscripts is virtually comparable to that found among soldiers suffering from psychological problems of a different nature: slightly more than half of the homesick individuals as well as of the persons with other psychological problems suffered from one or more personality disorders, whereas this was the case among only 17% of the healthy controls. The prevalences of the DSM-III-R dependent, avoidant and obsessive-compulsive personality disorders and personality disorder traits and the ICD-10 anankastic personality disorder and the ICD-10 anankastic, anxious and dependent personality disorder traits were significantly higher among the homesick soldiers than among both control groups.

In addition, homesick persons scored significantly higher than both control groups on the ICD-10 paranoid personality disorder scale. Finally, the homesick group appeared to be significantly less antisocial than the psychiatric controls, whereas the prevalences of the ICD-10 dissocial personality disorders were equal in both problematic groups. The high level of personality pathology among the homesick might be due to the way homesickness has been operationalized: all of the items of the 9-item checklist except the first one, which assesses the desire to go home, describe symptoms of major depression. It is well known that the comorbidity between depressive disorders and especially the dependent and avoidant personality disorders is relatively high (van den Brink, 1989).

The aim of the second study was to investigate the link between homesickness and personality disorders in a group of females. In contrast to the former study among males, this study operationalized homesickness by means of self-report and a distinction was made between chronic and episodic homesickness. Both homesick groups showed in general markedly more signs of personality pathology than the healthy controls irrespective of whether one was in an actual state of homesickness or not. The percentage of females suffering from one or more disorders was for both homesick groups approximately 40%. In contrast, only about 16% of the healthy controls suffered from one or more disorders. DSM-III-R paranoid, avoidant and dependent and the ICD-10 anankastic, anxious and dependent personality disorders appeared to be the most prevalent disorders in both types of homesick females. In addition, the prevalence of the passive aggressive disorder was relatively high among the chronic homesick females.

Although homesick females, more so than homesick males, t were found to be hostile (see also Voolstra, 1992), homesickness appeared to be incompatible with antisocial traits and behavior in females. This suggests that those who suffer from chronic feelings of homesickness do not tend to behave in an openly aggressive way. In other words, homesick individuals tend to internalize rather than externalize problems. This tendency to internalizing behavior was also found by Thurber (1995) among a group of homesick preadolescent and adolescent boys.

The high level of personality pathology among homesick females is consistent with results of the study on personality pathology among homesick males, despite the fact that the latter study used a different population and operationalized homesickness by means of the 9-item checklist, covering both actual homesickness experiences and symptoms of major depression, which could have resulted in a bias towards more severe personality pathology. To summarize, the conclusion seems warranted that homesickness is associated with personality pathology, irrespective of sex, age, the way homesickness has been operationalized and assessed, or whether one is in an actual state of homesickness or not. More precisely, our results suggest that homesickness is associated with traits of the anankastic/obsessive-compulsive, dependent and avoidant/anxious personality disorders and with a high level of rigidity, subassertiveness and introversion and a low level of dominance. In other words, homesick persons experience a strong need for personal control and for the support from familiar persons, together with a high level of social anxiety. These characteristics may render functioning in and adaptation to a strange, new environment with unfamiliar persons rather difficult and distress provoking, in particular when separation is out of the individual's control.

Homesickness and Attachment

Eurelings-Bontekoe *et al.* (2003) studied the association between homesickness proneness, personality disorders and the perceived quality of attachment among 128 first year university students. The results of this study showed that homesickness-proneness is in particular associated with features of the DSM-IV/ICD-10 avoidant/anxious personality disorders and, in addition, with a perceived high level of parental support and protection by the parents. This implies that those individuals who are anxious and avoidant and who highly value the support and protection of their parents have a greater risk of developing homesickness.

However, given the cross-sectional nature of the data it remained unclear whether a strong reliance on parental support and parental overprotection should be regarded as an etiological factor in the development of anxious and avoidant traits and homesickness proneness, or whether these traits have reinforced the reliance on parental support and protection. It is to be expected that a high level of dependency upon the support of the parents interacts with a high level of anxiety and avoidance resulting in homesickness proneness, i.e., a failure to separate from the parents and to adapt to a novel situation after having left the parental home. The results of this study pointed to the necessity to further explore the link between homesickness-proneness and attachment with instruments using a different conceptualisation of attachment. A possible instrument could be the Relationship Scales Questionnaire, developed by Griffin and Bartholomew (1994). The RSQ distinguishes, in addition to one secure, favourable attachment style, three types of problematic attachment-styles: (1) fearful attachment, (2) preoccupied attachment and (3) dismissing attachment. It was thereby hypothesised that homesick individuals are characterised by a preoccupied or fearful style of attachment, implying a negative, helpless image of the self combined with either a positive image of the other in case of the preoccupied style or a negative model of other in case of the fearful attachment style. In a study among 573 international students from 48 different countries on the association between the strength of "Sense of Place", attachment styles and adjustment difficulties after relocation Eurelings-Bontekoe & Ota (in preparation) found that individuals with either a "fearful" or a "preoccupied" attachment style are "at risk" of developing adaptation difficulties immediately after relocation. In addition, persons who ascribe a significant portion of their identity to belonging to the "place they come from" and who *simultaneously* report a fearful or, to a lesser extent, preoccupied attachment style seem to experience the most adjustment difficulties after relocation. These individuals appear to experience increasing difficulty over time in connecting with and fitting into their new environment. These results suggest that professionals involved with the internationally mobile should be extra alert to persons with especially a fearful attachment style and a strong Sense of Place: they are likely to be so rigidly rooted to a former place called "home" that any chance of adjusting to and accepting their new place seems slim. Attachment security, on the other hand, provides the best long-term means for metabolizing the challenges of the relocation, regardless of the strength of Sense of Place.

Experiences of homesick females

Extensive discussions with 21 homesick women from the female study groups gave us the opportunity to obtain more in-depth information and to shed some more light on the results. Fourteen (66%) of these women had experienced their early environment as neglecting; the remaining seven had experienced overconcern. In addition, eight (38%) had experienced the sudden death of a parent or a sibling during childhood, which subsequently led to the (once true, but now irrational) basic assumption that you should never leave the persons you love, because they may leave you suddenly and unexpectedly at any moment in time.

More than half of the women had been sent to boarding school. These women felt they were sent away, because they were not loved or wanted by their parents. Virtually all of the women reported their present situation to be an ambiguous one: on the one hand they felt very attached to and dependent upon others, feeling a strong responsibility for the well-being of their partners or parents and for the harmony in the family, whereas on the other hand they reported to feel pressured, angry and unsatisfied with their situation and showed a strong desire to be more independent and individualistic. Feelings of anger and dissatisfaction seemed however difficult to handle and difficult to express. Perhaps homesickness, in particular episodic (holidays-related) homesickness, may have a function in this respect. For example, one woman suffering from homesickness during holidays told us that what she disliked most about going on holidays was that she felt forced to spend every hour with her partner and family. Another woman got homesick whenever on holidays with the family because her husband, who never had time to participate in doing the household, did not want to help doing the household during holidays either. Because holidays confronted her with the fact that she had an inflexible, 'unloving' husband, she wanted to stay at home where she felt less aware of this fact.

Results suggest that among approximately 50% of homesick individuals the vulnerability to develop homesickness is structurally anchored in personality and is probably related to early developmental factors. The women's stories revealed that most of these women had insecure attachment experiences during childhood. It seemed as if the homesick women had become afraid of loosing (the love, support and approval of) those who are close to them. Being independent, assertive or *openly* aggressive could lead to a confrontation and hence to feared rejection. Instead, making oneself dependent upon the partner or family gives one the 'reassurance' of not being abandoned. This fear of rejection may not only account for the high prevalence of the passive aggressive and dependent personality disorders but also for the high prevalence of the avoidant personality disorder: avoidant people are generally unwilling to enter into relationships unless given an unusual strong guarantee of uncritical acceptance. Results of the studies on attachment and homesickness empirically underpin the importance of an insecure attachment style, in particular a fearful attachment style as a predictor for homesickness and allocation difficulties.

A psychodynamic frame of reference

Although unusual in homesickness research and perhaps speculative, I nevertheless would like to propose a psychodynamic theoretical frame of reference for the here presented findings and observations. More precisely, I would like to emphasize the link between homesickness and separation anxiety, which results from anxious attachment and narcissistic vulnerability. These conditions may both originate from adverse family experiences during childhood, such as (threats of) abandonment or rejection by parents or to a parent's or sibling's illness or death for which the child feels responsible (Murray Parkes *et al.*, 1991). Although both anxious attachment as well as a high narcissistic vulnerability may give rise to symptoms other than homesickness, such as for instance agoraphobia (de Ruiter, 1992) and severe depression (Kernberg, 1986), it will be argued that homesickness may be another possible manifestation of these conditions.

Homesickness as a manifestation of separation anxiety

DSM-IV has included homesickness as one possible manifestation of separation anxiety disorder, noting that some children with separation anxiety disorder become distressed especially after separation (Thurber, 1995). From a psychodynamic point of view, separation anxiety may be considered as a psychopathological condition pointing to attachment disturbances. This may develop itself during the processes of separation and individuation, which at an early age may manifest itself for instance in school phobia and a dislike of school-excursions. Infringements of the mother-infant tie, for whatever reasons, may give rise to separation anxiety. Failure of the mother to play her part as a reliable need fulfilling and comfort giving person will cause breakdown in individuation and autonomy or depression and the development of highly ambivalent relationships. It is only after object constancy and individuation have been reached that the external absence of the object is substituted by the presence of a stable internal image and a lengthy separation can be tolerated without developing symptoms of distress. In addition, separation is only possible if one is able to tolerate and integrate aggressive feelings towards the parental figures. When, however, there are strong unintegrated, hence anxiety provoking hostile feelings directed towards the parents, this will result in the inability to separate: out of fear of loosing the attachment figure, these hostile feelings are not expressed and constructively utilized for separation (externalizing behavior), but, instead, are dealt with by clinging and dependent behavior and by defensive idealization of the parental figures. The aggressive side of the relationship is however denied, repressed or introjected, resulting in internalizing behavior such as social anxiety, subassertiveness and avoidance of social contacts, dependency, self blame and low self-esteem, all to ensure the safety of the objects 'threatened' by the individual's aggression. The process of individuation and separating from parental figures may last well into late adolescence and early adulthood. A very important issue during the second individuation process taking place during adolescence is deidealization of the parents. If it is successful, a progressively more mature mutually satisfying relationship with the parents emerges. The adolescent will at the same time be able to establish new and extrafamilial relationships and to share emotions with friend and lovers (Tyson & Tyson, 1990). It is very well possible that among those who suffer from severe homesickness this early process of separation-individuation from the parents has not been successful, which may have resulted in the development of a fearful and/or preoccupied attachment style, which in turn manifested itself initially in feelings of homesickness already at an early age and subsequently in enduring and life-long difficulties in separating from familiar persons and familiar environments in general. Insecure fearful attachment and the subsequent difficulties with separation will lead to recurrent feelings of homesickness each time a separation is necessary.

Homesickness as a possible manifestation of narcissistic vulnerability

In line with psychodynamic theory it could further be argued that the vulnerability to develop homesickness may be one possible manifestation of a narcissistically damaged, fragile sense of self. Narcissistic traits can develop when there are deviations from ideal rearing on either side: pampering (separation occurring too late) or neglecting (separation occurring too early), expecting too much or too little (Stone, 1993). The following characteristics are typical of narcissistically damaged people (Kernberg, 1986):

1. A constant search for symbiosis with ideal people in ideal relationships, which links to a profound tendency toward idealization. This search for symbiosis and idealization might interfere with the process of deidealization, so necessary for successful separation.
2. A profound need for personal control: the other person is forced to fulfill completely the narcissistically hurt persons' expectations and loss of control over the other is felt as loss of the sense of self. The motto seems to be: 'to control or being controlled.' This pronounced need for personal control might render adaptations to new situations, where control is less than usual, extremely difficult

and anxiety provoking, which may result in feelings of homesickness. Feelings of homesickness might in turn be considered as an attempt to reassume control over the situation. For instance, homesick conscripts are allowed to return home and females, becoming homesick when on holidays more or less force the family to interrupt holidays and return home. This strong need for control might explain the high prevalence of obsessive compulsive and anankastic personality traits and the high level of rigidity found to be characteristic of people suffering from homesickness.

3. Another characteristic of the narcissistically wounded person is his/her pronounced need to depend upon others for love, admiration and social support, while at the same time these needs can hardly be satisfied; the slightest insult will be subjectively interpreted as abandonment and blame. A considerable number of narcissistic people is constantly in a state of *"angry dependency"* and hypervigilant to the slightest hurt to self-esteem (Gabbard, 1990). These features of narcissism might as well explain the simultaneous presence of dependent and avoidant personality traits and the presence and feelings of anger among homesick subjects.

Diagnostic and therapeutic considerations

We presume that a psychodynamic developmental perspective on homesickness might be of value as a guideline with respect to the clinical management of this condition and complementary to the more commonly applied behavioral techniques, such as controlled breathing, (Larbig et al., , 1979), social skills training, active and physical activities, thought stopping and 'time-out for worry' (Vingerhoets et al., 1993; Van Tilburg et al., 1996), rational emotive therapy (Chartoff, see Vingerhoets et al., 1993) and writing about homesickness on a daily basis (Pennebaker, 1990).

Regarding the early detection of homesickness proneness a brief "front door" screening could take place by assessing the strength of an individual's bond with the former place he lived in together with his or her attachment style, by using measures like the RSQ (Griffin & Bartholomew, 1994). If identity is mainly determined by being part of the former place and there is, simultaneously a fearful or preoccupied attachment style, adjustment difficulties may be expected. This type of assessment could offer an efficient early warning system to flag those individuals likely to experience significant difficulties in relocation, thereby allowing for the implementation of interventions earlier in the moving process for those who most need support.

With respect to the clinical detection of homesickness, the following may be of importance: far more persons admit to suffer or have been suffering from homesickness if they have to answer questions such as "Were you ever homesick?" or "Do you feel homesick at the moment?", than in case of a spontaneous report (Fisher, 1988). It seems as if there is a threshold to label feelings of distress and

192

depression spontaneously as homesickness, which might be related to culturally and individually determined differences in the degree of acceptability and shamefulness of the labels 'depression' and 'homesickness.' This means that if a depressed patient is not asked directly about homesickness, the diagnosis 'homesickness' might be missed. If so, mental health care workers, working with patients who got depressed after a residential move, such as elderly, who had to leave their homes, or female patients who followed their husband to another city, might help the patients by labeling the depressive feeling as homesickness right away, thereby providing an explanation and a context for the depressive feelings, which in turn may make the depression less vague, less out of control and more understandable to the patient. Another advantage of narrowing the broad concept of depression to that of homesickness, when appropriate, is that it provides a distinct guideline and focus for the clinical management: the treatment may now directly and specifically focus on the feelings of homesickness and the specific issues related to these feelings as described in the next part rather than on depression in general, which might increase therapeutic efficacy.

An appropriate treatment could combine both the psychodynamic and the behavioral perspective and could aim at:

1. Confronting the person with his negative/aggressive feelings towards his/her partner and parents and increasing the tolerance for and the integration of these feelings. It might be useful to clarify to the patient that being homesick might serve two functions at the same time: expression of negative feelings and of the experienced powerlessness and at the same time an attempt to ward off these feelings. Assertiveness training might prove to be helpful in learning how to express negative feelings in a modulated and more appropriate fashion.
2. Confronting the person with the defensive character of idealization, of 'giving without taking' and of the strong feelings of responsibility for the other one's well-being.
3. Clarifying and challenging the cognitive beliefs about the necessity of being dependent and having total control by explaining how they once were adaptive, but now maladaptive.
4. Increasing feelings of safety in the new environment.
5. Increasing social skills and social contacts.
6. Loosening the tie with the former environment and increasing emotional investment in the new environment.
7. Increasing firmness of identity, self-esteem and autonomy and decreasing narcissistic vulnerability and dependency by encouraging the persons own sense of ability and confronting the person with his or her (hidden) wish to function independently.

Finally, since severe, long lasting homesickness is likely to be related to early developmental factors as an insecure, fearful attachment style and since early attachment patterns are quite firmly rooted in personality, it seems likely that this type of severe homesickness is rather intractable. The main aim of therapy could be to provide the patient with support and with information as how to cope best with this deep-seated personal vulnerability.

References

American Psychiatric Association (1987). *Diagnostic and statistical manual of mental disorders. DSM-III-R (3rd ed. revised)*. Washington, DC: American Psychiatric Association.

American Psychiatric Association (1994). *Diagnostic and statistical manual of mental disorders. DSM-IV*. Washington, DC: American Psychiatric Association.

Brewin, C. R., Furnham, A., & Howes, M. (1989). Demographic and psychological determinants of homesickness and confiding among students. *British Journal of Psychology, 80,* 467-477.

Brink, W. van den (1989). *Meting van DSM-III-R persoonlijkheids-pathologie. Betrouwbaarheid en validiteit van de SIDP-R en as II van de DSM*. PhD thesis, University of Groningen, The Netherlands.

Carden, A. I., & Feicht, R. (1991). Homesickness among American and Turkish college students. *Journal of Cross-Cultural Psychology, 22,* 418-428.

Cloninger, C. R., Przybeck, T. R., Svrakic, D. M., & Wetzel, R. D. (1994). *The Temperament and Character Inventory (TCI): A guide to its development and use*. St. Louis, MO: Center for Psychobiology of Personality, Washington University.

Cohen, S., & Syme, S. L. (1985). Issues in the study and application of social support. In: S. Cohen & S. L. Syme (Eds.), *Social support and health* (pp 3-22). Orlando, FL: Academic Press.

Diekstra, R. F. W., Duijsens, I. J., Eurelings-Bontekoe, E. H. M., & Ouwersloot, G. (1993). *International personality disorder examination, IPDE, version 1.1. Interview manual*. Lisse:, the Netherlands: Swets & Zeitlinger.

Dijkstra, S. J., & Hendrix, M. J. J. L. (1983). Heimwee, een verkenning [Homesickness, an exploration]. *De Psycholoog, 18,* 3-10.

Duijsens, I. J., Eurelings-Bontekoe, E. H. M., Diekstra, R. F. W., & Ouwersloot, G. (1993a). *Vragenlijst voor Kenmerken van de Persoonlijkheid (VKP)*. Lisse, The Netherlands: Swets & Zeitlinger.

Duijsens, I. J., Eurelings-Bontekoe, E. H. M., Diekstra, R. F. W., & Ouwersloot, G. (1993b). *VKP. Preliminary manual*. Lisse, The Netherlands: Swets & Zeitlinger.

Duijsens, I. J., Eurelings-Bontekoe, E. H. M., & Diekstra, R. F. W. (1996). The VKP, a self report instrument for DSM-III-R and ICD-10 Personality disorders: Construction and psychometric properties. *Personality and Individual Differences, 20,* 171-182.

Duijsens, I. J., Bruinsma, M., Jansen, S. J. T., Eurelings-Bontekoe, E. H. M., & Diekstra, R. F. W. (1996). Agreement between self-report and semi-structured interviewing in the Assessment of Personality Disorders. *Personality and Individual Differences, 21,* 271-270.

Eurelings-Bontekoe, E. H. M., Vingerhoets, A. J. J. M., & Fontijn, T. (1994). Personality and behavioural antecedents of homesickness. *Personality and Individual Differences, 16,* 229-235.

Eurelings-Bontekoe, E. H. M., Verschuur, M., Koudstaal, A., van der Sar, S., & Duijsens, I. J. (1995). Construction of a Homesickness Questionnaire: preliminary results. *Personality and Individual Differences, 19,* 319-325.

Eurelings-Bontekoe, E. H. M., Tolsma, A., Verschuur, M., & Vingerhoets, A. J. J. M. (1996). Construction of a Homesickness Questionnaire using a female population with two types of self reported homesickness. Preliminary Results. *Personality and Individual Differences, 20,* 415-421.

Eurelings-Bontekoe, E. H. M., Duijsens, I. J., & Verschuur, M. (1996). Prevalence of DSM-III-R and ICD-10 personality disorders among military conscripts suffering from homesickness. *Personality and Individual Differences, 21,* 431-440.

Eurelings-Bontekoe, E. H. M., Brouwers, E., Verschuur, M., & Duijsens, I. J. (1998). DSM-III-R and ICD-10 personality disorder features among women experiencing two types of self reported homesickness. An exploratory study. *British Journal of Psychology, 89,* 405-416.

Eurelings-Bontekoe, E. H. M., Brouwers, E. P. M., & Verschuur, M. J.(2000). Homesickness among foreign employees of a high tech company in the Netherlands. *Environment and Behavior, 32,* 443-456.

Eurelings-Bontekoe, E. H. M., Verschuur, M. J., Steensma-De Jong, M., & Ter Heide, J. J. (2003). Features of DSM-IV and ICD-10 personality disorders and perceived quality of parental attachment among homesickness-prone first year university students. *Unpublished manuscript.*

Eurelings-Bontekoe, E. H. M., Ota, D., & Verschuur, M. J. (in preparation). Ambiguous grief. The role of sense of place and attachment style in the adjustment of mobile adolescents.

Eurelings-Bontekoe, E. H. M. (in press). Social support in personality disordered patients. A multidimensional approach to assessment and treatment. In: B. Rörhle & A. R. Laireiter (Eds.), *Soziale Unterstützung und Psychotherapie.* Berlin, Germany: DGTV Verlag.

Fisher, S. (1988). Leaving home: Homesickness and the psychological effects of change and transition. In: S. Fisher & J. Reason (Eds.), *Handbook of life stress, cognition and health.* New York: Wiley and Sons.

Fisher, S. (1989). *Homesickness, cognition and health.* London: Erlbaum.

Gabbard, G. (1990). *Psychodynamic psychiatry in clinical practice.* Washington DC: American Psychiatric Press.

Gasselberger, K. (1982). Depressionsfördernde soziale und territoriale Faktoren von Heimweh-reaktionen [Social and territorial factors as a trigger for depression]. *Zeitschrift für Klinische Psychologie: Forschung und Praxis, 11,* 186-200.

Glickauf-Hughes, C., & Wells, M (1997). *Object-relations Psychotherapy. An individualized and interactive approach to diagnosis and treatment.* Northvale, NJ: Jason Aronson Inc.

Gruijters, I. (1992). *Heimwee en situatiekenmerken* [Homesickness and situational characteristics]. Unpublished M.A. thesis. Tilburg, The Netherlands.: Tilburg University.

Heller, K. (1979). The effects of social support: Prevention and treatment implications. In: A. P. Goldstein & F. H. Kanfer (Eds.), *Maximizing treatment gains: Transfer enhancement in psychotherapy* (pp 353-382). New York: Academic Press.

Heller, K., & Swindle, R. W. (1983). Social network, perceived social support and coping with stress. In: R. D. Felner, L. A. Jason, J. Moritsugund, & S. S. Farber (Eds.), *Preventive psychology; Research and practice in community intervention* (pp 87-103). New York: Pergamon Press.

Hobfoll, S. E., & Stokes, J. P. (1988). The process and mechanics of social support. In: S. W. Duck (Ed.), *Handbook of personal relationships.* New York: Wiley and Sons.

Kernberg, O. F. (1986). *Severe personality disorders.* New Haven, CT: Yale University Press.

Larbig, W. C., Xenakis, C., & Sato Onishi (1979). Psychosomatische Symptome und funktionelle Beschwerden bei Arbeitnehmern im Ausland- Japaner und Griechen in Deutschland, Deutsche im Ausland [Psychosomatic symptoms and functional complaints among persons working abroad: Japanees and Greek working in Germany, Germans working abroad]. *Zeitschrift für Psychosomatische Medizin und Psychoanalyse, 25,* 49-63.

Lu, L. (1990). Adaptation to British universities: Homesickness and mental health of Chinese students. *Counseling Psychology Quarterly, 3,* 225-232.

Murray Parkes, C., Stevenson-Hinde, J., & Marris, P. (1991). *Attachment across the life cycle.* London/New York: Routledge.

Pennebaker, J. W., Colder, M., & Sharp, L. K. (1990). Accelerating the coping process. *Journal of Personality and Social Psychology, 58,* 528-537.

Stone, M. H. (1993). *Abnormalities of Personality. Within and beyond the realm of treatment.* New York: Norton.

Ruiter, C. de (1992). Agorafobie en angstig-ambivalente gehechtheid: Suggesties voor de gedragstherapie [Agoraphobia and anxious-ambivalent attachment: Suggestions for behavioral therapy]. *Gedragstherapie, 25,* 69-91.

Tyson, Ph., & Tyson, R. L. (1990). *Psychoanalytic theories of development. An integration.* New Haven, CT: Yale University Press.

Thurber, C. A. (1995). The experience and expression of homesickness in preadolescent and adolescent boys. *Child Development, 66,* 1162-1178.

Van Tilburg, M. A. L., Vingerhoets, A. J. J. M., & van Heck, G. L. (1996). Homesickness: A review of the literature. *Psychological Medicine, 26,* 899-912.

Verschuur, M. J., Eurelings-Bontekoe, E. H. M., & Spinhoven, Ph. (2001). Construction and Validation of the Homesickness Vulnerability Questionnaire. *Personality and Individual Differences, 30,* 11-19.

Verschuur, M. J., Eurelings-Bontekoe, E. H. M., & Spinhoven, Ph. (2003). Homesickness, Temperament & Character. *Personality and Individual Differences, 35,* 757-770.

Verschuur, M. J., Eurelings-Bontekoe, E. H. M., & Spinhoven, Ph. (2004). Associations among homesickness, anger, anxiety, and depression. *Psychological Reports, 94,* 1155-1170.

Vingerhoets, A. J. J. M., van Heck, G. L., Gruijters, I., Thijs, H., & Voolstra, A. (1993). Heimwee. Een literatuuroverzicht [Homesickness: A review of the literature]. *Gedrag en Gezondheid, 21,* 227-237.

Voolstra, A. (1992). *Heimwee en persoonlijkheid* [Homesickness and personality]. Unpublished doctoral thesis. Tilburg, The Netherlands: Tilburg University.

West, M., Rose, M. S., & Sheldon-Keller, A. (1994). Assessment of patterns of insecure attachment in adults and application to dependent and schizoid personality disorders. *Journal of Personality Disorders 8,* 249-256.

World Health Organization (1993). *The ICD-10 classification of mental and behavioral disorders. Diagnostic criteria for research.* Geneva, Switzerland: World Health Organization.

13 Health Issues in International Tourism: The Role of Health Behavior, Stress and Adaptation

AD VINGERHOETS, NANDA SANDERS, WENDELA KUPER

Introduction

In the last decades, people from western countries travel increasingly and more often abroad, visit exotic places, and come into contact with different cultures (cf. Cossar, 2000; Cossar & Reid, 1989). For example, according to recent figures from the Dutch Tourism Office and the Dutch Central Statistical Office, approximately 81% of the Dutch population spend their annual vacation away from home and 39% go abroad for a longer period (CBS, 2004). Worldwide, the number of international tourists increased from 26 million in 1949 to 429 million in 1990 (Cossar, 2000). The increase in the number of international tourists is paralleled by an increased number of contacts with emergency centers, which are encumbered by travelers with serious mental or physical health problems, who in some cases need to be repatriated. This number probably only reflects the top of the iceberg where tourists' health problems are concerned, since the more frequent but less dramatic forms of somatic and psychic health problems associated with traveling/ being abroad will not be reported and can only be investigated in specific studies (e.g., Cossar et al., 1990; Page et al., 1994).

The aims of the present contribution are twofold. Firstly, we want to give a brief review of the minor and major health problems typically faced by the international traveler. We will also identify and briefly discuss the health risks and the adverse health practices of international tourists. Secondly, we will argue that tourists may be at greater risk because their resistance may be lowered due to exposure to typical holiday stressors and because of the physiological challenge of adaptation to the new holiday environment. There is little doubt that many of the associated health problems can in principle be prevented, since most problems are caused by taking inadequate health precautions. We agree with authors like Cossar (1996) and Page et al. (1994) when they state that the time is ripe for more specific scientific investigation into the issue of international traveling and the related health aspects. The above-mentioned increase in the numbers of international tourists and business travelers has not been paralleled by an equal interest on the part of investigators into the inherent health issues. Our aim is to provide a health psychological basis for health promotion campaigns for the international tourist aimed at reducing the number of incidents. Our discussion will focus mainly on the health psychological aspects instead of on merely medical or epidemiological points of view, like, for example, in the studies of Cossar and Reid (1989) and Pasini (1989). For a more extensive discussion of travel medicine, the reader is recommended to consult the recent volume Travel medicine and migrant health (Lockie *et al.*, 2000). For the specific psychiatric aspects of traveling, the reader is referred to the chapter by Monden in this volume.

The health risks of international travelers

The traveler seems to be vulnerable to health hazards on account of the very nature of the travel itself and because of being in a new environment (Costar, 1996). Traveling implies being exposed to new cultures and new experiences. We assume that the traveler's ability to cope with such changes depends on his (pre-)existing mental and physical state of health, a factor which in turn is, at least partly, influenced by demographic variables, personality factors and health behavior.

The health risks of the international tourist are manifold and diverse. Traveling may be associated with sustaining possibly serious injuries due to traffic accidents, or with putting up with minor but rather annoying health problems like travel sickness and jet lag. Abundant use of alcoholic beverages and recreational drugs are not uncommon. Sun tanning may be excessive. Sleep patterns may be disturbed and practicing unprotected sex has its inherent health risks. There might be further exposure to unfamiliar pathogens, which may form a serious threat to one's health status, because of the lack of natural resistance we have to such micro-organisms. We shall discuss below these problems in more detail devoting attention to the stressors associated with traveling and vacations. Finally, a discussion of some aspects of modern stress theories will be presented, which we feel are relevant to the holiday situation.

The journey

Whereas public transport and air travel may be generally thought of as safe modes of transport, traveling by car seems to carry more risks. Drivers often fail to rest sufficiently before and during the long journeys to their holiday destinations, which may sometimes result in a dangerous combination of sleepiness, inclement weather and hectic or unknown traffic situations. It has been established that the efficiency of car driving is affected by ambient temperature. Both cold (< 50° F) and hot (> 90° F) temperatures may negatively affect driving performance because grip strength is reduced and muscle dexterity impaired. In addition, there is diminished and less sensitive tactile discrimination and poorer vigilance and tracking performance. It is common practice for youngsters to buy themselves (very) cheap but unsafe 'holiday' cars. Unanticipated traffic jams, the behavior of impatient and bored fellow travelers or the aggression of fellow road users may turn the journey into a rather stressful experience. This is not to speak of the possible accidents, breakdowns, or travel-sickness among journey fellow travelers, all of which may make heavy demands on one's adaptational resources. Finally, there is some evidence that carbon monoxide and oxidants in the blood of drivers may negatively affect mental responsiveness. For a review of these factors, the reader is referred to Bell *et al.* (1996). In addition, driving with a caravan might enhance the risk of myocardial infarction during the first two days of one's vacation travel.

Although air travel may be considered a safe way of transport, it does not preclude the occurrence of health problems. A common cold may turn a potentially pleasant flight into a very painful and stressful event. Unstable atmospheric conditions may facilitate the development of travel-sickness, characterized by nausea and vomiting. These health problems are generally not too serious and as far as is known hardly any research has so far focused on these aspects of traveling (see for further information on motion sickness Bick, 1983; Dobie & May, 1995; and Reason & Brand, 1975). By contrast, more is known about jet lag, which results from the rapid crossing of time zones. The recent (relevant) literature is summarized below.

Crossing time zones
In former times one used to travel by boat or by train and the transition to another time zone went gradually. Nowadays, airplanes travel fast and cross time zones forcing travelers to adapt to new times. Jet lag or 'time zone fatigue' can be regarded as an entirely self-inflicted condition resulting from transmeridian air travel. It is often accompanied by several subjective symptoms, including difficulties with concentration, fatigue, disorientation, loss of appetite, gastrointestinal disturbances, and lightheadedness.

Air travelers also frequently report experiencing delayed sleep phase syndrome after flying eastwards and transient advanced sleep phase syndrome after flying westwards (Lewy *et al.*, 1996). There are important individual differences in the type and severity of the symptoms that one experiences. It is not yet clear whether repeated time zone transitions always induce the same symptoms within an individual. On the other hand, it has been established that the severity of the symptoms increases with the number of time zones crossed. When crossing more than six time zones it will take four to eight days to adapt to the new time zone situation. Flying eastwards demands longer periods of readjustment and is more tiresome than flying westwards. These eastward bound travelers have great difficulty falling asleep before 1.00 a.m. Data gathered from experiments with shift-work schedules further suggest that extroverts adapt faster than introverts. The so-called 'evening types' may also be expected to cope better with time shifts than the 'morning types.' Finally, older travelers suffer more from these symptoms.

In the adaptation phase many biological rhythms have to be readjusted some of which will adapt at a slower rate than others. Body temperature, for example, takes more time to adjust to a new time zone than do some hormonal rhythms. During this adaptation phase the human body is more vulnerable to infectious agents. Reviews on this subject have been written by McFarland (1975), Redfern (1989), and Redfern *et al.* (1994).

Alcohol consumption

The adverse effects of alcohol abuse are well known and include impairment of cognitive, perceptual and motor functions for several hours. Long-term heavy drinking is associated with serious health problems like cirrhosis, some forms of cancer, hypertension and heart and brain damage. During their holidays many people consume more alcohol than they normally would, which can lead to recklessness and all kinds of careless behavior, which considerably increases the risk of becoming involved in accidents or conflicts (Sanders *et al.*, 1996). In addition, alcohol can have adverse effects on several travel-related complications, including motion sickness, heat exhaustion, and jet lag (cf. Lange & McCune, 1989). Even relatively small increases can contribute to acute ventricular fibrillation, also known as the 'holiday heart syndrome' (Baars & Tjia, 1990). The symptoms of the holiday heart syndrome-patient include palpitation of the heart, shortness of breath, atypical pain on the chest, dizziness and fainting.

Excessive exposure to the sun

Excessive exposure to sunlight predisposes people to premature skin ageing, skin cancer and to cataract development (Cossar, 1996). The power of the sunlight can be amplified by the effects of water, snow, sand, altitude and latitude. Tanning is considered an enjoyable pastime related to leisure time activity; it is often associated with increased feelings of health and well being, as well as with high self-esteem, fashion and sexuality (Weston, 1996). From 11 a.m. till 3 p.m. direct exposure to the sun should be avoided. During this period the sun is nearest to the earth and ultra violet light is at its most damaging state. Protective clothing, gradual exposure to sunlight and using appropriate sunscreens are all good protective measures against sunburn and skin cancer.

Exposure to unfamiliar pathogens

Animals (humans included) living in a stable environment are able to react relatively rapidly to the continuously changing threat of parasites. However, traveling involves being exposed to new and unfamiliar micro-organisms, which can seriously threaten one's health. How dramatic these effects may be is best illustrated by reports on the effects of native Americans' exposure to viruses from the Old World, such as smallpox, measles, and influenza. It has been established that native American civilizations were primarily struck down by newly introduced diseases of this kind. No less than 90 to 95% of the total indigenous American population has been killed as a consequence of lack of immunological protection against these pathogens. In addition, statistics on British military personnel show a mortality rate of 11.5 per 1,000 among males living in England between 1817 and 1936, whereas the corresponding figure for the English troops stationed in the African Gold Coast was 668 per 1,000. More recent data collected from a retrospective study carried out among 1427 Scottish missionaries who worked abroad between 1873 and 1929 showed that 25% had to return prematurely because of personal or family ill health and a further 11% died in service. Significant differences were found in the numbers affected by adverse health, depending on the period of time, the specific area, and the personal level of medical knowledge (Cossar, 1987, 2000).

Nowadays, we do not simply depend on our inherited immunological resources. We are able to artificially decrease susceptibility to disease by having vaccinations and taking other medication. It is thus desirable to prepare oneself adequately when one travels to regions with specific pathogens.

Hygiene and protection against pathogens

Most complaints of international tourists are related to alimentary issues (diarrhea and/or vomiting). Cartwright (1992) analyzed data on self-reported health problems gathered from as many as 2,756,321 questionnaires, completed during summer seasons from 1984 to 1991. The symptoms of diarrhea often commence during the first few days after arrival in a high-risk area. During the first week the traveler seems to be at highest risk of developing diarrhea. Similar variations between countries were observed over the years. Low incidence rates of such alimentary problems were experienced from Italy and Florida (< 5%), whereas Turkey, Tunisia, and the Dominican Republic had rates of respectively 23%, 34% and 40%. What was also remarkable was the decrease in the peak incidence between the years 1984 and 1986 (15%) dropping to 6% in 1989. It is not entirely clear what mechanisms accounted for this remarkable reduction.

Traveler's diarrhea is essentially a condition that can be prevented, for instance by keeping high standards of health behavior, in particular, those aspects, which are, concerned with the safe provision of water supplies, food and sewage disposal systems (Cartwright, 1996). The traveler is exposed to more risks when he travels to less developed countries, but many safety measures can be taken to prevent diarrhea by, for example washing one's hands after going to the toilet and before handling any food. Food that might possibly be contaminated has to be avoided. One can conclude that the traveler has a great personal responsibility to maintain high levels of hygiene. The highest frequencies of such health problems were reported by the younger age group (20 - 29 years, 48%) in a study by Cossar et al. (1990) with the lowest rates being among those aged 60 and older (20%). Smokers reported more symptoms episodes than non-smokers, but no sex differences were reported.

Other examples of preventable disease conditions associated with traveling are malaria and hepatitis. Malarial parasites are injected into the human bloodstream when one has been bitten by an infected mosquito. The infection produces subsequent attacks of fever varying in severity and frequency. The number of people suffering from malaria is increasing. The solutions proposed in the last century have included using pesticides like DDT, and providing medical treatment with anti-malaria drugs (Rudkin & Hall, 1996). The malarial parasites have not been destroyed by the widespread use of chemical pesticides. Instead they have now developed high genetic resistance to these insecticides. The use of such insecticides has also had negative side effects on other insects. Malarial parasites have also become resistant to anti-malarial prophylaxis. The traveler should take precautions to minimize mosquito bites, because no current antimalarial measures can guarantee absolute protection (Cossar, 1996). Possible preventive measures include taking preventive medication, covering skin with clothing and using mosquito nets over the bed. A final remark concerns the recent observation that antimalaria medication may increase the risk of mental health problems in tourists.

Hepatitis is a viral disease in which the liver becomes inflamed and unable to function properly. The symptoms are like persistent flu and a yellowing of the skin takes place. There are two types of hepatitis: Hepatitis A, which appears to be transmitted when food, water and utensils are contaminated and Hepatitis B which is transmitted by the transfusion of infected blood and by the sharing of contaminated needles by drug addicts. The traveler is more at risk of developing hepatitis A, infectious hepatitis. A possible preventive measure is vaccination before the onset of the journey. Again, it can be said that one should be careful with contaminated food and water.

Sexually transmitted diseases (STD) form another category of preventable diseases sometimes associated with holiday making. Lately there has been an increased interest in the sexual behavior of holidaymakers and expatriates based on concerns related to the HIV/AIDS pandemic (De Graaf et al., 1996; Gillies & Slack, 1996). AIDS is an infectious disease caused by the human immunodeficiency virus (HIV) and it is spread through shared contact with blood and semen. This viral agent attacks the immune system, most notably the helper T-cells. AIDS is an epidemic; its annual mortality rate is alarming. Many millions of people around the world are already infected with the HIV virus and a great majority of these people will eventually die as a result of AIDS (Osborn, 1988). There is the fear in regions of relatively low incidence of HIV/AIDS that traveling to areas of higher incidence may have a substantial impact on the spread of the disease. In the United Kingdom approximately 75% of the heterosexual AIDS/HIV patients have acquired the disease abroad. Although these figures are extremely high for blacks and Asian/oriental males (> 97%), the figures are also impressive for white males (66.8%), while only 26.8% of the white female patients had been exposed to the virus abroad. Studies in the United Kingdom have revealed that the following factors are associated with sexual risk behavior while abroad: traveling without a sexual partner, being male, of the younger age group, increased alcohol consumption and recreational drug use, traveling abroad for longer periods, and having a sexually active lifestyle (Clift, 1996). The spread of STD has thus become associated with travel and tourism. Traveling induces a feeling of freedom, which results in less responsible behavior among tourists (cf. Eiser & Ford, 1995). Especially where alcohol is involved, people seem to forget the risks of HIV/AIDS.

A number of countries, especially in South-East Asia, are well known for their sex tourism. It is not exactly known why so many sex tourists travel to these countries, but one can think of reasons like the sexual novelty and being away from the social constrictions of home. The prevalence of HIV/AIDS is very high among prostitutes in these regions because they lack knowledge on preventive measures for STD. Having unprotected sexual intercourse with these prostitutes is highly risking. Although sex tourism is a significant source of foreign currency income for many of these countries, the severity of the increasing health problems, especially where AIDS is concerned, has forced governments to take action. In Thailand, for example, large-scale health education programs have been set up for prostitutes in order to promote the use of condoms. Up until now, little can be said about the effectiveness of the campaigns.

To summarize, there is ample evidence that for a subgroup of holidaymakers there is a significantly increased tendency to engage in unsafe sex (cf. Gillies & Slack, 1996; Eiser & Ford, 1995). Later on we will argue that the risk of disease might be even greater during holiday periods than in the home situation if the immune system has been weakened by an unhealthy lifestyle and the possible stress of adaptation to the holiday situation.

Climatic and atmospheric conditions
Although it is somewhat beyond the scope of this chapter, we nevertheless want to mention briefly the possible effects of (excessive) heat and cold on the human body. Among the most important effects are heat exhaustion, heat stroke, heath asthenia, and myocardial infarction, resulting from excessive demands made by the body's cooling mechanism on the cardiovascular system. Exposure to extreme cold can lead to conditions such as frostbite and hypothermia. Additional health risks are associated with stays in high-altitude areas and activities like diving under high air-pressure conditions. Alcohol and drugs may significantly interact with these conditions to result in clinically significant health problems (Lange & McCune, 1989).

Acute and serious health conditions
The health problems listed above – except for AIDS – mainly concern acute and less serious threats to one's health or else the possible negative health effects may manifest themselves in the long run. However, data from Dutch emergency centers indicates that tourists also contract more serious diseases. Heart diseases, fractures and concussion are among the most frequently mentioned reasons for contacting the emergency services. Within this category, myocardial infarction is the foremost diagnosis and reason for repatriation. Myocardial infarction is caused by atherosclerosis, narrowing of the arterial walls due to plaque formation that reduces the flow of blood through the arteries and interferes with the passage of nutrients from capillaries to the cells. The temporary deprivation of oxygen supply and nutrients causes chest pain or angina pectoris. The occurrence of an infarction can best be seen as a complex interplay between biological, psychological and social factors (see Kop *et al.*, 2003). Myocardial infarction is a condition that results from months or years of narrowing of the arteries. However, what is more important in the

context of this contribution is the fact that recent publications show that certain acute factors may also play a role in triggering these cardiac events. These acute factors not only include physical environmental factors, but also psychosocial triggers (Mittleman et al., 1995).

In collaboration with emergency centers Kop et al. (2003) had compared the psychosocial profiles of patients who develop the first symptoms of myocardial infarction when on holiday and those of cardiac patients who manifested their first cardiac symptoms in the normal home situation. They came to conclude that the incidence of MI during vacation is highest during the first two days of vacation. Risk for MI may be increased by vacation activities such as adverse driving conditions and less luxurious accommodations. Individuals with known vulnerability for MI may therefore likely benefit from minimizing physical and emotional challenges specifically related to vacation travel.

Psychosocial factors and vulnerability to disease

We have summarized above the potential health threats when one is on holiday. These health threats are partly connected to the new environment (e.g., to new pathogens) and partly to 'typical' vacation behavior (alcohol abuse, sexual promiscuity) and to the typical holiday stressors. In the remainder of this chapter we want to argue that the transition to a new environment may have additional negative effects on a person's natural resistance to disease. It may thus be speculated that an individual engaging in drinking and promiscuous sex in the familiar home environment may be less at risk health-wise than when on holiday. Our arguments are mainly based on current evidence on the effects of life changes and other health status psychosocial factors. In addition, attention will be devoted to topics like daily stressors, but also to the further social demands and to unmet expectations.

Why people go on holiday
People might differ quite a lot in their wishes, desires and motives for a holiday, depending on their underlying needs. The behavior that is shown on holiday is directed to satisfy these needs (Maslow, 1970; Iso-Ahola, 1983; Mill & Morrison, 1985; Pearce, 1982; Rubenstein, 1980). Several investigators have assessed the motives for going on holiday. Some of the most important and most frequently mentioned reasons for going on holiday are the following (Clift & Clark, 1995; Mill & Morrison, 1985; Rubenstein, 1980):

1. *Relaxation.* Physical or mental relaxation is for many people the most important motive for going on holiday. One needs time off to take rest, to recharge one's batteries, and to get revitalized.
2. *Protection.* Security reasons can also be a reason. People who do dangerous work (e.g., police officers, firemen, military servicemen) seek feelings of peace and protection during their holiday.

3. *Affection.* People may go on holiday because they want to meet new people or because they want to strengthen existing friendships. Couples with marital problems may want to revitalize their relationship or get to know their children better.

4. *Status.* Choosing exclusive destinations might heighten one's status. Such holiday destinations might give such people greater prestige in particular social circles.

5. *Self discovery.* Some want to explore their (unknown) capacities and try to find themselves.

6. *Intellectual enrichment.* Some travelers want to know and learn more about the world. These travelers have a genuine interest in the places they visit and they want to explore those places. They may be interested in the food, the culture or the way of life of the local people.

7. *Vacation for beauty.* Aesthetical experiences may be a further important motive for holidaymakers. Both the splendid nature and the architecture and culture of a given holiday destination may be attractive to subgroups of tourists.

8. *Exotic adventure.* People may seek excitement, exotic adventure, danger and sexual escapades.

9. *Health.* Health tourism can be defined as the deliberate choice of destinations or tourist facilities that offer health care services, such as medical examinations, special diets, special medical treatment (spas!) and examinations (Goodrich, 1993).

On the basis of these motives and preferences, the following categories of tourists can be identified (Pearce, 1982). The *exploitative travelers* are those who are hardly aware of their vacation environment. They only seek shallow contacts with the locals. Nature, culture nor the local population is the reason for choosing a specific destination. What is most important to them is that everything is much cheaper than in the home country.

By contrast, for the second group of tourists, the *high contact travelers*, social contact with the locals is the most important aspect. These kinds of holidaymakers want to know more about the local people, their habits, behavior and daily life. They do not join guided tours and tend to avoid places and events especially designed for tourists. Their main aim is to interact with the local population and to go their own way. Travelers who do not spend much money, who are not status minded and who are in search of the meaning of life are referred to as *spiritual travelers*. The 'hippie' belongs to this category, as do all the volunteers who work in developing countries during their holidays. The *environmental travelers* are holidaymakers whose focus is on adventure, social interaction and the environment. They are physically active but do not forget the needs of others. The fifth and last group of travelers is the *pleasure-first travelers*, who want status, souvenirs and pleasure. These are the 'real' prototype tourists, who take many pictures, prefer to eat what they eat at home, buy presents in the souvenir shops, and spend a lot of money on tourist attractions and activities. In short, there would appear to be important differences between individuals where their motivation for going on holiday is concerned. In addition, many holiday destinations have their specific profile. For example, some destinations focus on the nightlife, others on nature, and others on culture.

Rubenstein (1980) argues that "few of us succeed in achieving any remarkable transformations while on vacation and, alas, we carry the same psychological baggage with us, wherever we go." This is illustrated by the finding that workaholics take their work with them, health nuts engage in health activities and sports, but that those who enjoy their work most also appreciate their vacations best. Most holidaymakers thus usually fail to undergo any remarkable psychological transformations while on holiday, which would imply that it is important for tourists, choosing their destination, to take into account their personality and motives. As in any other domain of our social world the aim in this context should also be to have an optimal person-vacation environment fit. In the next paragraph, we will devote some attention to this issue.

French et al. (1982) have formulated their Person-Environment Fit approach, which, especially in the occupational setting, has been studied extensively. Later on, the model was applied in a wider and more general context to psychosocial stress (cf. Howell et al., 1995; see also Buffum, 1987-88; O'Connor & Vallerand, 1994). The interaction between specific characteristics of the person and specific features of the environment is so important and unique that it is considered to be the most relevant variable in the development of health problems. Hettema (1979), as an advocate of the interactionistic approach to personality, also dwells on the importance of the relationship between the individual and his/her environment, in particular the strategies that may be applied to restore the possible disequilibrium between the environment and the person. Within public health, it is more common to include in the model the variables agent, host, and environment (e.g., Susser, 1973).

Another approach within the stress research field is to focus on life events. Although the original theoretical position taken by Holmes and Rahe (1967) has been challenged, it is nevertheless important to devote attention to it. Holmes and Rahe regarded adjustment as the critical factor: how many 'units' of adjustment does exposure to a certain situation require, independently of whether it is appraised as negative (e.g., the death of a spouse, job loss) or positive (e.g., marriage, holiday). Their hypothesis is that the more effort one puts into adjustment processes, the more vulnerable one will be to contracting disease. Thus, the more adjustment a certain holiday destination requires, the more likely it is that the general resistance to disease is diminished. The results of more recent studies further suggest that the negative health effects may be even worse if the individual does not receive adequate social support from his or her network, which of course is often limited when one is on vacation abroad or if the individual concerned does not possess adequate coping strategies (see also the contribution by Monden in this volume).

The items in the Social Readjustment Rating Scale further refer to changes in living conditions, recreation, residency, social activities, and in eating and sleeping habits. In addition, it contains one specific item on vacation. This list was based on research finding, indicating what kinds of events relatively often precede the onset of disease and/or the seeking of medical advice.

Since the early eighties there has been increased interest in the measurement of daily stressors and their impact on physical and mental health. Evidence shows significant correlations between daily stressor exposure and distress (e.g., DeLongis *et al.*, 1982) and more objective indices of disturbed biological functioning (e.g., Brantley *et al.*, 1988; Jabaaij *et al.*, 1993). There is no reason to assume that typical minor vacation stressors should have a different impact from everyday stressors. Although systematic research is lacking, the following list presented by Rosenblat and Russell (1975) may give a good impression of the kind of problems that may arise during holidays.

1. Family members are forced to spend much of the time together, whereas in the home situation the different family members engage in many different activities like going to school, working, shopping, attending meetings, taking exercise, etc. At home, each family member has greater space to live in and possesses his own radio and TV. This separation insulates family members from one another's moodiness, noises, distracting activities, and preferences for temperature and specific stimulation and provides privacy.

2. Sharing territories. Whereas in the home situation there are often implicit or explicit rules about functioning in the family and one's place in the household (e.g., where to sit at the dinner table, etc.), entering into a new living space means that everybody has to struggle for their own territory. Disputes may arise over who may sit where, who has the right to switch the radio on or off, who has to sleep where and with whom, etc. Research suggests that people traveling with nuclear family members generally experience fewer difficulties than those who are accompanied by non co-resident relatives or friends.

3. Another aspect is that families have usually worked out the division of household chores. During a vacation those responsible for typical household activities may want a rest from such daily routines. In addition, there may be new activities that need to be allocated to someone.

4. Traveling with children. Many parents know from firsthand experience the problems and inconveniences that are inextricably linked to traveling with children, like the lack of interest children may have for some tourist attractions, inconvenient toilet timing, etc.

5. Travelers may be confronted with 'typical' holiday problems that may tax their adaptational demands. Some of the most frequently reported problems are: car breakdowns, illness, crowded camp sites and touristic attractions, noise and other disturbances created by fellow campers, etc. Much to their surprise, Rosenblatt and Russell (1975) found that holidaymakers experiencing bad weather reported less anger and tension than people who had good weather. They wonder whether this result may have to do with collectively blaming the weather for the disappointment, having to make fewer decisions, do less fast driving, having fewer physical demands and getting more sleep.

6. In addition to the above-mentioned issues, one should not forget the daily problems related to feelings of loss (Fisher, 1989) concerning a pet, family, friends, or loved objects. Loss of identity may be another important determinant of health problems during holidays (Monden, 1988).

7. A vacation is something that is, to a very large extent, idealized. It is associated with high expectations, like seeking total revitalization, wanting ideal weather and anticipating a coming together of all the good things in life. Such expectations can easily lead to great dissatisfaction, which in turn may initiate a blaming of self or family members. When going on holiday it is thus better to have realistic expectations and so ward off potential problems. Many people consider their vacations to be very important and attach much value to traveling. They are regarded as necessary; vacations provide an essential escape valve (Rubenstein, 1980). You should rejoice at having a holiday: a break from one's boring daily life. By definition almost, vacations are not associated with accidents, problems and ill health. However, there is often a significant gap between vacation fantasy and reality. Nevertheless, by far the majority of people are very optimistic about vacations and report having great expectations.

There is accumulating evidence to suggest that experiencing these kinds of events and accumulating daily stressors may disturb endocrine functioning (catecholamines, cortisol, neuropeptides). Affected hormonal processes may in their turn influence cardiovascular and immune functions that may then mediate changes in health status (Cohen & Herbert, 1996). Which specific disease one will be confronted with depends on genetic, lifestyle (smoking, alcohol consumption, etc.) and environmental factors (exposure). Recent developments in psychoimmunology have yielded evidence to suggest that the susceptibility to immune related diseases, including infectious diseases, some kinds of cancer, allergies, and autoimmune disease may be increased after exposure to demanding and emotional situations. Spending one's holiday in exotic countries may thus (a) facilitate unhealthy behavior in specific groups; (b) lead to an increase in the vulnerability to disease, in particular where there is a misfit between the personality and the environment, and (c) result in the exposure of the person to unfamiliar pathogens. These three factors put together may facilitate pathophysiological processes that may seriously endanger one's health status.

A final group of people that deserves attention in this context are those who suffer from "*leisure sickness.*" Although leisure and vacation are generally associated with feelings of relaxation and well-being, there is evidence that some people feel ill and develop symptoms especially during weekends and vacations (Vingerhoets *et al.*, 2002). Little is known about the background of these people, although *workaholic* features may be a risk factor. In addition, there is a lack of clarity and strong need for more research on the specific responsible mechanisms.

Conclusion

In this chapter we have dealt with international tourism from the perspective of health psychology. Traveling carries with it some inherent risks for minor and major health problems. Most of them are preventable, because they are associated with specific risk behaviors, e.g., exposure to ultraviolet rays, unprotected sexual behavior, which are not specifically related to vacations (cf. Dembert *et al.*, 1986). In addition, there are (mental) health problems, which are specifically related to traveling, such as jet lag and exposure to unfamiliar pathogens. We would further argue that going on holiday implies making adaptive efforts, which may render the traveler more vulnerable to disease.

Making adequate preparation and adhering to good health habits can prevent a lot of problems. This does not merely mean having the right vaccinations and using sun blocks, but also carefully choosing a destination that fits your personality best. The better the traveler-environment fit, the better the well-being will be and the lower the risk of disease. The value of a vacation will increase significantly when the balance between the positive experiences outweighs the avoidable (health) problems and difficulties. This may be a new challenge for both health promotion teams and travel agents.

References

Baars, M. W., & Tjia, M. W. (1990). Alcohol en hartritmestoornissen [Alcohol and cardiac arrhythmias]. *Tijdschrift voor Alcohol, Drugs en andere Psychotrope Stoffen, 16*, 105-109.

Bell, P. A., Greene, T. C., Fisher, J. D., & Baum, A. (1996). *Environmental psychology* (4th ed.). Fort Worth, TX: Harcourt Brace.

Bick, P. A. (1983). Physiological and psychological correlates of motion sickness. *British Journal of Medical Psychology, 56*, 189-196.

Brantley, P. J., Dietz, L. S., McKnight, G. T., Jones, G. N., & Tulley, R. (1988). Convergence between the Daily Stress Inventory and endocrine measures of stress. *Journal of Clinical and Consulting Psychology, 56*, 549-551.

Buffum, W. E. (1987-88). Measuring person-environment fit in nursing homes. *Journal of Social Service Research, 11*, 35-54.

Cartwright, R. Y. (1996). Travelers' diarrhoea. In: S. Clift & S. J. Page (Eds.), *Health and the international tourist* (pp. 44-66). London: Routledge.

Cartwright, R. Y. (1992). The epidemiology of travelers' diarrhoea in British package holiday tourists. *PHLS Microbiology Digest, 9*, 121-124.

CBS (2005). *Toerisme en recreatie in cijfers: 2004*. Voorburg/Heerlen, The Netherlands: Centraal Bureau voor de Statistiek.

Clift, S., & Clark, N. (1995). Dimensions of holiday experience and their implications for health: A study of British tourists in Malta. *Travel, Lifestyles and Health Working Paper, No 8*. Canterbury, UK: Canterbury Christ Church College.

Cohen, S., & Herbert, T. B. (1996). Health psychology. Psychological factors and physical disease from the perspective of human psychoneuroimmunology. *Annual Review of Psychology, 47*, 113-142.

Cossar, J. H. (2000). Historical aspects of travel medicine. In: C. Lockie, E. Walker, L. Calvert, J. Coassar, R. Knill-Jones, & F. Raeside (Eds.), *Travel medicine and migrant health* (pp. 3-23). Edinburgh, Scotland: Churchill Livingstone.

Cossar, J. H. (1996). Travelers' health: A medical perspective. In: S. Clift & S. J. Page (Eds.), *Health and the international tourist* (pp. 23-43). London: Routledge.

Cossar, J. H. (1987). *Studies on illnesses associated with travel.* MD thesis. Glasgow: University of Glasgow.

Cossar, J. H., & Reid, D. (1989). Health hazards in international travel. *World Health Statistics Quarterly, 42*, 61-69.

Cossar, J. H., Reid, D., Fallon, R. J., Bell, E. J., Riding, M. H., Follett, E. A. C., Dow, B. C., Mitchell, S., & Grist, N. R. (1990). A cumulative review of studies on travelers, their experience of illness and the implications of these findings. *Journal of Infection, 21*, 27-42.

De Graaf, R., Van Zessen, G., Houweling, H. (1996). Nederlanders in aids-endemische gebieden [Dutch people in AIDS-endemic areas]. *SOA-bulletin, 17*, 12-14.

DeLongis, A., Coyne, J. C., Dakof, G., Folkman, S., & Lazarus, R. S. (1982). Relationships of daily hassles, uplifts, and major life events to health status. *Health Psychology, 1*, 119-136.

Dembert, M. L., Baemmert, R. J., Weinberg, W. G., Ledbetter, E. K., Fraser, J. R., Keith, J. F., & Taylor, W. H. (1986). Medical advice for foreign travel. *Military Medicine, 151*, 211-220.

Dobie, T. G., & May, J. G. (1995). The effectiveness of a motion sickness counselling programme. *British Journal of Clinical Psychology, 34*, 301-311.

Eiser, J. R., & Ford, N. (1995). Sexual relationships on holiday: A case of situational disinhibition? *Journal of Social and Personal Relationships, 12*, 323-339.

Fisher, S. (1989). *Homesickness, cognition, and health.* Hove, UK: Erlbaum.

French, J. R. P. Jr., Caplan, R. D., & Van Harrison, R. (1982). *The mechanism of job stress and strain.* Chichester, UK: Wiley.

Gillies, P., & Slack, R. (1996). Context and culture in HIV prevention. The importance of holidays? In: S. Clift & S. J. Page (Eds.), *Health and the international tourist.* London: Routledge.

Goodrich, J. N. (1993). Socialist Cuba: A study of health tourism. *Journal of Travel Research, 32*, 36-40.

Hettema, P. J. (1979). *Personality and adaptation.* Amsterdam: North-Holland Publishing Co.

Holmes, T. H., & Rahe, R. H. (1967). The Social Readjustment Scale. *Journal of Psychosomatic Research, 11*, 213-218.

Howell, R. H., Krantz, D. S., & Barnard, M. (1995). Person-environment interactions are alive and well in health psychology. *Psychology & Health, 10*, 281-284.

Iso-Ahola, S. E. (1983). Towards a social psychology of recreational travel. *Leisure Studies, 2*, 45-56

Jabaaij, L., Grosheide, P., Heijtink, R., Duivenvoorden, H., Ballieux, R., & Vingerhoets, A. (1993). The influence of perceived psychological stress and distress on antibody response to low dose rDNA hepatitis B vaccine. *Journal of Psychosomatic Research, 37*, 361-369.

Kop W. J., Vingerhoets A. J. J. M., Kruithof G. J., & Gottdiener J. S. (2003) Risk factors for myocardial infarction during vacation travel. *Psychosomatic Medicine, 65*, 396-401.

Lange, W. R., & McCune, B. A. (1989). Substance abuse and international travel. *Advances in Alcohol & Substance Abuse 8*, 37-51.

Lewy, A. J., Ahmed, S., & Sack, R. L. (1996). Phase shifting in the human circadian clock using melatonin. *Behavioral Brain Research 73*, 131-134.

Lockie, C., Walker, E., Calvert, L., Coassar, J., Knill-Jones, R. & Raeside, F. (Eds.). (2000). *Travel medicine and migrant health.* Edinburgh, Scotland: Churchill Livingstone.

Maslow, A. M. (1970). *Motivation and personality.* New York: Harper & Row.

McFarland, R. A. (1975). Air travel across time zones. *American Scientist, 63,* 23-30.

Mill, R. C., & Morrison, A. M. (1985). *The tourism system: An introductory text.* Englewood Cliffs, NJ: Prentice-Hall.

Mittleman, M. A., Maclure, M., Sherwood, J. B., Mulry, R. P., Tofler, G. H., Jacobs, S. C., Friedman, R., Benson, H., & Muller, J. E. (1995). Triggering of acute myocardial infarction onset by episodes of anger. *Circulation 92,* 1720-1725.

Monden, M. A. H. (1988). De repatriëring van psychotische patiënten vanuit hun buitenlands vakantie-adres [The repatriation of psychotic patients from holiday destinations abroad]. *Nederlands Tijdschrift voor de Geneeskunde, 132,* 1492-1494.

O'Connor, B. P., & Vallerand, R. J. (1994). Motivation, self-determination, and person-environment fit as predictors of psychological adjustment among nursing home residents. *Psychology and Aging, 9,* 189-194.

Osborn, J. E. (1988). The AIDS epidemic: Six years. In: L. Breslow, J. E. Fielding, & L. B. Lave (Eds.), *Annual Review of Public Health, 9.* Palo Alto, CA: Annual Reviews.

Page, S. J., Clift, S., & Clark, N. (1994). Tourist health: The precautions, behaviour and health problems of British tourists in Malta. In: A. V. Seaton (Ed.), *Tourism. The state of the art.* Chichester, UK: Wiley.

Pasini, W. (1989). Tourist health as a new branch of public health. *World Health Statistics Quarterly, 42,* 77-84.

Pearce, P. L. (1982). *The social psychology of tourist behaviour.* Oxford, UK: Pergamon Press.

Reason, J. T., & Brand, J. J. (1975). *Motion sickness.* London: Academic Press.

Redfern, P. H. (1989). `Jet-lag': Strategies for prevention and cure. *Human Psychopharmacology, 4,* 159-168.

Redfern, P. H., Minors, D., & Waterhouse, J. (1994). Circadian rhythms, jet lag, and chronobiotics: An overview. *Chronobiology International, 11,* 253-265.

Rosenblatt, P. C., & Russell, M. G. (1975). The social psychology of potential problems in family vacation travel. *The Family Coordinator, 24,* 209-215.

Rubenstein, C. (1980). Vacations. Expectations, satisfactions, frustrations, fantasies. *Psychology Today,* 62-76.

Rudkin, B., & Hall, C. M. (1996). Off the beaten track: The health implications of the development of special-interest tourism activities in South-East Asia and the South Pacific. In: S. Clift & S. J. Page (Eds.), *Health and the international tourist* (pp. 89-107). London: Routledge.

Sanders, N., Kuper, W., & Vingerhoets, A. (1996). Wat zoekt u op vakantie? *Psychologie, 14,* 72-75.

Susser, M. (1973). *Causal thinking in the health sciences. Concepts and strategies in epidemiology.* New York: Oxford University Press.

Vingerhoets, A. J. J. M., Van Huigevoort, M., & Van Heck, G. L. (2002). Leisure sickness: A pilot study on its prevalence, phenomenology, and background. *Psychotherapy and Psychosomatics, 71,* 311-317.

Weston, R. (1996). Have fun in the sun: Protect yourself from skin damage. In: S. Clift & S. J. Page (Eds.), *Health and the international tourist* (pp. 235-259). London: Routledge.

14   Development of Psychopathology in International Tourists

Marcel A.H. Monden

Introduction

Each year many western habitants take a holiday abroad. Worldwide the tourism flow is growing. In general, holidays are associated with positive experiences. Holidays are thought of as being a welcome change for today's hectic life. Many of us feel free and relaxed when on a holiday. However, problems can and do arise. In period from 1994 until 2004, there was an increase of approximately 23,500 to about 45,000 in the number of requests for assistance by Dutch international tourists. Surprisingly, the number of requests associated with psychic problems remained rather constant (approximately 500) over this period. Psychoses and other forms of severe psychopathology are not exceptional. It is clear that the development of psychopathology is not restricted to one's own habitat. However, very little is known about the causes and consequences of developing psychopathologies abroad.

This chapter focuses on possible causes, treatment and repatriation of those who develop psychopathologies when on a holiday abroad. In addition, a theoretical framework will be presented. First, however, two cases will be described, to give the reader an impression of the kind of psychiatric problems alarm centers are confronted with.

Two cases

Case A

A 23-year-old woman went on a honeymoon. She delivered the mail for several years. Until a few days before her marriage she did her job, because she wanted to save as much days as possible for their honeymoon to South America. She married her husband, a physiotherapist, on Friday and they left for South America on Saturday. At their destination, the bridal suite appeared to be double booked and they were transferred to another room. On the second day her purse, containing her valuables, was stolen. The next two days she hardly got any sleep and on the fourth day she became agitated and paranoid, resulting one day later in a psychosis. With the exception of her husband, everyone she was confronted with was brutalized. She walked around the hotel and harassed the other guests. A Dutch alarm center was contacted and two days later she flew back, accompanied by a nurse. Back in The Netherlands she was admitted to a hospital. Two months later she was dismissed in a good condition and took up her job again.

Case B

A 36-year-old man made a trip to Florence, Italy to recuperate from a stressful period in the Netherlands. In the train to Florence he became paranoid and thought that someone wanted to poison him. He was also convinced that the Mafia was after him. At the hotel he threw away his passport and locked himself into his room. That night he flung the T.V.-set out of the window of his room on the 10th floor. It was a miracle that no one got hurt. An Italian doctor sedated him, but the next day his condition got worse. The Dutch alarm center was contacted and a psychiatrist flew to Florence where he was confronted with a severely psychotic man, who had no prior history of psychosis. The man received medication and was flown to the Netherlands on a stretcher where he was admitted to hospital. Six days later he got over his amnesia and his psychotic state was no longer evident. The diagnosis was: a transient psychotic reaction. After being dismissed from hospital he went into psychotherapeutic treatment.

Both were healthy persons with no prior history of any psychological or psychiatric symptoms. In these two cases the holiday itself may be considered to have contributed significantly to the development of psychopathology.

Theories

The development of psychopathology and psychiatric problems during travel have only been sporadically described in the scientific literature. As early as in 1900 Freud wrote in his *Traumdeutung* about his mental problems on his travels to Rome. For years he traveled no further than Trasimeno. When he finally reached Rome he wrote in his letters to Fliess that this event meant a "Höhepunkt des Lebens." In 1919 Ferenczi (1964) introduced the term 'Ferialneurose,' indicating that there is a specific psychological state of mind when people travel. However, until now there are no theories, which explicitly address the issue of development of psychopathology during travel (see also Jones, 2000). Therefore, the focus in this contribution will be on psychodynamic and psychoanalytic theories concerning the development of psychopathology in general, and stress theories, which might explain why the travel situation evokes psychopathologies more easily than the home environment. Changes in circadian rhythm influence mood and may also facilitate the development of mood diseases. Phase advance of sleep or limiting its duration has an effect on depression. Sleep deprivation may improve depression as well as exposure to light (Van den Hoofdakker & Beersma, 1988; Wehr *et al.*, 1988). Sleep deprivation is further known to act in some cases as a final common pathway in the genesis of mania (Wehr *et al.*, 1987).

From a psychoanalytical point of view the basis for developing psycho-pathology is often found in disturbances in childhood. It is generally hypothesized that the younger the age, at which psychological disturbances develop, the worse the problems in adulthood will be. In my opinion Mahler's theory (1975) is the best applicable theoretical approach for the development of psychopathology during travel. In the remainder of this paragraph I will discuss the four stages of Mahler's separation-individuation theory and its consequences with respect to traveling. The following four phases are distinguished in Mahler's theory:

1. *Differentiation* (5-10 months). The child starts to differentiate between mother and non-mother. The absolute dependence on mother diminishes which may involve curiosity and fear.

2. *Practicing* (10-16 months). The child explores the world with the mother as the home base in a lustful way: the world is his oyster. Separation anxieties are common in this phase. The role of the mother is very important, as she must allow her child to explore the environment.

3. *Rapprochement* (16-24 months). The infant is now a toddler; it is more aware of its physical separation from his mother, which dampens its mood of elation. The child tries to bridge the gap between itself and mother. If mother's efforts to help the toddler are not perceived as helpful, tantrums are characteristic. Mahler considers the rapprochement crisis as very important for a healthy development of the self. The child wants to be soothed by the mother and yet is not able to accept her help. The solution of this crisis takes place when the child's skills improve and the child is able to get gratification from doing things, like helping mother.

4. *Consolidation and object constancy* (24-36 months; but may also be considered open ended because a persons may struggle his or her whole life to attain object constancy). The child now can cope better with mother's absence and is able to substitute it. The child may also begin to feel more comfortable when the mother is absent, because it knows that the separation is only temporary. There is a gradual internalization of the image of the mother as being reliable and stable. Through increasing verbal skills and a better sense of time the child can tolerate delay and endure separations from his or her mother.

The third sub-phase is the most important one, because in many cases the basis for an unsolved intra-psychic conflict is developed in this phase. Characteristic for the third phase is the fear of loosing love of the mother. This fear is indirectly related to the ambivalence concerning the mother. If the ambivalence is too great, the child may split his object world and create a good and a bad mother. A bad mother image may diminish the child's self-esteem. The split may cause projection; the good mother is experienced in the outer world. This may result in an infantile neurosis or neurosis in adulthood.

According to Groen (1980), Mahler identifies two kinds of child self-esteem: its own omnipotence and that of the mother, eventually developing into the feeling of own autonomy and emotional object constancy. Sandler (1960) highlights the importance of the feeling of safety in the third phase. He introduces a safety principle along with a reality and lust principle. Safety is closely related to the guardian presence of mother. When the fourth sub-phase is reached, the feeling of safety will come from the inside and is less dependent on the outer world. If this is not the case, safety must be found in a safe environment.

An unresolved psychic conflict in the third phase can cause psychopathology during travel in adulthood, because during travel a safe environment no longer exists (Groen, 1980). The unstable object constancy is also threatened by going elsewhere. If the third sub-phase was problematic, the mother may be experienced as a blockade in the separation process. Traveling may be conceived as leaving the mother in an aggressive way, or the projected good or even ideal mother turns out to be disappointing once abroad. Separation may have a negative effect on the self-esteem with depressive states as a consequence. Disintegration and depression may also develop when one goes on a holiday in a weak narcistic balance. This is quite often seen among people traveling alone. Rümke (1957) describes 5 cases where traveling contributes to the development of psychiatric symptoms. The origin of these symptoms is mainly psychodynamically interpreted.

I will now turn to more recent stress theories explaining the development of psychopathology during traveling. Holidays by definition imply a change of environment, meaning that one has to adjust to new routines and procedures and unknown people (Fisher, 1989; Jones, 2000). In terms of adaptation, one tries to change either the environment or oneself so that there is a better fit with one's needs (Hosman, 1991). The subjective and objective personal characteristic features as well as the subjective and objective environment characteristic features may be changed in order to accomplish this improvement in person-environment fit (French et al., 1974). One may distinguish phylogenetic and biological, psychological, and social adaptation mechanisms (Hosman, 1991). For people on holiday the psychological and social adaptation mechanisms are most important to cope with all the typical changes and events associated with travel.

Successful personal adaptation depends on three aspects: effective coping mechanisms, the motivation to deal with the demands of the new environment, and psychological balance. Psychological and physical stress during travel affects the adaptation process. This stress becomes real and dangerous if the person fails to adapt because of s/he is not able to cope adequately with the altered circumstances (Totman, 1988). Fisher's chapter in this volume describes five theoretical explanations concerning feelings of discomfort when people change their old environment for a new one: Loss, Interruption, Control, Role Change, and Conflict. These factors might elicit all kinds of anxieties possibly resulting in the development of psychopathologies. Here I will discuss several stress-eliciting factors which are specific to travel situations and which might influence emotional (in)stability during a holiday.

Culture shock
If the culture in the new country is very different from one's own culture, the traveler might feel shocked and overwhelmed (see the chapter by Furnham in this volume).

Culturally based behaviors like manners, habits, nonverbal behavior, language, etc., are dramatically different and the traveler might feel him/herself unable to communicate and behave in an appropriate and clear manner. This experience can be very stressful, leading to all kinds of anxieties. For example, Magherini (1992) describes a particular acute psychotic reaction in art-loving tourists visiting Florence. These reactions are mainly associated with a latent mental or psychiatric disturbance that manifests itself as a reaction to paintings of battles or masterpieces and culminates in the full-blown so-called Florence or Stendhal syndrome.

Another example of a psychiatric syndrome associated with culture shock is the Jerusalem syndrome described by Bar-El *et al.* (2000) and Witztum and Kalian (1999). According to these authors this syndrome is a unique acute psychotic state. He identifies three main categories of the syndrome. Type I refers to individuals already diagnosed as having a psychosis before their visit to Israel. Type II involves people with mental disorders such as personality disorders or an obsession with a fixed idea, but who do not have a clear mental illness; their strange thoughts and ideas fall short of delusional or psychotic dimensions. The type III form is the most fascinating one because it describes individuals with no previous history of mental illness, who fall victim to a psychotic episode while in Israel (and especially while in Jerusalem), recover fairly spontaneously, and then, once back home, again apparently enjoy normality. Bar-El and colleagues failed to arrive at a broader empirical base because none of his 42 type III patients did respond to his questionnaire and attempts to obtain information by telephone produced the same disappointing result.

Identity
The individual might feel the urge to take on new roles when on holiday, as existing roles do no longer apply. If the individual fails to change his or her own role, a feeling of having lost one's identity might result. As mentioned before, complicating factors are difficulties in separation and individuation, which may facilitate the development of identity problems especially in adolescence.

Negative events
Most persons are very optimistic about their holidays. In a study of Rubenstein (1980) 91% of the respondents indicated that nothing can spoil their holiday. Travel manuals raise great expectations (Lundberg, 1990). Many holiday situations will not fulfill these high expectations and dissatisfaction might result. Furthermore, negatively perceived events are more difficult to cope with during a holiday, because of the inability to rely on routines, habits and social networks. Thus, one is more vulnerable when on a holiday and stressors will more easily be perceived of as threats instead of challenges.

Social relationships
When traveling a large part of the social network of an individual is left behind. Confronted with problems during a holiday an individual has diminished possibilities

to rely on social contacts. If the individual lacks the social abilities and assertive behavior necessary to initiate new social contacts and mobilize social support when needed in the holiday situation, strong anxieties and emotional instability might result.

The voyage

The voyage itself might be stressful (Flinn, 1961; Fisher, 1989). A good preparation promotes adaptation (Fisher, 1989). Furthermore, privacy, personal space and territory issues might influence the perceived stressfulness of the voyage (Fridgen, 1984). Those traveling alone, unaccompanied are more vulnerable to developing psychological problems (Flinn, 1961). Shapiro (1976) mentions jet lag as a factor. Time zone changes of a minimum of two hours may induce symptoms of depression or mania in predisposed individuals. Two studies show that significantly more people traveling eastward showed symptoms of mania whereas significantly more people traveling westward showed symptoms of depression (Young, 1995; Jauhar, 1982). More detailed information is found in Vingerhoets *et al.*'s contribution to this volume.

Somatic conditions

Tropical diseases may also cause psychiatric symptoms. Examples are malaria (Prakash, 1990), the cerebral form of typhus, the South African forms of trypanosomiasis causing sleeping sickness, the cerebral form of tape worm (Obrador, 1948) and AIDS.

A simple stimulus-response model does not suffice to explain psychic decompensation due to stress exposure. Other vulnerability factors such as neuroticism, self-esteem, locus of control, coping and social support are also important. Personality factors might influence the labeling of stressful encounters in challenges or threats. Coping strategies and quality and quantity of social support determine how able one is to cope successfully with the demands of the new environment. Some other factors are:

1. *Previous experience with holidays.* Experience with holidays lessens the threat of leaving the familiar environment (Fisher, 1989). If one has been on a vacation before, one knows what to expect (Mazurky, 1989). In addition, information provided by others with relevant travel experiences may also be helpful to make holidays less threatening (Iso-Ahola, 1983). On the other hand, the motive for a holiday may be narcistic. It makes nice conversation and even much status in one's social network if one has traveled far away.
2. *Length of the holiday.* The longer the holiday lasts, the more difficult it will be to be away from the familiar environment (Monden & Meester, 1994).
3. *Activities.* The more distractions, the less one thinks about home and the quicker one adjusts to a new environment (Fisher, 1989). Inactivity and monotony may promote the development of psychological problems during a holiday (Flinn, 1961; Shapiro, 1976).

4. *Sex.* More men than women prefer the safe environment of a place where they have been before (Rubenstein, 1980). Furthermore, marked differences have been reported between men and women in psychiatric syndromes. In women the prevalence of psychic disturbances is higher than in men. More women than men suffer from depressions, whereas in men personality disorders are more prevalent (Jenkins, 1991).

5. *Age.* Older people tend to choose less active holidays and more distant travel destinations than younger people, who choose adventurous holidays (Mill & Morrison, 1985). In addition, it has been found that psychic decompensations generally are more prevalent among older than among younger people (Jacobs & Bijl, 1992).

6. *Training and education.* Persons with a higher education have more opportunities to select their favorite destinations (Mill & Morrison, 1985). In addition, they tend to adapt better when traveling (Jones, 2000).

7. *Marital status.* Marital status is associated with the risk of developing psychological problems (Gove, 1972). Generally, being married is associated with less psychological problems. On the other hand, it has been suggested that during a holiday, partners need to consider each other more than at home and this might lead to more relational problems when traveling.

8. *Loss.* Those who decompensate often had exit or loss events before their holiday like the death of a spouse, divorce or an accident. This may also facilitate the onset of psychiatric syndromes (Goodyer, 1988).

So far, a wide variety of factors have been discussed, which might increase psychological distress during holidays, like anxieties, depression and homesickness. If high levels of psychological distress coincide with a personal basis for psychopathology in personality and/or early childhood, psychological disturbances and psychic decompensation might occur. However, many important issues regarding developing psychopathologies abroad are still unresolved. For instance, which personality characteristics are found in those developing psychopathologies abroad? Which psychiatric problems are specifically found in the holiday situation? Would those who did decompensate during travel also have decompensated when they would have stayed at home? Are those who decompensate during travel predominantly recidivists who relapse during stressful periods? In the reminder of this chapter some findings of a study on psychopathology in international tourists will be summarized.

Research

Monden and Meester (1994) conducted an exploratory study on psychiatric patients repatriated by a Dutch alarm center. During the period of January 1985 until December 1989 all files of the patients who approached the alarm center with psychiatric problems were reviewed. In these files information was collected on sex, age, holiday destination, days between the departure and the report to the alarm center. In addition, it was recorded whether these patients traveled alone or in a group and if they had needed professional guidance for their return home. The diagnosis, according to the Diagnostic and Statistical Manual of mental disorders (DSM-III-R; APA, 1987), was made on the basis of all the information given by the persons involved in the treatment of the patient. Finally, it was coded whether it was a first decompensation or a relapse.

The files of 393 patients were reviewed. Thirteen of them were excluded from analysis due to inadequate or incomplete information. Of the remaining 380, 154 were males with an average age of 36 ($SD = 17$) and 226 were females with an average age of 37 ($SD = 19$). The calls came from 43 different countries. The majority of them were from Spain and Greece (43.5%). The patients approached the alarm center on average after 10.2 days ($SD = 14.29$). Fifty-five percent traveled alone and 45% in a group. People were considered to travel in a group if they could actually call upon other people in case of difficulties or emergencies. As many as 35% had their first psychiatric decompensation, whereas the remaining 65% experienced a relapse. The most frequently reported disorder was paranoid disorder (21.1%). Depressions covered 18.9%, anxiety disorders 13.9%, and bipolar disorder 10.8%. Schizophrenia was diagnosed in 8.4% of the cases, all relapses. Finally, there was a group of miscellaneous diagnoses (25.8%) including organic mental disorders, somatoform disorders, dissociative disorders, and impulse control disorders.

About one third thus suffered from a depression or an anxiety disorder. This is probably due to the neurotic constellation that makes people sensitive to depressions and anxieties in strange surroundings. They may experience a lack of structure in their daily routine and an inability to cope with new situations.

In a follow-up study of Sanders (1995), similar results had been found. In contrast, Shapiro (1976) found 75% of the identified cases to be schizophrenic in her study on an international airport. Compared to the 8.4% in the study of Monden and Meester (1994) this is a remarkable difference. There might have been differences in the diagnosis of schizophrenic disorder in these two studies. However, even if all psychotic patients had been considered schizophrenic, this would have resulted in only 40.4% being diagnosed as schizophrenic in the study by Monden and Meester (1994). It might be speculated that the prospect of flying or leaving one's familiar environment is a potent trigger for the onset of psychotic symptoms. As a consequence, it would be less likely for schizophrenic people to reach their holiday destination.

It was striking that almost half of the case reported by Monden and Meester (1994) came from Greece and Spain, while according to data of the Dutch Bureau of Tourism only approximately 15% of the Dutch tourists go these countries. Whereas the majority of the Dutch tourists go to France, there were only few reports from this country. This may be explained by the fact that most Dutch people travel to France in their own car, while coaches and airplanes are favorite modes of transportation to Spain and Greece, respectively. When on holiday in Spain and Greece one is therefore unable to return home early in case of psychological problems because of booked return tickets. However, this does not exclude other explanations, e.g., do predisposed people have a preference for Spain and Greece above France? Or is France more similar to the Netherlands and does it require less adaptation?

Of all cases involved in Monden and Meester's (1994) study, 35% had to be repatriated. Ninety percent went by commercial aircraft and 10% by other means of transport, such as by taxi or ambulance, which was only possible when the distance was less than approximately 1000 miles.

Unfortunately, there are only a few studies on the relationship between travel and psychic decompensation. Langen et al. (1997) did research on "honeymoon psychosis" in Japanese tourists going to Hawaii. They present 16 cases of Japanese honeymooners who required emergency psychiatric intervention. If honeymooners would have similar incidence rates of psychiatric emergencies as other Japanese tourists, only 5 such cases would have been expected. It is fascinating that the investigators did not find any case of non-Japanese honeymooners. Ten of the 16 had a past psychiatric history and 13 out of 16 presented with psychotic symptoms. Nine of them had an arranged marriage and the authors suggest that this arranged marriage may be a predisposing factor to "honeymoon psychosis". Further factors are marriage, travel, time change, immersion in a new culture and the pressure from expectations at home.

Jones (2000) reviews research among expatriates, some of it dating back to 1890. For example, between 1890 and 1908, 1000 missionaries were examined. Forty percent of them did discontinue their assignments, and in 40% this was due to mental health issues.

Odegaard (1932) and Malzberg and Lee (1940) established that psychiatric syndromes are more frequent among immigrants than among locals. In a similar way, the loss of objects by moving within the own country may also induce psychopathologies. For example, Meloy (1998) describes that immigration or culture shock, with the loss of aspects of the own culture, may be considered as an important predisposing factor of stalking.

Still many interesting questions remain unanswered. For example, is there a difference between decompensating for the first time versus experiencing a relapse while traveling? And, to what extent is the holiday situation a necessary factor for the development of decompensation?

Repatriating patients: historical review

Repatriation of physically ill persons by ground transportation has been reported as early as in the 19th century during the siege of Paris. In 1910, before World War I there were plans in the U.S. to adapt an airplane for the transportation of somatic patients. In 1915 the Serbian army was the first to start the actual transportation of patients (Jones, 1980). After World War I larger planes were adapted for this purpose. However, the crash of an airplane in Maryland in 1921, resulting in the loss of seven patient's lives, seriously delayed this development. At that time one did not yet think of transporting psychiatric patients.

With the start in 1928 of the Royal Flying Doctor Service in Australia, the standard of aeromedical transportation significantly improved. In 1936 the Germans successfully flew their wounded soldiers out of Spain and in 1940 thousands injured servicemen were evacuated from Poland. Before World War II no records are found of the transportation of psychiatric patients anywhere in the world. The reluctance to transport psychiatric patients was mainly due to the perceived danger caused by suicidal patients in the narrow compartment of the plane.

During World War II the first transportations of psychiatric patients were executed, mainly by boat. There were only a few pharmacological alternatives available for sedating, therefore violent patients had to be confined to the hold of the ship. Jones (1980) reported a death rate of 638 per 100.000. At the end of World War II transportation of psychiatric patients by air was started. Delays due to technical problems or the aircraft sometimes confronted the accompanying psychiatrist with unrestrained, unsedated, confused and sometimes aggressive psychotics.

The introduction of paraldehyde and later chlorpromazine made it possible to transport patients in a more efficient way. The Vietnam conflict provided extensive test material for the modern aeromedical evacuation system. The slogan became: "If the patient can be transported at all, the patient should be transported by air." The greater part of the experience in aeromedical transport originates from military sources. By 1970 the transport of psychiatric patients by commercial airplanes became standard procedure.

Commercial repatriation today

To give the reader an impression of the process of repatriation, a brief description of a Dutch repatriation protocol will be given. When developing problems abroad, Dutch people can contact one of six alarm centers. These alarm centers handle psychiatric, somatic, and practical (like break-down of a car) problems abroad for clients of insurance companies. These alarm centers can be reached by telephone 24 hours a day. Counselors who can handle cases with psychic problems are always available. Reports of psychic problems are made by a wide variety of people such as doctors in the holiday country, relatives of the patient, friends, the hostess of the travel agency and, occasionally, even the Office of Foreign Affairs. The counselor makes an inventory of the problems, the circumstances, whether there has ever been any psychiatric treatment in The Netherlands and the name of the family doctor. This seems an easy task but is often difficult due to language problems. Information about the medical history of the patient by a foreign doctor or nurse is often inadequate. Therefore, consultation with the family doctor and, if possible, with the treating psychiatrists or psychologists in The Netherlands is indispensable in order to determine the treating strategy and management of the particular case. The doctor of the alarm center plays an important role in the decision-making. It is very important to know if the patient receives adequate treatment. Patients might refuse treatment or it may be impossible to arrange adequate treatment abroad. If so, the decision to repatriate a patient is speeded.

Based on the state of the patient the following categories can be distinguished (Monden & Wester, 1995):

A.   Patients who are not admitted to hospital. These patients often suffer from reactive symptoms such as anxieties or depressions.

B.   Patients who are admitted to hospitals but stay in open wards. This is frequently the case with personality disordered patients.

C.   Patients who stay in closed wards of psychiatric hospitals but are able to communicate with the staff. These patients often suffer from mild psychotic states without aggression or agitation.

D.   Patients who stay in closed wards and have to be nursed with severe medication, isolation or fixation. This often concerns severely psychotic persons who are aggressive or who suffer from personality disorders with a lot of acting out.

Group A does not need guided repatriation; group B may sometimes be guided home by family or friends; only group C and D need professionally guided repatriation. Waldeck (1984) gives valuable guidelines for the indications and execution of repatriation.

Once the decision to repatriate has been made, a specialized transport company is contacted. This company takes care of the actual repatriation. Mostly the relief workers of the transport company leave within a few hours after the report has been made. There is an extensive network with companies abroad, which can support the relief workers after they have arrived at their destination. This is certainly the case in Switzerland, Spain and France. Upon arrival, the relief worker immediately contacts the patient, because it is often of great importance for the patient to be able to communicate in his or her own language.

On the first contact with the patient it has to be decided whether it is possible to return by plane. Because of the limited space available for crisis intervention in a plane, there may be extra problems for severely disturbed and phobic patients. Furthermore, it is considered whether the patient needs any medication and whether he or she has to be admitted to a hospital in The Netherlands. In this phase, there is always contact, if possible, with the treating psychiatrist in The Netherlands concerning the above mentioned decisions.

The relief worker never flies back with the patient on the same day. He or she takes some time to get to know the patient, because repatriation always implies a very intensive contact with the patient. In order to be allowed to fly, the airline company has to give a medical O.K. Then, if all the terms are met, the relief worker picks up the patient the next day and travels to the airport by taxi. When entering the plane the purser is informed so that in case of an emergency quick action can be taken. In flight psychiatric emergencies should, if possible, be avoided. Although the frequency is much lower than that of other medical emergencies in-flight, the public is likely to be less tolerant to such incidents. Seriously dangerous incidents in the air are statistically rare, but have a high public impact (Gordon et al., 2004). The flight itself is preferably made by business or first class in order to avoid extra irritation for the patient, certainly if he or she is suffering from a paranoid psychosis.

After arrival at the airport in The Netherlands the patient is transported by taxi to his or her family, the family doctor, the counseling institute or the psychiatric hospital and the repatriation is finished.

Green (2000) describes the method of repatriating psychiatric patients to the United Kingdom and this is not different from the Dutch method accept for some legal aspects. Section 86 of the 1983 Mental Health Act allows the Home Secretary to authorize "the removal of alien patients" to another country. In-flight repatriation may in future be more complicated due to threats of terrorism and the spread of diseases like SARS (Gordon et al., 2004).

Conclusion

Psychic decompensation abroad is a serious problem. Currently, in The Netherlands alarm centers annually receive reports of about 300 people with serious psychic or psychiatric problems. Repatriation of these patients requires a specific approach. For the group of recidivists, more preventive actions are needed with regard to traveling abroad. Unfortunately, until now there are no theories concerning the development of psychopathologies abroad which can guide research, repatriation, and preventive actions. In addition, as only a few studies have focused on these issues very little is known about decompensations abroad. Therefore, more theory-driven research is needed which compare decompensation during travel and at home in order to reveal important aspects of psychic decompensation during travel.

References

American Psychiatric Association (1987). *Diagnostic and Statistical Manual of Mental Disorders*. Washington, DC: APA.

Bar-El, Y., Durst, R., Katz, G., Zislin, J., Strauss, Z., & Knobler, H. Y. (2000). Jerusalem syndrome. *The British Journal of Psychiatry, 176*, 86-90.

Ferenczi, S. (1964). *Sonntagsneurosen in Bausteine zur Psychoanalyse, II*. Bern, Switzerland: Hans Huber.

Fisher, S. (1989). *Homesickness, cognition & health*. East Sussex: Lawrence Erlbaum.

Flinn, D. E. (1961). Transient psychotic reactions during travel. *American Journal of Psychiatry, 119*, 173-174.

French, J. R. P., Rodgers, W. L., & Cobb, S. (1974). Adjustment as person-environment fit. In: G. V. Coelho, D. A. Hamburg, & J.E. Adams (Eds.), *Coping and Adaptation.* New York: Basic Press.

Freud, S. (1900). *Die Traumdeutung.* G.W.II-III. Londen: Imago Publisher.

Fridgen, J. D. (1984). Environmental psychology and tourism. *Annals of Tourism Research, 11*, 19-39.

Gordon, H., Kingham, M., & Goodwin, T. (2004). Air travel by passengers with mental disorder. *Psychiatric Bulletin 28,* 295-297.

Goodyer, I. M. (1988). Stress in childhood and adolescence. In: S. Fisher & J. Reason (Eds.), *The handbook of life stress, cognition and health.* Chichester, UK: Wiley.

Gove, W. R. (1972). The relationship between sex roles, mental illness and marital status. *Social Forces, 51,* 34-44.

Green, L., & Nayani, T. (2000). Repatriating psychiatric patients. *Psychiatric Bulletin, 24,* 405-408

Groen, J. (1980). Vacantie: een psycho-analytische visie [Vacation: A psycho-analytical vision]. *MGV, 8/80,* 619-630.

Hoofdakker, R. H. van den, & Beersma, D. G. M. (1988). On the contribution of sleep wake physiology to the Explanation and the treatment of depression. *Acta Psychiatrica Scandinavica, supplementum 341,* 53-71.

Hosman, C. M. H. (1991). *Adaptatie en gezondheid: een integratieve benadering* [Adaptation and health: An integrative approach]. Paper presented at the Symposium on Clinical Psychology. Nijmegen, The Netherlands.

Iso-Ahola, S. E. (1983). Towards a social psychology of recreational travel. *Leisure Studies, 2,* 45-56.

Jacobs, C. M. V. W., & Bijl, R. V. (1992). *GGZ in getallen 1992. Kwantitatief overzicht van de geestelijke gezondheidszorg; instellingen, zorgcircuits, trends 1980-2000.* [GGZ in numbers in 1992. Quantitative overview of the mental health care; institutions, care circuit, trends 1980-2000]. Utrecht, The Netherlands: NCGV.

Jauhar, P., & Weller, M. P. (1982). Psychiatric morbidity and time zone changes; A study of patients from Heathrow airport. *British Journal of Psychiatry, 156,* 594-595.

Jenkins, R. (1991). Demographic aspects of stress. In: C. L. Cooper & R. Payne (Eds.), *Personality and stress; individual differences in the stress process.* Chichester, UK: John Wiley & Sons.

Jones, M. (2000). Psychological aspects of travel and the long-term expatriate. In: C. Lockie, E. Walker, L. Calvert, J. Cossar, R. Knill-Jonmes, & F. Raeside (Eds.), *Travel medicine and migrant health* (pp. 115-141). Edinburgh: Churchill & Livingstone

Lundberg, D. E. (1990). *The tourist business* (6th ed.). New York: Van Nostrand Reinhold.

Langen, D., Streltzer, J., & Mutsuoki, K. (1997). Honeymoon psychosis in Japanese tourists to Hawaii. *Cultural Diversity and Mental Health, 3,* 171-174.

Magherini, G. (1992). *Syndrome di Stendhal.* Milan, Italy: Fettrilini.

Mahler, M. S. (1966). Notes on the development of basic moods. In: R. M. Loewenstein (Ed.), *Psychoanalysis, a general psychology* (pp. 152-160). New York: International University Press.

Mahler, M. S. (1975). *The psychological birth of the human infant.* New York: Basic Books.

Malzberg, B., & Lee, L. S. (1940). *Migration and mental disease: a study of first admissions to hospital for mental disease.* New York: Social Science Research Council.

Mazurky, D. (1989). Past experiences and future tourism decisions. *Annals of Tourism Research, 16,* 333-344.

Meloy, J. R. (1998). *The psychology of stalking: Clinical and forensic perspectives.* San Diego, CA: Academic Press.

Mill, R. C., & Morrison, A. M. (1985). *The tourism system: An introductory text.* Englewood Cliffs, NJ: Prentice-Hall.

Monden, M. A. H., & Meester, W. J. T. (1994). Psychiatric decompensation during a holiday in a foreign country. *Nederlands Tijdschrift Geneeskunde, 138*, 1520-1523.

Monden, M. A. H., & Wester, J. P. J. (1995). Repatriation of psychiatric patients. *Nederlands Militair Geneeskundig Tijdschrift, 48*, 29-56, 36-41.

Obrador, S. (1948). Clinical aspects of cerebral cysticercosis. *Archives of Neurology and Psychiatry, 59*, 457-468.

Odegaard, O. (1932). Emigration and insanity: a study of mental disease among Norwegian born population of Minnesota. *Acta Psychiatrica et Neurologica, Supplement 14.*

Rubenstein, C. (1980). Vacations. Expectations, satisfactions, frustrations, fantasies. *Psychology Today, May*, 62-76.

Rümke, H. C. (1957). Vakantiereizen als conditionerende factor bij het ontstaan van psychische stoornissen [Holiday travel as a conditioning factor for the development of psychic disturbances]. *Nederlands Tijdschrift voor Geneeskunde, 101*, 1525-1530.

Sanders, N. (1995). *Psychische decompensatie tijdens vakantie in het buitenland* [Psychic decompensation during a holiday abroad]. Unpublished doctoral thesis., Tilburg, The Netherlands: Tilburg University.

Sandler, J. (1960). The background of safety. *International Journal of Psychoanalysis, 41*, 352-356.

Shapiro, S. (1976). A study of psychiatric syndromes manifested on an international airport. *Comprehensive Psychiatry, 17*, 453-456.

Totman, R. (1988). Stress, language and illness. In: S. Fisher & J. Reason (Eds.), *The handbook of life stress cognition and health.* Chichester, UK: John Wiley and Sons.

Waldeck, K.J. J. (1984). *Medische repartriering van Nederlandse toeristen.* [Medical repatriation of Dutch tourists]. Unpublished Phd. Thesis. Utrecht University, The Netherlands.

Wehr, T. A., Rosenthal, N. E., & Sack, D. A. (1988). Environmental and behavioural influences on affective illness. *Acta Psychiatrica Scandinavica, supplementum 341*, 44-52.

Wehr, T. A., Sack, D. A., & Rosenthal, N. E. (1987). Sleep reduction as a final common pathway in the genesis of mania. *American Journal of Psychiatry, 144*, 201-204.

Witztum, E., & Kalian, M. (1999). The "Jerusalem syndrome" – fantasy and reality. A survey of accounts from the 19th century to the end of the second millennium. *Israelian Journal of Psychiatry and Related Sciences, 36*, 260-271.

Young, D. M. (1995). Psychiatric morbidity in travelers to Honolulu, Hawaii. *Comprehensive Psychiatry, 36*, 224-228.

TITELS VERSCHENEN BINNEN DE AAA-SERIE

Andriessen, L. en Schönberger, E. *The Apollonian Clockwork*, 2005 (ISBN 90 5356 856 5)

Appel, R. en Muysken, P. *Language Contact and Bilingualism*, 2005 (ISBN 90 5356 857 3)

Bal, M. *Reading Rembrandt*, 2005 (ISBN 90 5356 858 1)

Bennis, H. *Gaps and Dummies*, 2005 (ISBN 90 5356 859 x)

Blom, H. *De muiterij op De Zeven Provinciën*, 2005 (ISBN 90 5356 844 1)

Dehue, T. *De regels van het vak*, 2005 (ISBN 90 5356 845 x)

Engbersen, G. *Publieke bijstandsgeheimen*, 2005 (ISBN 90 5356 852 2)

Engbersen, G.; Schuyt, K.; Timmer, J. en Waarden, F. van *Cultures of Unemployment*, 2005 (ISBN 90 5356 846 8)

Goedegebuure, J. *De schrift herschreven*, 2005 (ISBN 90 5356 847 6)

Goedegebuure, J. *De veelvervige rok*, 2005 (ISBN 90 5356 848 4)

Hugenholtz, B. *Auteursrecht op informatie*, 2005 (ISBN 90 5356 849 2)

Idema, H. en Haft, L. *Chinese letterkunde*, 2005 (ISBN 90 5356 842 5)

Janssens, J. *De middeleeuwen zijn anders*, 2005 (ISBN 90 5356 850 6)

Kohnstamm, D. *Ik ben ik*, 2005 (ISBN 90 5356 853 0)

Komter, A. *Omstreden gelijkheid*, 2005 (ISBN 90 5356 854 9)

Meijer, M. *In tekst gevat*, 2005 (ISBN 90 5356 855 7)

Oostindie, G. *Ethnicity in the Caribbean*, 2005 (ISBN 90 5356 851 4)

Pinkster, H. *On Latin Adverbs*, 2005 (ISBN 90 5356 843 3)

Tilburg, M. van en Vingerhoets, A. *Psychological Aspects of Geographical Moves*, 2005 (ISBN 90 5356 860 3)